Intermediate Macroeconomics with Chinese Perspectives

This is an intermediate-level macroeconomics textbook for undergraduate students who wish to gain some exposure to the Chinese economy while learning macroeconomics. And this is a truly "intermediate-level" textbook since it provides a calculus treatment of the standard intermediate macroeconomic theories such as the Solow models, IS-LM models, and so on. Students in many countries need an alternative macroeconomics textbook that is less American-centric than the existing ones. In particular, students in many developing countries need to learn about theories (e.g., the Lewis model of economic development) and cases (the Asian Financial Crisis) that are relevant to developing countries but are ignored in mainstream English textbooks. The use of calculus makes the textbook concise without sacrificing depth. And most importantly, after some training, students would feel comfortable with applying mathematics, the "engine of inquiry," to macroeconomic analysis.

Junhui Qian is Professor of Economics at Antai College of Economics and Management, Shanghai Jiao Tong University, China. He obtained a Ph.D. degree in Economics in 2007 from Rice University. His research areas include econometrics, international finance, and the Chinese economy. He has published academic papers in top international journals such as the *Journal of Econometrics* and co-edited *Financial Systems at the Crossroads: Lessons for China* with Wing T. Woo, Yingli Pan, and Jeffrey D. Sachs. He teaches a wide variety of courses including macroeconomics, econometrics, and the Chinese economy.

Intermediate Macroeconomics with Chinese Perspectives

A Calculus-based Approach

Junhui Qian
Shanghai Jiao Tong University, China

CAMBRIDGE
UNIVERSITY PRESS

Shaftesbury Road, Cambridge CB2 8EA, United Kingdom

One Liberty Plaza, 20th Floor, New York, NY 10006, USA

477 Williamstown Road, Port Melbourne, VIC 3207, Australia

314–321, 3rd Floor, Plot 3, Splendor Forum, Jasola District Centre,
New Delhi – 110025, India

103 Penang Road, #05–06/07, Visioncrest Commercial, Singapore 238467

Cambridge University Press is part of Cambridge University Press & Assessment,
a department of the University of Cambridge.

We share the University's mission to contribute to society through the pursuit of
education, learning and research at the highest international levels of excellence.

www.cambridge.org
Information on this title: www.cambridge.org/9781009193955

DOI: 10.1017/9781009193979

First published 2023

A catalogue record for this publication is available from the British Library.

A Cataloging-in-Publication data record for this book is available from the Library of Congress

ISBN 978-1-009-19395-5 Hardback
ISBN 978-1-009-19396-2 Paperback

Contents

Figures

Tables

Preface

I began teaching intermediate macroeconomics in 2013 at Shanghai Jiao Tong University. Before long, I set about writing lecture notes for my students, in which I used to provide additional case studies about the Chinese economy and discuss models relevant to developing economies like China but ignored in the mainstream Western textbooks. These notes also used a heavier dose of mathematics than other intermediate-level textbooks. They served to make students feel comfortable with applying mathematics, the *engine of inquiry*, to macroeconomic problems. After seven years of accumulation and improvement, these notes have become a book.

Cases in the book are by no means Chinese only. The title of the book may well be intermediate macroeconomics with *global perspectives*. But I am determined to avoid American-centricism when selecting case studies. For example, the 1997–1998 Asian Financial Crisis was a minor shock to the American economy. Consequently, it is rarely covered in mainstream textbooks. But it was a pivotal event for many East Asian countries, including China. Thus this book provides a case study of the crisis following the discussion of the Mundell–Fleming model.

I also take a Chinese or global perspective when I select models to cover in this relatively short book. An important criterion is *relevance* to developing economies, which are in the majority in the world. For example, I provide a detailed account of the Lewis model of economic development since it is relevant to the analysis of industrialization and urbanization of formerly agricultural economies. Indeed, the term *Lewis turning point* frequently appears in the Chinese popular press. And the model is technically tractable, fitting well into an intermediate-level textbook.

I hope that my selection of cases and models will make the book better connected to students in China and other countries in Asia. And I hope a better connection may give students stronger motivation to study macroeconomics. Outside Asia, the book may also help students who want to gain some exposure to the Chinese economy while learning macroeconomics. By some measure (e.g., industrial output), the Chinese economy is already the largest in the world; consequently, economists of the future cannot afford to be ignorant about it.

As the first edition, it almost surely contains errors. Please let me know if you discover any typos or mistakes. Please visit `http://jhqian.org/macrobook` for teaching and learning materials.

1

Introduction

1.1 What Is Macroeconomics About?

In contrast to microeconomics, which studies the behavior of individuals and firms, macroeconomics studies the economy as a whole.

Macroeconomics seeks to understand the causes and consequences of "business cycles" and why some countries achieve long-term economic growth while others do not. A better understanding may lead to better policy making on the part of the government, whether the objective is to promote growth and employment or to smooth business cycles. For market participants, a better understanding of macroeconomics helps to form better expectations on the future evolution of the economy and government policies. Finally, for general citizens, a better understanding of macroeconomics leads to more productive discussions and debates on government policy making.

A better understanding of macroeconomics leads to better management of the economy, which in turn leads to a better economy. A better economy is important not just for the satisfaction of material needs. A stably growing economy leads not only to better living for millions of people, but also to a better society. As Guanzi of ancient China says, "when the granaries are full, the people follow appropriate rules of conduct, and when there is enough to eat and wear, the people know honor and shame."[1] In contrast, recent world history teaches us that economic depressions often breed political radicalism, extremism, and wars, which always make human lives cheap and miserable. In poverty and misery, human morality and dignity are bound to decay, overwhelmed by more basic and urgent human desires such as survival.

The fact that macroeconomics studies the economy as a whole has some important implications. First, macroeconomics must rely on aggregation. We must measure the economy using aggregated variables suc as gross domestic product (GDP), the consumer price index (CPI) and so on. Macroeconomists must also rely on aggregated concepts such as aggregate demand, aggregate supply, and representative firm, among others.

Second, the economic meaning of aggregated variables is not necessarily the same as its microeconomic counterpart. For example, the price of a certain good, in microeconomics, is relative. A rise in the price of a good signals an increased attractiveness of the good relative to other alternatives, holding the supply fixed. But the aggregated price, or the general price level (e.g., CPI), is nothing but an index. A rise in the aggregated price indicates inflation or the loss of purchasing power of money. The absolute value of the aggregated price does not have economic meaning, as it is meaningless to compare different price indices such as CPI and GDP deflator. The price indices contain information in their variations only over time.

As a direct consequence, some familiar laws of microeconomics cannot automatically carry to macroeconomics. For example, the demand curve in microeconomics is almost always downward sloping: Demand increases as the price declines. But in macroeconomics, the aggregate demand does not necessarily increase as the general price level declines. Some classical economists, for example, may argue that the aggregated demand does not depend on the general price level at all since consumers can see through the *veil of money*. Inflation would not fool consumers to buy less, and deflation would not fool them to buy more. Even for those who support the downward-sloping aggregate demand curve, they do not take it for granted. Keynes, for example, would argue that a decline in the price level increases the real money supply, which reduces the real interest rate and stimulates the aggregate demand.

Third, macroeconomic analysis is inherently general-equilibrium analysis since macroeconomic equilibrium, in which the aggregate demand matches the aggregate supply, is necessarily a general equilibrium in all markets. Partial-equilibrium analysis, which is productive in microeconomics, has no place in macroeconomics. The problem of unemployment, for example, cannot be separately analyzed in the labor market, holding other markets (e.g., the goods market) constant. The goods market simply cannot be held constant when the labor market shifts, since the level of employment and wage affects both aggregate demand and supply in the goods market.

Finally, it is often more reasonable to use the behavioral approach in macroeconomic modeling.[2] That is, we do not need to assume that people are rational, having rational expectations and so on. Even when everyone in the economy behaves rationally, as a whole they may exhibit strong irrationality. The history of Wall Street alone offers many such examples. Besides, the economy as a whole has structural constraints that individuals do not have. For example, a rational individual may smooth his consumption to the extent that the variation of current income has a small effect on current consumption. In macroeconomics, however, the current total consumption must depend crucially on the current total income due to the simple fact that consumption expenditure generates income to the sellers of consumption goods.

In the rest of this chapter, we first describe how different types of economies work. Then we describe how, in general terms, economists use models to understand the economy. In the end, we briefly talk about the history of macroeconomic thoughts.

1.2 How Do Economies Work?

The economy is an integrated part of society. It addresses the production and distribution of material goods and services for individuals in society. For an economy to work for society, it must find ways to solve three fundamental problems: (1) What and how many goods and services should be produced? (2) How should resources that are scarce and have alternative uses be used in producing these goods and services? (3) For whom are they produced? The first two problems are related to production, and the third is related to distribution.

There are several conceptual forms of economy, each of which solves the aforementioned problems in distinct ways. The most primitive is the economy of instinct, in which bees and ants, for example, solve these problems by instinct. Early human societies, according to Karl Marx and Friedrich Engels, may solve the problems in the form of primitive communism. As human societies grow and become more complex, the market economy emerges to solve such problems using the "invisible hand" of the market. Finally, in the twentieth century, a group of countries (including China) experimented with the planned economy or command economy, which relied on administrative commands to solve these three problems.

Note that these are very stylized conceptual forms of economy. With the possible exception of the economy of instinct, these forms only exist in theory. Reality is much more complex. In the following, we describe in more detail the market economy and the planned economy. Understanding these two stylized economies helps us understand the mixed economy, which is arguably closer to what we have in reality.

1.2.1 The Market Economy

A market economy relies on voluntary transactions to solve the three fundamental problems. As the demand for some goods and services increases, consumers bid up their prices, which induce suppliers to produce more. To produce more of the demanded goods and services, suppliers bid up prices of required inputs (labor, capital, land, energy, metals, etc.). The increased prices then lead to the reallocation of these resources for production. Workers receive their compensation for the supply of labor, owners of capital get paid for the supply of capital, and owners of the firms claim the residual profit. Capable workers or those with sought-after skills receive more; shrewd or/and lucky capitalists and entrepreneurs survive and become rich. All of them are consumers of goods and services in the economy.

In a market economy, price plays a crucial role. Prices signal the supply and demand condition in the market of consumer goods and services. Prices also signal the relative scarcity of factor inputs (i.e., labor and capital), thus inducing factor suppliers to increase or decrease their supply. Without any coercion, prices direct resources to be used in producing millions of goods and services demanded by millions of consumers with different tastes and preferences.

The market of a market economy, however, cannot function by itself. For the market to work, that is, transactions should be fair (no cheating) and fast (no unbearable delay), there should be strong protection of property rights, efficient enforcement of contracts, efficient means of money settlement, and so on. The government, which provides the legal and monetary infrastructure, is indispensable for the functioning of the market economy.

The government also restricts the domain that the market can operate. Some voluntary transactions should never happen; that is, there are things money should not buy. For example, human beings should not be on sale, child labor should not be employed, and political rights should not be for sale. The ground for such restrictions of the market is moral. There are moral limits on the market.

And the government's role is often much bigger than restricting and safe-guarding voluntary transactions. Due to various reasons (externality, monopoly, information asymmetry, etc.), the "free market" has severe limitations in running the economy. Examples abound: Without government expenditure, the market alone would undersupply public goods (e.g., defense and public security); without government regulation, the market would oversupply public "bads" (e.g., pollution); without antitrust policies, monopolies may emerge and lead to undersupply of goods and services with distortional prices; and without proper regulation of the financial industry, the market may experience violent boom/bust cycles.

Finally, the government has compelling reasons to intervene in income distribution and to conduct welfare policies. For one, the market value of labor can be unfair. For example, the salary of "supermanagers" of big corporations can be hundreds of times of what nurses can earn. Such differences in pay arguably cannot be justified by differences in contributions to society. For another, if the government does not conduct transfer payment (taxing the rich and providing welfare benefits to the poor), the distribution of income and wealth in a free-market economy may be dangerously unequal.

1.2.2 Planned Economy

From 1953 to 1978, China experimented with the planned economy, modeled after the former Soviet Union. Historically speaking, China's adoption of the planned economy was somewhat inevitable. After World War II, there appeared to be a consensus among economists that the planned economy could work. And given the success of the Soviet wartime economy, many even argued that the planned economy was better than the "chaotic" market economy, especially for developing countries. Paul Samuelson, arguably the "foremost academic economist of the 20th century" (*New York Times*), repeatedly wrote in his textbook that the Soviet economy was growing faster than that of the United States.

Given such views by mainstream economists, even if Chinese leaders had turned to the West for ideas, they would still choose a planned economy since China lagged far behind the advanced economies, and the Chinese people were desperate to build a powerful industrialized nation. Of course, Chinese leaders did not really turn to the West for ideas. The apparent success of the Soviet experience was convincing enough. The rest of China's history was a gigantic social and economic experiment, or with the benefit of hindsight, a gigantic gamble.

The new republic soon removed almost all market activities from the economy. The government nationalized private firms and started to direct production according to government plans. Factory managers were more like government officials than business decision makers. In fact, managers had no power to hire or fire workers, no power to select resource inputs, and no power to reward workers. The government determined what and how much goods and services would be produced, what resources would be used in production, and how final goods and services would be distributed.

In the countryside, the government collectivized farms. Farmers were organized into "communes," working for meager pay. Indeed, to support investment in heavy industry, the government suppressed rural demand by setting an exorbitantly low price for farm products. And to prevent farmers from leaving communes for cities, the government established the household registration system. Rural status, under the household registration system, made it impossible for farmers to migrate to the cities. They had to remain in their commune and work on the collective's land. Since farmers no longer claimed the "residual" profit of farming, they did not have any incentive to work hard, let alone invest.

Prices in the planned economy no longer directed resource allocation. They were still in place for the mere purpose of accounting. Prices are highly distortional. Wages were very low, even for industrial workers. Prices of consumer goods were also very low, to the extent that the government had to issue "ration coupons" to regulate sales. Almost every consumer good, from grain to meat to clothes, was on ration. The prices for industrial goods were comparatively high, keeping heavy industry viable.

The gigantic experiment of the economic planning turned out to be a gigantic failure. In particular, the Great Leap Forward, a misguided industrialization campaign, resulted in huge waste in the use of labor and capital, paving the way for a disastrous famine in 1959–1961. Making matters worse, political campaigns and revolutions persisted, disrupting the economy. For nearly thirty years, Chinese people had to live with extreme scarcity of consumer goods. The planned economy failed to make the nation rich. Neither did it industrialize China. By the end of the

1970s, China was still an agricultural economy, and there was a strong consensus for economic reforms. In retrospect, Hayek was right that market activities are essential for aggregating diffuse private knowledge and that the system of market prices is too valuable to dispense with.

From 1978, the Chinese government started to let the market play more and more important roles. The so-called Reform and Open-Up has led to a China Miracle that has transformed a stagnant agricultural economy into a modern industrial economy. As the Chinese economy becomes one of the largest in the world, hundreds of millions of ordinary people have been lifted out of poverty.

1.2.3 Mixed Economy

The current economic model of China can be more precisely described as a mixed economy, where both the market and the government play important roles in solving the fundamental economic problems. It is worth noting that in advanced Western economies, government also plays important roles. It is the author's opinion that China's socialist market economy and Western market economies differ only in degree, not in category.

In a mixed economy, the government typically plays the following roles. First, the government should provide public goods such as national defense and public security, and quasipublic goods such as infrastructure and education. The private sector tends to undersupply public goods because the private cost of supplying public goods exceeds the total benefit to the public.

Second, since the private sector tends to oversupply "public bads" (e.g., pollution), the government is responsible for imposing penalties and costs on the provision of public bads and protecting public interests. A typical example is protection of the environment. The government is responsible for maintaining environmental standards for farming and manufacturing, ensuring sustainable development.

Third, the government is responsible for promoting economic growth. The government may invest in infrastructure, public education, scientific research, and so on. In China, local governments often actively attract private investment from other regions or countries, which stimulates the growth of the local economy. They may offer lower taxes and land fees and even facilitate bank lending for firms.

Fourth, to alleviate income inequality, or as social insurance, the government may make transfer payments to the disadvantaged groups such as the elderly, the unemployed, and so on. To balance regional differences in the public-good provision, the central government may make transfer payments to less-developed provinces and cities.

Fifth, the government is responsible for regulating financial institutions (e.g., banks, security firms, insurance companies, and others), fighting against financial crime, and protecting retail savers and investors from misinformation and fraud.

Sixth, the government also implements macroprudential measures to reduce "systemic risk" in the financial system. Unchecked "animal spirits" in the financial industry may easily lead to excessive leverage, bubbles, and financial crises. In a modern economy, a healthy financial industry is indispensable for the provision of financing and risk-sharing products for firms and households. Financial crises, with widespread failure of financial institutions, almost always lead to economic crises.

Seventh, the government is responsible for conducting fiscal and monetary policies. Even with a robust financial sector, economic cycles are inevitable. Fiscal and monetary policies, if rightly conducted, can take the steam out of an overheating economy and give a backstop to an economy in freefall.

Finally, the government may also directly own and manage state-owned enterprises (SOEs). China's central and local governments control a large number of SOEs, a legacy of the era of the planned economy. Since the 1980s, China has been continuously reforming its state sector.

1.3   Macroeconomic Modeling

We "know" the economy as a whole through macroeconomic variables (GDP, inflation, etc.), which are measurements of the economy from different dimensions or perspectives. We "understand" the economy using models that define functional relationships between macroeconomic variables. Key macroeconomic variables include GDP, (un)employment, inflation, interest rates, exchange rates, and so on.

There are two sets of variables in any model: endogenous variables and exogenous variables. Endogenous variables are variables whose values are determined within the model, while exogenous variables are those whose values are given outside the model, say, by the experimenter. Figure 1.1 graphically illustrates a macroeconomic model, with investment and inflation as endogenous variables and money supply as an exogenous variable.

A macroeconomic model is a toy economy with which we can do virtual experiments. A typical virtual experiment goes like this: If we change the money supply (Figure 1.1), how do endogenous variables (investment and inflation) change?

The macroeconomic model is most often expressed in a set of equations involving both endogenous and exogenous variables. Solving the model is nothing but solving the set of equations, that is, representing endogenous variables with exogenous variables. Mathematically speaking, endogenous variables are unknowns, and exogenous variables are considered known.

A typical modeling exercise starts from some puzzle, a phenomenon that cannot be (adequately) explained by old models. For example, the occurrence of the Great

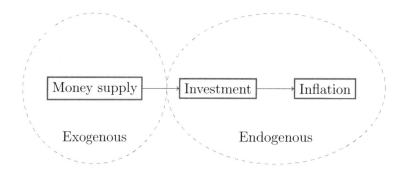

Figure 1.1 A graphic illustration of a macroeconomic model.

Depression, which is impossible in classical models, prompted John Maynard Keynes to propose his revolutionary theory.

A model succeeds when the virtual experiments on the model yield predictions that are consistent with data. In this way, the model can "explain" changes in some endogenous variable with changes in exogenous variables. In other words, the model characterizes *a* causal relationship between endogenous and exogenous variables.

For example, suppose that we observe a positive correlation between money supply and inflation. The correlation does not tell us anything about whether the money supply causes inflation. It may be that a third variable causes both unemployment and inflation, making them correlated. Now we construct a model that involves both money supply and inflation, treating the former as exogenous and the latter as endogenous to the model, as in Figure 1.1. With this model, we can perform virtual experiments. Specifically, we increase the money supply and see what happens to inflation. If inflation increases as well (consistent with data), then we say that the model characterizes a causal relationship between money supply and inflation. In fact, the model in Figure 1.1 provides a mechanism of how changes in money supply lead to changes in inflation: An increase in money supply leads to more investment, which in turn drives up inflation. In short, this model offers an economic explanation of inflation.

Of course, we should also perform other experiments on the model. For example, we might investigate how investment and inflation relate to each other when money supply behaves as the data. If the additional prediction is not consistent with data, we would have less confidence in the model. In such a case, we set out to improve the model in some way or propose a new model. If the additional prediction is also consistent with data, we would be more confident in the model.

There is a crucial difference between models in economics and those in natural sciences. In the natural sciences, a new model replaces an old one when the former is more general, meaning that the new model can explain facts that the old model cannot explain. In economics, however, new models rarely replace old ones. Instead, they add to the ever-richer set of models, each of which may give us insights in some particular settings. Economics is an arsenal of models.

Often it is a challenge to select one of the models available for analyzing a particular problem. It takes science to propose and evaluate models, but it takes art to choose an appropriate model in a particular setting. The default answer to an economic question should be: It depends. There is no definite answer since the setting where an economic question arises is almost always complex, so much so that there is uncertainty whether a model's assumptions would hold. It is thus important to have observations that are as accurate and complete as possible. And it is important to be humble.

1.4   A Brief History of Macroeconomics

Macroeconomics was born in the ruins of the Great Depression, at a time when classical economics failed to recommend any policy responses to the widespread misery even in advanced countries. John Maynard Keynes, in his magnum opus *General Theory of Employment, Interest and Money*, offered a theory that explained why the Great Depression could occur and what governments could do. Keynes challenged many classical assumptions, such as flexibility of price and rationality of individuals. He started to look at the economy as a whole and, thus, introduced many important macroeconomic concepts such as the aggregate demand, aggregate supply, marginal propensity to consume, multipliers, and so on. Only after the Keynesian revolution did economists find it necessary to have a separate discipline within economics – macroeconomics – different from microeconomics, which mainly deals with individual behavior.[3]

Before Keynes, there were already discussions of problems that we call macroeconomic problems. For example, there were many versions of the quantity theory of money, including Irving Fisher's formulation (1867–1947):

$$M \cdot V = P \cdot Y,$$

where M is money supply, V is the velocity of money, P is price, and Y is the real value of aggregate transactions (real GDP). In classical thinking, prices (and wages) are assumed to be flexible, and both V and Y are assumed to be constant. So an increase in money supply (M) would bring a proportional increase in the price level (P). It is in this sense that classical economists regarded money as a "veil" over the real economy: Money is exogenously given and does not have any impact on real activities.

For another example, the business cycles were well studied by the Austrian School. The Austrian theory of business cycles regards bank credit as the key to understanding economic fluctuations. The Austrians argued that the prevailing interest rates were too low, for which the central bank was to blame. The low level of interest rate encouraged businesses to take loans and overinvest in capital goods, resulting in booms and busts.

Keynes was an original thinker and wrote in his own unique style, making his *General Theory* difficult to read, even for professional economists. This opens the way for different interpretations of *General Theory*. The neoclassical Keynesians, notably John R. Hicks (1904–1989) and Paul A. Samuelson (1915–2009), offered an interpretation that soon dominated the academic and policy circles. They combined Keynes's macroeconomics with neoclassical economics and produced the so-called "neoclassical synthesis." In addition, Samuelson was instrumental for establishing a new pattern for economic teaching and research: economic theories expressed in formal, mathematical models.

At the same time, large-scale econometric models were developed for macro-economic forecasts and policy evaluations. These models may employ hundreds of regression equations. An important one of these is the Phillips curve, named after A.W.H. Phillips, who found an inverse relationship between wage inflation and unemployment. The Phillips curve gave support to policies that combat unemployment by creating inflation using fiscal and monetary policies.

This doctrine was then challenged by monetarism, which was championed by Milton Friedman. Friedman argued that there would be no long-run trade-off between inflation and unemployment since people would expect inflation following stimulus measures. In contradiction to his contemporary Keynesians, Friedman argued that monetary policy mattered and that fiscal policy might fail. During the great inflation era of the 1970s, monetarism was successful in explaining why inflation happened with a persistently high unemployment rate. A famous doctrine of monetarism is "inflation is always and everywhere a monetary phenomenon."

New classical economists, notably Robert Lucas, further challenged the Keynesians on the methodological front. The new classicals emphasized the "microeconomic foundation" of macroeconomics. They built models of representative rational agent with "rational expectations." Large-scale econometric models were discredited since the empirical relationship (reduced model) might break down when the underlying structural model changes (Lucas's critique). Moreover, Edward C. Prescott and Finn E. Kydland propose the real business cycle (RBC) theory, which argued that business cycles might be efficient responses to exogenous shocks. The model that the RBC theorists employed, the dynamic stochastic general equilibrium (DSGE) model, soon became the dominant framework of macroeconomic modeling in academia.

Monetarism, new classical, and RBC all shared the same view that the market economy was inherently self-correcting and that government interventions (aggregate demand management) were at least unnecessary, if not harmful. Keynesianism, in contrast, held that the market economy was inherently unstable and that aggregate-demand management would help to stabilize the unstable economy.

Despite the attacks by monetarists, new classicals, and RBC theorists, Keynesianism is still well alive today. On the one hand, some new Keynesians investigate how market imperfections occur, e.g., sticky-price, asymmetric information, and so on. These imperfections lay the "microeconomic foundation" that makes the economy unstable. On the other hand, the Global Financial Crisis (GFC) has dealt a blow to the notion of self-correcting market forces. After GFC, indeed, post-Keynesian economists such as Hyman Minsky received widespread recognition on their analysis of recurring financial crises.

1.5 Concluding Remarks

Macroeconomics is the study of the economy as a whole. The Chinese economy is a mixed economy, where both the market and government play important roles. To explain macroeconomic phenomena, economists rely on models that define functional relationships between endogenous and exogenous variables.

A model is, in a sense, always wrong, since it is necessarily an abstraction from reality. It is valuable as long as it sheds light on one or two questions. As we can see in the previous section, there are many schools of thought in the evolution of macroeconomics. Different schools differ in the modeling assumptions, sometimes not easily verifiable, about the world. In which school should we believe? The obvious answer should be none. We may have a prior opinion, but we should not religiously believe in any "ism." We should confront theory with facts and tests, and even when we settle on a seemingly satisfactory model, we should use it cautiously. In macroeconomics, as in other sciences, there is no absolute, unchanging truth, but tentative and temporary understanding. Research improves such understanding in a dynamic and evolutionary manner.

Notes

[1] 管子：仓廪实则知礼节，衣食足则知荣辱。

[2] George A. Akerlof once said, "If there is any subject in economics which should be behavioral, it is macroeconomics." In *Behavioral Macroeconomics and Macroeconomic Behavior*, by George A. Akerlof, a lecture delivered in Stockholm, Sweden, on December 8, 2001, when Akerlof received the Bank of Sweden Prize in Economic Sciences in Memory of Alfred Nobel.

[3] Although Ragnar Frisch (1895–1973), a Norwegian economist, invented the terms "macroeconomics" as well as "microeconomics" as early as in 1933, the category of macroeconomics entered the consciousness of economists as a result of the publication of Keynes's *General Theory of Employment Interest and Money* in 1936.

2

Macroeconomic Data

Seek truth from facts. – a Chinese idiom [1]

2.1 Introduction

We know about our economy through the measurement of some key macroeconomic variables such as the gross domestic product (GDP), consumer price index (CPI), unemployment rate, and so on. Each of these variables measures one dimension of the economy. For example, GDP measures the total size of the economy, CPI measures the overall price level, and the unemployment rate measures the extent of labor utilization.

On each dimension of our economy, there may be more than one relevant variable. For example, the gross national income (GNI) is also a good measurement of the total size of the economy. Often these variables complement each other in describing a certain dimension of the economy. For example, GDP emphasizes geographic boundaries of output, while GNI emphasizes national claim of income. Looking at both GDP and GNI may give us a clearer picture of the size of the economy.

To each variable, there is also a time dimension. So macroeconomic data are invariably a time series, or "realizations" of stochastic processes. The variation of a macroeconomic variable on the time dimension characterizes the dynamics of the economy. For example, the percentage change in GDP characterizes the speed at which the economy grows in size. For another example, the percentage change in CPI characterizes inflation or the speed at which money loses purchasing power.

Macroeconomic data are often systematically collected and compiled by national statistical bureaus, central banks, and other government agencies. In particular, GDP is a direct product of national income accounting, which is to measure the economic activity of a nation using a consistent system of accounting techniques.

From 1952 to 1992, China used the Material Product System (MPS), which was the prevalent system in socialist countries back then. In 1992, China formally adopted the System of National Accounting (SNA), which was the system used in Western countries. There are two major differences between MPS and SNA. First, as the name suggests, MPS counts only goods, exclusive of service. Second, SNA uses market prices in the valuation of goods and services, while MPS has to rely on administered prices.

Macroeconomic data can be very general in scope. Any data that help us gauge the state of the economy can be called macroeconomic data. In addition to data from government agencies, macroeconomic data can also include market quotes for interest rates, exchange rates, and so on. Indexes that are based on surveys, such as purchasing managers' indexes (PMI), are also macroeconomic data. It is also well known that output data from key industries can be reliable indicators of the state of the economy. For example, in China, the electricity consumption, volume of rail cargo, and total bank loans are all valuable indicators of the economy.

In this chapter, we focus on the principles and rules for computing four of the most important macroeconomic variables: GDP, CPI, unemployment rate, and money supply.

2.2   National Income Accounting

National income accounting is a set of principles and procedures for the measurement of total income and output in an economy. GDP and its components are arguably the most important statistics in national income accounting. The national income accounting also produces flow-of-funds and balance-of-payments tables. Here we focus on GDP and its components.

2.2.1   Nominal GDP

GDP is a measure of the size of the economy. There are three ways to view and calculate GDP:

(i) The production view: the total market value of final goods and services produced in the economy

(ii) The income view: the total income generated from all transactions involving final goods and services produced in the economy

(iii) The expenditure view: the total expenditure on the economy's output of final goods and services

Note that, in theory, GDP calculated from each of the preceding views (namely, production-based GDP, income-based GDP, and expenditure-based GDP) should be equal to each other. In practice, however, they are different from each other since they use different data sources and statistical procedures. Their differences are called *statistical discrepancies*.[2] Generally speaking, GDP based on production and expenditure is more reliable and timely.

Using the production approach, we formally define (nominal) GDP as the market value of all final goods and services produced within an economy in a given period (e.g., a quarter). Mathematically, we have

$$\text{GDP}_t = \sum_{i=1}^{M} q_{it} p_{it}, \qquad (2.1)$$

where q_{it} and p_{it} are quantity and price, respectively, of the ith item produced in period t. Note that p_{it} in (2.1) are current prices that change with time. We call the GDP calculated as in (2.1) the "nominal GDP," in contrast to the "real GDP" that we will introduce later.

Example: An Economy of Two Trees

Consider an economy of two trees, an apple and an orange tree. If the apple tree produces 20 apples and the orange tree produces 10 oranges in 2020, with their market prices 0.5 and 1.0 CNY (Chinese Yuan[3]), respectively, then the GDP of the twin-tree economy is

$$20 \times 0.5 + 10 \times 1.0 = 20 \text{ CNY}.$$

Note that (2.1) only counts final goods and services. Intermediate goods, which are parts of final goods, are not individually counted, to avoid double accounting. It is clear that

$$
\begin{aligned}
\text{GDP} \;&=\; \text{value of final goods and services produced} \\
&=\; \text{sum of value added at all stages of production.}
\end{aligned}
$$

To avoid repeated accounting, transactions of used goods are also not counted in GDP, and sales of goods in inventory do not add to GDP. To understand the latter point, suppose that Shanghai Motors produces a car in China but does not manage to sell it this year. Instead, Shanghai Motors puts the car into inventory and plans to sell it next year. The national accounting considers the unsold car as an "investment" in this year. When Shanghai Motors sells the car next year, the sale will not add to next year's GDP.

Note also that in computing GDP, we use market prices, when available, to calculate the value of goods and services. When market prices are not available, we use imputed prices, which are estimates of market prices. For example, to calculate the value of housing service, it is common to impute the rent people have to pay to their landlords, who may be themselves if they own their homes. The calculation of the value of government services, such as law enforcement and firefighting, also requires imputation. Typically, the national accounts value these government services in GDP by the wages paid to the public servants.

What GDP Does Not Include

One may argue that "services" of durable goods, such as cars and refrigerators, should also be valued in GDP, but these are omitted for convenience. There are also good reasons to include the value of domestic work performed by housewives and househusbands, such as cooking and washing, into GDP. Typically, however, these are also omitted in practice.

GDP calculation also omits goods and services in the underground economy. The underground economic activity can be substantial. People have incentives to "hide" transactions either because these transactions are illegal or for tax-avoidance purposes. Illegal transactions include illegal drug trade, human trafficking, and so on. For minor services such as housekeeping, the tax administration has little incentive to enforce taxation.

As can be seen, GDP is an inaccurate measure of the size of the economy. Besides, although the general framework for GDP computation is the same across countries, substantial differences exist in detail. As a consequence, comparing GDP across countries can be misleading. However, if the rules of calculation do not change over time, comparisons along the time dimension are meaningful.

2.2.2   Real GDP

Recall that in (2.1), we calculate GDP using current prices and obtain a nominal GDP. The nominal GDP changes over time because either there are changes in the amount (real value) of goods and services or there are changes in the prices of those goods and services.

In contrast, real GDP (or constant-price GDP) measures the value of final goods and services at constant prices,

$$\text{RGDP}_t = \sum_{i=1}^{M} q_{it} p_{i,t_0}, \tag{2.2}$$

where t_0 stands for the *base year* and p_{i,t_0} is constant over time for each i. Taking real measurements is essential for gauging the growth or improvement in living quality (e.g., real wage). And using nominal and real GDP, we can define the GDP deflator (or implicit price deflator for GDP) as follows: $P_t \equiv \text{GDP}_t / \text{RGDP}_t$. As we will see later in the chapter, the GDP deflator is a measure of the general price level.

One principle of calculating real GDP is that the base year should not be too distant, ensuring that prices are not too out of date. For example, the cell phone

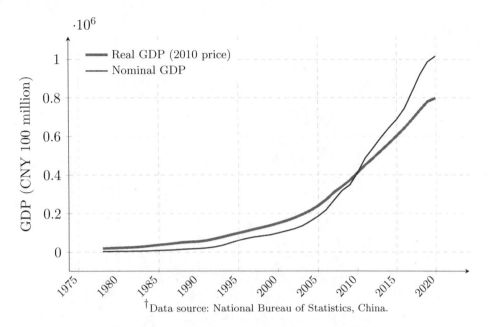

Figure 2.1 China's real and nominal GDP.

was a rare product 30 years ago and was very expensive. It would be absurd to use the price of cell phones 30 years ago to calculate the value of cell-phone output in today's GDP. In China, the National Bureau of Statistics changes the base year every five years for the calculation of real GDP.

Since 1995, the USA has been using chain-weighted measures of real GDP growth. For each year, the chain-weighted GDP growth rate is the average of two real GDP growth rates. For example, in 2020, there are two real GDP growth rates: the growth rate using 2019 prices and the growth rate using 2020 prices.

Figure 2.1 shows the real and nominal GDP of China from 1978 to 2020. Since the base year of real GDP is 2010, the lines of real and nominal GDPs cross in the year 2010. We can see in the graph that China experiences rapid growth during the over 30-year period. The growth of nominal GDP is, of course, higher than that of real GDP, reflecting a rising price level. Figure 2.2 shows the quarterly year-over-year (YoY) growth rate of real GDP from 1992 to 2020. GDP is typically reported every quarter. The quarterly YoY growth rate is calculated as

$$R_t = \log\left(\frac{\text{RGDP}_t}{\text{RGDP}_{t-4}}\right),$$

where t denotes a quarter. The YoY growth rate naturally filters out seasonality.

Table 2.1 shows the GDP and GDP per capita of the largest 10 economies in the world. Note that although China has become the second largest economy, it still lags far behind high-income countries such as the USA and Japan in terms of GDP per capita. And note that GDP per capita is a measure of average income (since GDP is total income) or the standard of living for average citizens.

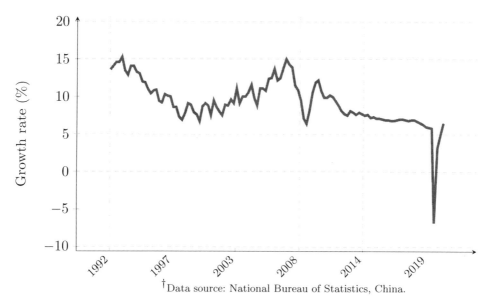

†Data source: National Bureau of Statistics, China.

Figure 2.2 Real GDP growth of China (quarterly).

2.2.3   Components of GDP

From the expenditure view, we may roughly decompose GDP into four components: consumption (C), investment (I), government spending (G), and net export (X). Let Y denote GDP. By definition we have

$$Y = C + I + G + X. \qquad (2.3)$$

We call this equation the national income accounts identity.

Consumption Expenditure (C)

The consumption component measures the value of all goods and services bought by households. It includes the value of durable goods, nondurable goods, and service. Durable goods are those that last a long time, such as cars, refrigerators, and so on. Nondurable goods last a relatively short time, e.g., food and clothing. Service refers to the work done for consumers by individuals and firms, such as housing, dry cleaning, air travel, and so on.

Investment Expenditure (I)

The investment component measures the value of total spending on goods bought for future use. There are two types of investment: one is the fixed investment, which adds to the capital stock; the other is inventory investment, which adds to the inventory.

Table 2.1 The 10 largest economies in 2020.

Country	GDP (trillion USD)	GDP per capita (USD)
United States of America	21,040.0	63,000.0
China	14,736.2	10,238.3
Japan	4,985.8	39,420.4
Germany	3,790.2	45,237.9
United Kingdom	2,706.2	39,711.9
India	2,679.6	1,941.7
France	2,605.2	38,564.6
Italy	1,885.2	31,179.9
Canada	1,643.4	43,542.4
Korea, Republic of	1,630.3	31,798.9

[†]Data source: United Nations Conference of Trade and Development (UNCTAD) Statistics.

The fixed investment conducted by firms is called business fixed investment, which is spending on plants and equipment that firms will use to produce goods and services. The fixed investment conducted by individuals and families is called residential fixed investment, which mainly consists of spending on apartments and houses.

The fixed investment would increase the stock of capital. For firms, capital is one of the most important factors of production. The more capital a firm has, the higher the capacity the firm has for future production. In aggregate, this is also true: The more capital we have in the country, the higher the potential we have for future production and consumption. Capital, however, depreciates. For example, machines wear and break down eventually. So investment in new capital is essential for maintaining and increasing the stock of capital.

For example, suppose that on January 1, 2016, an economy has a capital stock worth 500. During 2016, there is a fixed investment worth 100 with depreciation worth 20. Then at the end of 2016, the economy has a capital stock worth $500 + 100 - 20 = 580$.

Concepts: Stock and Flow

In economics and accounting, it is important to distinguish the *stock* variables and the *flow* variables. The stock variable measures the quantity at particular time points, while the flow variable measures the change in a given period. We also call stock variables *level* variables.

In business accounting, the balance sheet tabulates stock variables such as debt, equity, and so on. And both the income statement and the cash flow statement tabulate flow variables such as revenue, profit, cash inflow, wage layout, and so on.

In national accounting, GDP is a flow variable, since it measures the domestic output in a given period. The unit of annual GDP is Yuan/year. In contrast, the capital stock in a country is a stock variable with the unit Yuan.

We can meaningfully compare a stock variable with another stock variable, and a flow variable with another flow variable. However, it would be meaningless to compare a stock variable with a flow variable, since the stock variable and the flow variable have different units. Nonetheless, it sometimes makes sense to calculate the ratio of a stock variable to a flow variable. For example, we often compare the ratio of total national debt to GDP. Since the unit of the ratio is year, the ratio can be understood as the number of years the country would take to pay off the debt, if all income (GDP) is devoted to debt payoff.

An apartment or house is a special piece of capital. We purchase houses for future consumption of "housing service." Spending on new houses is thus investment, not consumption. The housing service the house provides, however, is consumption. Note that it is not "repeated accounting" that we count both the spending on new houses and rents. All fixed investments are supposed to generate future returns. Business fixed investments generate future profits, and residential fixed investments generate rent incomes.

The inventory investment component measures the change in the value of unsold outputs (if not spoilable, such as vegetables) that are placed into inventory, whether or not the inventory buildup is intentional. Note that when a good in inventory (produced last year) is sold this year, the component of inventory investment declines by the value of the good. At the same time, if the good is purchased by households as consumption, then the consumption component of this year increases by the same amount, so that the sale of the good in inventory does not add to this year's GDP.

And note that inventory investment can be negative, which means that the inventory falls over the year. For example, if the inventory is worth 12 billion CNY

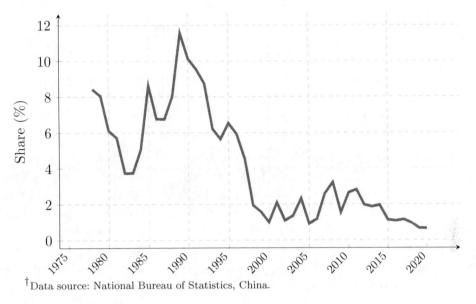

† Data source: National Bureau of Statistics, China.

Figure 2.3 Share of inventory investment in GDP.

at the beginning of the year, and 10 billion CNY at the end, then the inventory investment equals −2 billion CNY for the year.

Figure 2.3 shows the ratio of inventory investment to GDP in China. In the 1980s and the early 1990s, the share of inventory investment was high, implying that a substantial amount of factory output ended up unsold. We may understand this phenomenon by noting that China was in transition from a planned economy to a market economy in the 1980s and 1990s. In the 1980s and the early 1990s, the economy was still dominated by state-owned enterprises (SOEs), which would produce to fulfill "plans." They were largely guided by the visible hands of the government rather than the invisible hands of the market. As a result, there were big mismatches between production and demand in the economy. In the latter half of the 1990s, however, China made great progress in reforming its SOEs. The government privatized many small SOEs and reformed large SOEs into modern corporations. As a result, the managerial efficiency of corporate China improved dramatically. Even the remaining SOEs started to behave like business enterprises, constantly adjusting production according to market demand. Thus the share of inventory investment in GDP declined sharply to a healthy level.

Government Expenditure (G)

Government expenditure includes all government spending on goods and services. To avoid double accounting, G excludes "transfer payments" such as unemployment insurance payments. Transfer payments are, however, included in "government outlays" in the government budget.

Net Export (X)

Net export (X), or balance of trade, equals the total value of export minus that of import in a given period. Let EX denote the value of export and IM the value of import. Then $X = EX - IM$. Net export represents the net foreign expenditures on goods and services produced in our country. If it is positive, we say that the country has a *trade surplus*. Otherwise, we say that the country has a *trade deficit*.

Generally speaking, a trade surplus implies that the tradable sector of the country is competitive in the world. A moderate trade deficit, however, is not necessarily uncompetitive. The United States, for example, enjoys a special privilege in that other countries want to hold dollar-denominated financial assets. The US treasury bonds, in particular, are the dominant reserve assets held by other central banks. As a result, the USA persistently runs a trade deficit with the rest of the world. However, if the trade deficit becomes excessive and persistent, then some adjustment would have to occur; for example, the exchange rate would tend to depreciate.

A More Detailed Decomposition

Let C^d be the consumption of domestic goods and services, and let C^f be the consumption of imported goods and services. We have $C = C^d + C^f$. Similarly, we define I^d, I^f, G^d, and G^f, and we have $I = I^d + I^f$ and $G = G^d + G^f$. Note that $IM = C^f + I^f + G^f$. Now we have a more detailed decomposition of the total expenditure:

$$\begin{aligned} Y &= C + I + G + (EX - IM) \\ &= (C^d + C^f) + (I^d + I^f) + (G^d + G^f) + EX - (C^f + I^f + G^f). \end{aligned}$$

Note that C, I, and G include the value of both imported and domestically produced goods and services. For example, if I buy an imported car, then this purchase should be included in the calculation of C. However, this purchase does not affect GDP since the calculation of X removes the value of the imported car.

Table 2.2 shows China's decomposition of GDP on the expenditure side in 2020. The share of household consumption in GDP (C/Y) is 37.7% and the share of investment (I/Y) is 43.1%. In comparison, the US consumption and investment shares of 2020 are 67.2% and 17.4%, respectively. To understand the contrast between China and the US, note that it is typical for fast-growing economies to have high share of investment in GDP. But there is a caveat about Chinese investment data. While the investment component commonly refers to investment expenditure by private businesses and households, the investment component in China also includes investment expenditure made by the state sector (the government and the state-owned enterprises). As a result, the metric I/Y tends to make Chinese investment share higher than other countries.

Table 2.2 Expenditure components of China's GDP in 2020 (CNY trillion).

Total expenditure	102.59
Consumption	55.70
Household consumption	38.72
Government consumption	16.98
Investment	44.24
Fixed asset formation	43.57
Inventory investment	0.67
Net export	2.65

†Data source: National Bureau of Statistics, China.

Chinese data may also underestimate the share of consumption. First, the consumption of "housing service" is measured in China by multiplying the building cost by a depreciation rate (2% for urban houses and 3% for rural houses). This method underestimates the consumption of housing since the building cost is sometimes only a fraction of market value. Second, the official statistics do not account for household purchases that are paid for by company accounts and treated as investment.

2.2.4 Income Measures

Gross domestic income (GDI) is an alternative measure of the size of the economy. Since it is obtained by counting the incomes earned and costs incurred in production, we may call it income-based GDP. In theory, GDI should equal GDP, but they usually differ by a small *statistical discrepancy*,

$$\text{GDI} = \text{GDP} - \text{statistical discrepancy}.$$

As an income measure, GDI is not satisfactory because it does not count income earned from employment or investment in foreign countries. A better measure is GNI. The relationship between GNI and GDP is as follows:

$$\text{GNI} = \text{GDP} + \text{net factor payment from abroad}.$$

For large countries with diversified industries, GDP and GNI should be similar. In small countries with one or two dominant industries (e.g., oil), GDP and GNI can differ substantially from each other. Note that GNI is conceptually the same as gross national product (GNP). In international statistics, GNI has gradually replaced GNP.

Another measure of aggregate income is national income (NI), which is defined by

$$\begin{aligned} \text{NI} &= \text{GDI} + \text{net factor payment from abroad} - \text{depreciation} \\ &= \text{GNI} - \text{depreciation} - \text{statistical discrepancy} \end{aligned}$$

Furthermore, personal income is defined as the income received by all individuals or households from all sources (wage, dividend, interest, etc.) in a given period (e.g., a year). Disposable personable income (or simply, disposable income) is defined as the personal income minus personal tax and nontax payments.

2.3 Price and Inflation

In macroeconomics, price is often shorthand for the general price level in an economy. And inflation is a sustained increase in the general price level of goods and services over a time interval, such as a year. In this section, we discuss two popular measures of the general price level, consumer price index (CPI) and GDP deflator.

2.3.1 CPI

CPI is an index that measures the overall level of prices for consumers. A government agency (the National Bureau of Statistics in China, the Bureau of Labor Statistics in the US) first determines a basket of goods and services consumed by a typical or average household. Using the basket, the agency then computes an index,

$$\text{CPI}_t = c_0 \frac{\sum_i q_{i,t_0} p_{it}}{\sum_i q_{i,t_0} p_{i,t_0}}, \tag{2.4}$$

where p_{it} is the price of the ith item at time t, p_{i,t_0} is the price of the ith item at some base time t_0, q_{i,t_0} is the quantity of the ith item in the consumption basket at t_0, and c_0 is a constant. For example, we may choose $c_0 = 100$, implying that the level of CPI at time t_0 is 100.

Note that we may define the weight of expenditure on the ith item in the consumption basket as

$$w_i = \frac{q_{i,t_0} p_{i,t_0}}{\sum_i q_{i,t_0} p_{i,t_0}}.$$

The weight changes as the base year t_0 changes. But we omit the dependence of w_i on t_0 for the simplicity of notation. Then (2.4) can be written as

$$\text{CPI}_t = c_0 \sum_i w_i \frac{p_{it}}{p_{i,t_0}}. \tag{2.5}$$

That is, CPI is a *weighted average* of price ratios.

For example, the twin-tree economy produces and consumes all fruits of the apple tree and the orange tree. The following table shows the quantities and prices of the economy:

Year	Apple		Orange	
	Price	Quantity	Price	Quantity
2016	0.6	25	1.1	15
2015	0.5	20	1	10

Now we calculate the CPI of 2016 using the 2015 prices. That is, we use 2015 as the base year. According to the consumption of 2015, the weights in the consumption basket are as follows:

$$w_{apple} = \frac{0.5 \times 20}{0.5 \times 20 + 1 \times 10} = \frac{1}{2}, \quad w_{orange} = \frac{1 \times 10}{0.5 \times 20 + 1 \times 10} = \frac{1}{2}.$$

If $c_0 = 100$, which means $\text{CPI}_{2015} = 100$, then the CPI for 2016 is

$$\text{CPI}_{2016} = 100 \cdot \left(w_{apple} \cdot \frac{0.6}{0.5} + w_{orange} \cdot \frac{1.1}{1} \right) = 115.$$

Then the inflation in 2016 is $(115/100 - 1) \times 100\% = 15\%$.

The government typically reports inflation data every month. Within each year, inflation may exhibit seasonality. In China, for example, the price level typically reaches the high point during the Spring Festival every year. As a result, seasonal adjustment is often necessary before any analysis of inflation based on CPI.

To deal with the seasonality, China's National Bureau of Statistics (NBS) reports the following monthly CPI:

$$\text{CPI}_t = \sum_i w_i \left(\frac{p_{it}}{p_{i,t-12}} \right) \times 100. \tag{2.6}$$

Here the subscript t represents the month. The preceding statistic assigns 100 to the CPI of the same month in the previous year. It is straightforward to infer from the statistic the YoY inflation rate, the percentage change in CPI compared with the same month last year. If $\text{CPI}_{2020.9} = 103$, then we know that the YoY inflation rate for September 2020 is 3%. The YoY inflation rate does not eradicate the seasonality problem, because the Spring Festival may fall in different months (January or February). Furthermore, it loses information on month-to-month variation in CPI.

The statistics bureau determines the composition of the consumption basket and the weights assigned to each item by conducting household surveys. The composition of the basket has to change over time, as consumer behavior changes over time. For example, as income per capita increases, the proportion of income spent on food would fall (Engel's law). As a result, the share of food in the basket should decrease during economic growth. Even within the category of food, the share of grain would decrease, and that of meat would increase, as people's lives improve.

There are eight major categories of consumption expenditure in China's CPI basket: (1) food and beverages, (2) housing, (3) transportation and communications, (4) educational, cultural, and entertainment goods/services, (5) household goods/services, (6) health care, (7) apparel, and (8) other goods/services. For each of these eight major categories, there is a sub-CPI. From these sub-CPIs and the CPI for the entire basket, we can infer the CPI basket weights (or relative importance) for the eight categories, which China's NBS does not disclose. Table 2.3 shows the

Table 2.3 China's CPI basket weights (estimated, using 2016–2020 data).

Category	Weight (%)
Food and beverages	30.15
Housing	20.57
Transportation and communication	11.81
Educational, cultural, entertainment goods/services	11.36
Household goods/services	10.83
Health care	8.27
Apparel	3.83
Other goods/services	3.18

[†]Source: Author's own calculation.

Table 2.4 The US CPI basket weights (city average, 2017–2018 weights).

Category	Weight (%)
Food and beverages	15.157
Housing	42.385
Transportation	15.16
Recreation	5.797
Education and communication	6.810
Medical care	8.870
Apparel	2.663
Other goods/services	3.158

[†]Data source: U.S. Bureau of Labor Statistics.

estimated basket weights using 2016–2020 data (NBS adjusts weights every five years).

For comparison, Table 2.4 shows the weights for eight major categories of US consumption. It is notable that the US weight for *food and beverages* is much lower than the Chinese counterpart, consistent with what Engel's law predicts.

Why CPI Often Draws Criticism

The fact that a country calculates its CPI using one basket implies that the CPI reflects the price level facing the *average consumer* in the country. For a diverse country such as China or the US, this average consumer is elusive. Naturally, many people would feel that the CPI gives a biased measure of the living cost. In most cases, since price increases are more infuriating and newsworthy, people would feel that the CPI understates inflation systematically.

There are, however, good reasons to argue that CPI tends to overstate inflation. First, there is the so-called *substitution bias*. Since the CPI uses fixed weights, it cannot reflect consumers' ability to substitute with goods whose relative prices have fallen. In other words, when one item in the consumption basket becomes more expensive, the weight of this item should decrease. But the CPI calculation ignores this possibility.

Second, the introduction of new goods makes consumers better off and, in effect, increases the value of the money. But this does not reduce the CPI, also due to the fixed weights.

Third, quality improvements increase the value of the money, but they are also conveniently ignored.

Core CPI

A special and important sub-CPI is called *core* CPI, which is a price index for a consumer basket that excludes food and energy. The inflation of the core CPI is called *core inflation*. The rationale for using core inflation is that inflation is supposed to be *sustained* increase in the price level. But food and energy prices are largely dependent on some key commodities (corn, oil, etc.), the price of which may be volatile and transitory. Core inflation has become the preferred measure of inflation by major central banks. China's NBS does not report core inflation.

The US Federal Reserve prefers to use core personal consumption expenditures (PCE) price index. There are two main differences between the PCE price index and CPI. First, the CPI weight is based on a survey of what households are buying, while the PCE is based on surveys of what businesses are selling. For example, medical services paid for by employer-provided insurance are in PCE but not CPI. Second, the PCE attempts to account for substitution effects. When one good becomes more expensive and consumers buy less, its weight in PCE may decline, while the CPI weights remain fixed. As a result, the PCE inflation is in general lower than the CPI inflation. The core PCE, like core CPI, strips out food and energy components in the PCE basket.

2.3.2 GDP Deflator

There is another statistic that can be used to measure inflation, the GDP deflator. Recall that we define GDP deflator by

$$P_t = \frac{Y_t}{y_t} = \frac{\sum_i q_{it} p_{it}}{\sum_i q_{it} p_{i,t_0}}, \tag{2.7}$$

where Y_t is the nominal GDP and y_t is the real GDP with base year t_0. If we define

$$w_{it} = \frac{q_{it} p_{i,t_0}}{\sum_i q_{it} p_{i,t_0}},$$

then we obtain

$$P_t = \sum_i w_{it} \cdot \left(\frac{p_{it}}{p_{i,t_0}} \right),$$

which is also a weighted average of price ratios just like CPI.

However, there are three major differences between CPI and the GDP deflator. First, the baskets of goods and services are different. The basket for the GDP deflator contains all final goods and services produced domestically. The weight of each item is proportional to the total output of each item. But the CPI basket contains only those goods and services consumed by an "average consumer." The weight of each item is proportional to the consumption of the item by the average consumer. For example, an increase in the price of goods bought only by firms or the government will show up in the GDP deflator, but not in the CPI. For another example, imported consumer goods are not a part of GDP and therefore don't show up in the GDP deflator, but they are in the CPI basket. Second, the GDP deflator is available at the frequency as GDP, which is typically quarterly data, but CPI is typically monthly data. Third, the weight for the GDP deflator changes every quarter since the composition of output changes every time, while that for CPI changes much more slowly (roughly every five years in China).

Given a measure of the general price level, say P_t, we may calculate inflation by taking percentage change of P_t,

$$\pi_t = \frac{P_t - P_{t-1}}{P_{t-1}} = \frac{P_t}{P_{t-1}} - 1.$$

Or, we may take logarithm difference of P_t,

$$\pi'_t = \log\left(P_t / P_{t-1} \right),$$

where $\log(\cdot)$ is natural logarithm. Note that π is an approximation of π'_t since

$$\log\left(P_t / P_{t-1} \right) = \log\left(1 + \frac{P_t - P_{t-1}}{P_{t-1}} \right) \approx \frac{P_t - P_{t-1}}{P_{t-1}}.$$

Figure 2.4 shows the annual inflation in CPI and the GDP deflator. From 1979 to 2020, there are about eight cycles of inflation. The four inflation cycles before the mid-1990s are more volatile, while those after the mid-1990s are moderate. While CPI inflation and GDP deflator inflation generally move together in each cycle, there are substantial quantitative differences.

2.3.3   PPI

The producer price index (PPI) measures the (weighted) average changes of the prices received by domestic producers. In contrast to CPI, the PPI basket generally does not have full coverage of services. In China, the PPI basket includes industrial

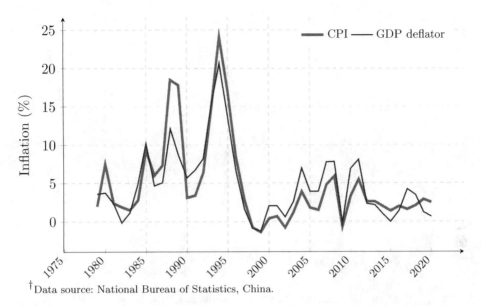

Figure 2.4 China's annual inflation in CPI and the GDP deflator.

goods only. The full name of China's PPI is the Producer Price Index for Industrial Products. Additional to the treatment of services, there are also several other major differences between PPI and CPI. First, the CPI basket includes imports, while the PPI basket does not (similar to the GDP deflator). Second, the PPI basket includes exports, while the CPI basket does not. Third, the PPI basket includes government purchases, while the CPI basket does not. Fourth, the PPI basket includes intermediate inputs to production, including fixed-asset investment, while the CPI basket does not. Finally, similar to the GDP deflator, the PPI weights change every month.

PPI is available at a monthly frequency. Because many industrial goods are inputs to the production of consumption goods, PPI is widely believed to be a leading indicator for CPI. In practice, however, this lead–lag relationship is not entirely obvious. And thanks to the differences in the coverage of goods and services, PPI and CPI can sometimes diverge (Figure 2.5).

2.4 Employment

In macroeconomics, employment is shorthand for total employment, which is the number of employees in the economy. The measure of employment typically excludes business owners, household employees, unpaid volunteers, and the unincorporated self-employed. Total employment is a measure of the utilization of human resources.

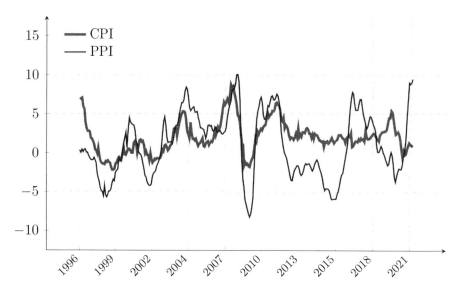

Figure 2.5 China's monthly inflation in CPI and PPI.

†Data source: National Bureau of Statistics, China.

2.4.1 Nonfarm Employment

Sometimes it is helpful to focus on nonfarm employment, the measure of employment that excludes farmers and farm employees. Changes in nonfarm employment give us valuable information on business cycles. For example, the monthly total nonfarm employment data of the US is a popular indicator of the US business cycles. The Automatic Data Processing (ADP) national employment report of the US, which tracks the US nonfarm private-sector employment, is also closely scrutinized by the capital market.

For developing countries such as China, changes in the share of nonfarm employment in total employment also reflect the pace of economic development. Economic development is almost synonymous with industrialization. As an agricultural economy develops, more and more people would leave the agricultural sector for the industrial or service sector. Consequently, the share of nonfarm employment may exhibit a secular upward trend, as we can see in Chinese data since the 1970s (Figure 2.6).

2.4.2 Unemployment Rate

We may define unemployment as the situation of someone above a specified age (say, fifteen) who wants to work but cannot find a job. If someone neither has a job nor is looking for one, then that person is not considered unemployed. Instead, we say that the individual has withdrawn from the labor force. We define the unemployment rate as the percentage of the labor force that is unemployed:

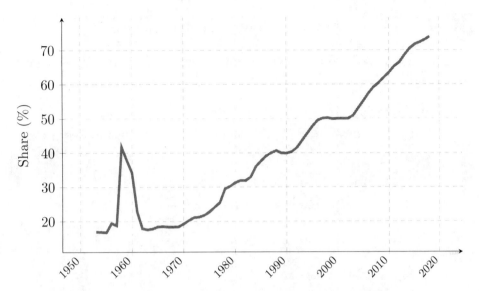

Figure 2.6 Share of nonfarm employment in China.

[†]Data source: National Bureau of Statistics, China.

$$\text{Unemployment rate} = \frac{\text{Number of the unemployed}}{\text{Labor force}}, \qquad (2.8)$$

where the *labor force* is the sum of the employed and the unemployed. The unemployment rate is a measure of how difficult it is to find a job. It is also a measure of how *tight* the labor market is. A high unemployment rate means that it is difficult for an unemployed worker to find a job. But it also means that it is easy for employers to find workers.

In China, there are two unemployment statistics. One is called the registered urban unemployment rate,[4] the other is the surveyed urban unemployment rate.[5] The former is known to be prone to underreport the unemployment rate, reflecting the fact that the unemployment insurance program is underdeveloped in China. The latter, which is based on monthly surveys, is more promising. But it is available only from 2018.

2.4.3 Labor-Force Participation Rate

A related ratio is the labor-force participation (LFP) rate, which is the percentage of the adult population who are in the labor force:

$$\text{Labor force participation rate} = \frac{\text{Labor force}}{\text{Adult population}}. \qquad (2.9)$$

China's Population and Labor Statistics

In 2019, China's population and labor statistics are as follows (unit: million):

$$1410.1 \text{ (population)} = 236.6 \text{ (children, age 0–14)} + 1173.5 \text{ (adults)}$$
$$811.0 \text{ (labor force)} = 774.7 \text{ (employed)} + 36.3 \text{ (unemployed)}$$

Then,

$$\text{Unemployment rate} = \frac{36.3}{811.0} = 4.5\%$$
$$\text{Labor-force participation rate} = \frac{811.0}{1173.5} = 69.1\%$$

[†]Data source: National Bureau of Statistics, China.

2.5   Money Supply

Traditionally, money includes physical cash (cash in short), central bank reserves (reserves in short), and bank deposits. Reserves are a central bank's liabilities held only by commerical banks. And bank deposits are commercial banks' liabilities held by individual or corporate savers. The supply of cash and reserves is controlled by the monetary authority (the central bank), which also records and publishes money supply data.

Different types of money differ mainly in liquidity. Cash is the most liquid money, while time deposits (or term deposits) are much less liquid. The fact that there are different types of money poses a problem for the measurement of the total money supply in the economy. Central banks use several measures (M0, M1, M2, etc.), classified from the narrowest to the broadest measurements. Narrow measures include the most liquid types of money, while broad measures include illiquid money.

Typically, the definitions of narrow money supply are similar in different countries. For example, M0 typically measures all physical currency. For another example, the base money (MB) is the value of all physical currency plus reserves (including required reserve and excess reserve). However, each central bank may use different names. For example, the Bank of England's "narrow money (M0)" roughly corresponds to MB in the US and China.

However, the definitions of broad money may differ substantially in each country. We can see this in Table 2.5, which tabulates the definitions of M0, M1, and M2 in the US and China. As a result of different definitions, it may be misleading to compare the supply of broad money across countries.

Table 2.5 The definitions of money supply and data (December 2020).

	China	US
M0	Physical currency (9.3 trillion CNY)	Physical currency (2.0 trillion USD)
M1	M0 + demand deposits (54.6 trillion CNY)	M0 + demand deposits + travelers checks + Other checkable deposits (17.8 trillion USD)
M2	M1 + saving deposits (202.3 trillion CNY)	M1 + Saving deposits (including money market deposits) + retail money market mutual fund balances + small time deposits (19.3 trillion USD)

[†]Data source: Wind Data Service (WIND).

2.6 Concluding Remarks

Macroeconomic data are important for the functioning of an economy. First, the availability of high-quality data helps firms and individuals to make decisions with more confidence. Among all decisions, the decision to invest is particularly fragile. It takes great courage to overcome the "fear of unknown" to invest. High-quality data, however, help investors to evaluate risk and reduce overall uncertainty in the economy.

Second, high-quality data are a necessary condition for successful policy making. Without high-quality data, it is impossible for policy makers to identify adverse trends in a timely manner and take appropriate measures. The effectiveness of macroeconomic management itself is an important piece of data for investors. The lack of high-quality data is an indicator for poor economic management, which discourages investment, especially foreign direct investment (FDI).

Third, high-quality data attract high-quality research. Effective policy making relies on the understanding of an economy, which further relies on economic research. High-quality data not only help *in-house* research in the central bank or other government agencies but also attract academic economists around the world to study the economy. The US, for example, receives dividends for its high-quality economic data.

For serious students of macroeconomics, familiarity with data is a prerequisite for understanding the economy. Keynes once said, "Good economists are scarce because the gift for using 'vigilant observation' to choose good models, although it does not require a highly specialized intellectual technique, appears to be a very rare one." The "vigilant observation" obviously refers to the familiarity with data.

Exercises

(1) Categorize each of the following transactions into one of four components of GDP of China: (household) consumption, investment, government consumption, and net export.

(a) Huawei sells a computer to the army.

(b) Huawei sells a computer to Taobao.

(c) Huawei sells a computer to a Chinese resident in Shanghai.

(d) Huawei sells a computer to a local government in Japan.

(e) Huawei produces a computer but fails to sell it this year (perhaps it can sell it next year).

(2) A farmer grows a ton of wheat and sells it to a miller for 500 CNY. The miller uses the wheat (the only input) to produce flour and sells the flour to a baker for 1,000 CNY. The baker uses the flour to make bread. Consumers buy this bread for 3,000 CNY.

(a) What is the value-added in each stage of the production of bread?

(b) If the farmer, miller, baker, and the consumers constitute an economy, what is the GDP for this economy?

(3) Find Chinese GDP data and list the shares of consumption, investment, government consumption, and net export in 1980, 1995, and 2010. (Note: Data are available at www.stats.gov.cn.)

(4) In the twin-tree economy, the production and consumption of apples and oranges are as follows:

Year	Apple Production	Apple Consumption	Orange Production	Orange Consumption
2016	25	20	15	12
2015	15	10	10	8

Note that the differences between "Production" and "Consumption" are exported. And the market prices for apples and oranges are as follows:

Year	Apple	Orange
2016	6	3
2015	5	2

(a) Compute the nominal GDP of the twin-tree economy for both 2015 and 2016.

(b) Compute the real GDP of 2016 using the 2015 price.

(c) Compute the CPI for 2016 using 2015 as the base year. (Let the CPI of 2015 be 100.)

(d) Compute the GDP deflator for 2016, using the 2015 price. (Let the GDP Deflator of 2015 be 100.)

(e) Compute the GDP deflator for 2015, using the 2016 price. (Let the GDP Deflator of 2016 be 100.)

(5) Find the nominal and real GDP of China, then calculate and plot the annual GDP deflator from 1978 to 2016. Compare the inflations of CPI and the GDP deflator.

(6) Suppose that an economy has 100 people, divided into nine groups:

Group	Description	Number of people
1	Have full-time jobs	30
2	Have one part-time job	10
3	Have two part-time jobs	5
4	Would like to work and are looking for jobs	10
5	Would like to work, but have given up looking	5
6	Running their own business	10
7	Retired	15
8	University students	5
9	Small children	10

(a) Compute the labor force and the labor force participation rate.

(b) Compute the unemployment rate.

Notes

[1] 实事求是

[2] In China's Statistical Year Book, GDP calculated from the production view is listed in table 3-1 (Gross Domestic Product, 国内生产总值), GDP calculated from the expenditure view is listed in table 3-11 (Gross Domestic Product by Expenditure Approach, 支出法国内生产总值). The National Bureau of Statistics does not directly report income-based GDP. But there are three ways to calculate it from other data: (i) aggregation of province data; (ii) the nonfinancial flow-of-funds table (非金融资金流量表); and (iii) the input–output table (intermediate use) (投入产出基本流量表, 中间使用部分). The quality of data for the provinces is poor. The quality of the other two is good, but they are available only with a significant delay.

[3] In foreign exchange markets, CNY represents the *onshore* Chinese Yuan, and CNH represents the *offshore* Chinese Yuan, which is traded mostly in Hong Kong and Singapore.

[4] 城镇登记失业率

[5] 城镇调查失业率

3

Classical Theory

3.1 Introduction

In this chapter, we study the economy as a whole under classical assumptions. Classical assumptions include the following: (1) people are individually rational, meaning that consumers maximize utilities and firms maximize profits; (2) prices (including wages and interest rates) are flexible, so that markets always clear; (3) markets for final goods/services and factor inputs are competitive; (4) and people have access to perfect information.

Under classical assumptions, the aggregate supply (AS) curve would be vertical since changes in the general price level cannot fool entrepreneurs to increase or cut output. Furthermore, competition between entrepreneurs will always push production to the point where almost all capital and labor are employed. This amounts to the same as the full employment of capital stock and labor supply.

Given a vertical AS, the demand side does not matter in the determination of the aggregate output. As the famous Say's law says, demand always accommodates supply. Indeed, if there are no fluctuations in factor inputs and productivity, then there would be no business cycles. In particular, there would be no unemployment problem, beyond a healthy "natural rate of unemployment." If one group of the population somehow reduces, their consumption, the rest will increase consumption at a lower price, keeping all factories running. It is a perfect world.

The assumption of flexible prices can be justified if we take a long-term view. Wages, for example, can be sticky in the short term but flexible in the long run. It is for this reason that classical economists may oppose government stimulus during recessions since prices and wages will adjust to bring the economy back to its potential level in the long run.

In this chapter, we assume as given both factor inputs (labor and capital) and the technology that transform inputs into outputs. That is, the "output potential" is assumed to be constant. We will leave to later chapters the study of economic growth.

3.2   The Output

In this section, we first introduce the macroeconomic concept of *technology*, which may be characterized by a production function. Then we present a classical AD-AS model to characterize the total output of the economy under classical assumptions.

3.2.1   Technology

Throughout the book, we assume that there are two factor inputs to the economy as a whole: capital and labor. We let K denote a measure of the capital stock, and let L denote the labor supply (either in the unit of working hours or the number of workers). And we use a production function F to characterize the "technology" of the economy, which is to transform K and L into an aggregate output (Y):

$$Y = F(K, L).$$

We should understand the "technology" of the whole economy in general terms. It is determined not only by the scientific and engineering know-how but also manufacturing organization, marketing skills, transportation, communication, and so on.

Assumptions on the Technology

The production function used in macroeconomics generally satisfies the following assumptions:

(a) Constant return to scale: for any $z > 0, F(zK, zL) = zY$.

(b) Increasing in both K and L:

$$F_1 \equiv \frac{\partial F}{\partial K} > 0, \quad \text{and} \quad F_2 \equiv \frac{\partial F}{\partial L} > 0.$$

(c) Decreasing marginal product of capital and labor:

$$F_{11} = \frac{\partial^2 F}{\partial K^2} < 0, \quad F_{22} = \frac{\partial^2 F}{\partial L^2} < 0.$$

(e) Capital–labor complementarity:

$$F_{12} = \frac{\partial^2 F}{\partial L \partial K} > 0.$$

Note that F_1 is the *marginal product of capital* (MPK) and F_2 is the *marginal product of labor* (MPL). It is readily accepted that, as in microeconomics, F should be increasing in both K and L, and that F should exhibit decreasing MPK and decreasing MPL. The capital–labor complementarity means that capital and labor are complementary inputs, in the sense that adding one of them would make the other more productive. Note that, for most production functions, $F_{12} = F_{21}$,[1] meaning that the effect of an additional unit of labor on the MPK is equal to the effect of an additional unit of capital on MPL.

The assumption of constant return to scale requires more argument. If F does not have constant return to scale, then the performance of an economy would depend on its size. (We may measure the performance of an economy by per capita GDP, average life expectancy, and so on.) If F has increasing return to scale, for example, big countries would have advantages. In our real world, however, there is no evidence that size plays any crucial role in the contest of economic performance in the per capita sense. High-income countries include big ones and small ones. The same is true for low-income countries.

Perhaps the most famous production function is the Cobb–Douglas function, which is given by

$$F(K, L) = AK^\alpha L^\beta,$$

where A is a constant that denotes the level of production efficiency. To satisfy the constant-return-to-scale assumption, we must impose $\alpha + \beta = 1$. As such, we rewrite the production function as

$$F(K, L) = AK^\alpha L^{1-\alpha}. \tag{3.1}$$

While the preceding production functions are static, we can easily make them dynamic, reflecting technological progress. Let A_t be the level of efficiency at time t. There are three ways to incorporate A_t into the production function:

- Labor augmenting: $Y_t = F(K_t, A_t L_t)$,

- Capital augmenting: $Y_t = F(A_t K_t, L_t)$,

- Total-factor augmenting: $Y_t = A_t F(K_t, L_t)$.

Another name for total-factor augmenting is *Hicks-neutral*. If technological progress is Hicks-neutral, then the marginal products of both factors increase at the same proportion. Obviously, the Cobb–Douglas technology in (3.1) is Hicks-neutral.

For simplicity, we assume in this chapter that both K and L are fixed, that $K = \bar{K}$ and $L = \bar{L}$, and that $F(\cdot, \cdot)$ is a fixed function. We define *output potential* as the level of total output that utilizes the current technology and all capital and labor. Letting $\bar{Y}$ denote output potential, we have

$$\bar{Y} = F(\bar{K}, \bar{L}).$$

3.2.2   A Classical AD-AS Model

Since macroeconomics studies the economy as a whole, it is useful to introduce the concepts of aggregate demand (AD) and aggregate supply (AS). AD is the "sum" of all demand for goods and services. We can decompose AD into four major components: consumption demand, investment demand, government demand, and net foreign demand. And the AS is the "sum" of all supply of goods and services. Both AD and AS are in the "real" sense: When we say AD or AS changes, it is the quantity of goods and services that changes.

The quotation marks around "sum," however, signify the difficulty of summation of heterogeneous goods and services. If there is only one good that consumers and firms desire, then AD is simply the total quantity of the good people want to buy. In reality, however, there are almost infinite different goods and services. To understand aggregate demand (supply) of heterogeneous goods and services, we may imagine adding up the value of these goods and services in demand (supply) using constant prices just as we do when calculating real GDP.

The AS Curve

Generally, both AD and AS may be functions of the general price level (P). The AD curve is a relationship between AD and the general price level (P). And the AS curve is a relationship between AS and P. We first discuss the AS curve, which is more important than the AD curve under classical assumptions.

Under classical assumptions (in particular, that people have access to full information and prices are flexible), the AS curve may be vertical. Firms in the classical world know the difference between changes in relative prices, to which they would respond by increasing production, and changes in the general price level, to which they do not respond. Hence the aggregate supply does not change with the general price level.

The vertical AS curve is contrary to the easy conjecture that the AS curve is upward sloping since supply curves for individual products are generally upward sloping. This gives us an example of the so-called fallacy of composition, which says that what is true for parts does not necessarily hold for the whole.

The next question is where the AS curve is located. We may conjecture that, in the classical world, competition between entrepreneurs will always push production *close to* the output potential ($\bar{Y}$ in Figure 3.1). Notice here that I use "close" to accommodate the fact that capacity utilization is always below the maximum level (e.g., due to option value of extra capacity) and that there is a natural level of unemployment (e.g., due to the fact that it takes time for people to switch jobs). To

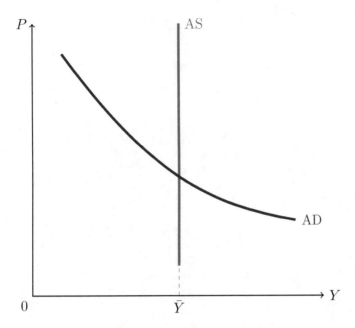

Figure 3.1 A classical AD-AS model.

put it more precisely, firms will expand production to the point where output ceases to be elastic, which is equivalent to the almost full employment of capital stock and labor supply.

The AD Curve

The AD curve is widely believed to be downward sloping. However, it does not follow from the microeconomic *law of demand*, which states that the demand curves for individual goods are generally downward sloping. We need a *macroeconomic argument* for this claim. One famous argument made by Arthur Pigou (1877–1959) is that as the general price level declines, the purchasing power of money holding increases. Becoming wealthier, money holders would increase spending, thus boosting aggregate demand. Since a decline in the price level corresponds to an increase in AD, we have a downward sloping AD curve.

The point where the AD curve crosses the AS curve gives the equilibrium of the economy, as shown in Figure 3.1. Since the AS curve is vertical, it solely determines the equilibrium output, which is equal to the output potential:

$$Y = \bar{Y} = F(\bar{K}, \bar{L}). \tag{3.2}$$

The shifting of the AD curve only changes the general price level. For example, if the government expands its welfare program, then the AD curve would shift to the right. That is, given any price level, the corresponding AD is bigger. As shown in Figure 3.2, the fiscal expansion would lead to inflation, while failing to raise output.

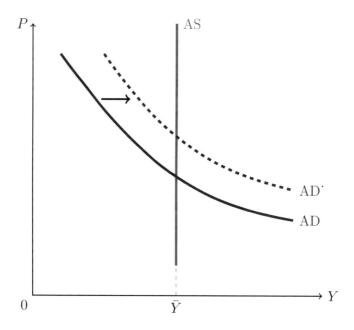

Figure 3.2 The effect of fiscal expansion in the classical AD-AS model.

That AD always matches AS at the level of output potential relies on the crucial assumption that prices are flexible. If the aggregate demand falls short (the AD curve shifts to the left), the price level immediately declines to ensure the balance between demand and supply at the output potential $\bar{Y}$. In the real world, it often takes time for firms to adjust prices and wages. That is, many prices are sticky in the short run. But eventually prices and wages will adjust. It is in this sense that we may call classical models in this chapter *long-run* models.

The AD curve may not slope downward. To counter Pigou's argument, suppose that a substantial number of people are in debt. Then a price decline would make their debt heavier in real terms and they become less willing to spend. The net effect of a price decline on the AD may be zero or even negative.

The case of zero net effect is interesting, since this corresponds to a vertical AD curve. In this case, since both AD and AS curves are vertical, they must overlap to make markets clear, as in Figure 3.3. Any point on the AS or AD curve is an equilibrium, corresponding to some general price level, which is indeterminate in this model. And to understand how the aggregate demand can accommodate aggregate supply at any price level, imagine that in a barter economy, people sell something to buy something else. As a result, we have the maxim "supply creates its own demand," a classical doctrine called Say's law.

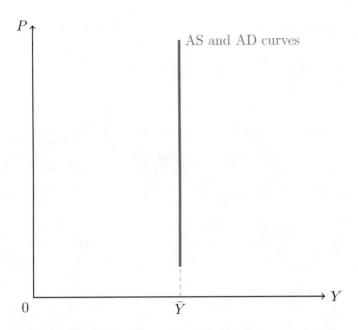

Figure 3.3 When both AD and AS curves are vertical.

3.3 Unemployment

As discussed previously, in an idealized world where classical assumptions hold, unemployment should be minimal. However, the unemployment rate would still be nonzero simply because it takes time for workers to switch jobs. For example, after a worker quits their job, they typically cannot find a new job immediately. It would take some time for the worker to search for vacancies, submit resumes, conduct interviews, and so on. Between quitting the old job and accepting a new job offer, the worker is unemployed.

We may call the minimal rate of unemployment existing in a healthy economy as the *national rate of unemployment*. In this section, we first present a simple model that relates the natural unemployment rate to the ease (difficulty) of finding and losing jobs. We then discuss the reason why it takes time to find jobs, which results in so-called frictional unemployment. Finally we discuss the structural unemployment arising from wage rigidity.

3.3.1   A Model of Natural Unemployment

Let L denote the labor force, E the number of the employed, and U the number of the unemployed. We know that $L = E + U$ and U/L is the unemployment rate.

Let s be the rate of job separation with $0 \leq s < 1$. We assume that in a given period (say, a month), there are sE of those employed losing their jobs. Note that if people who lost jobs can find jobs immediately, then $s = 0$. From a macroeconomic point of view, no one is losing a job when people can switch jobs instantly.

Similarly, let f denote the rate of job finding with $0 \leq f < 1$, and we assume that there are fU of the unemployed finding jobs in the same period.

And we assume that the job market is in a *steady state*, in which the number of job loss (sE) equals the number of job finding (fU):

$$sE = fU.$$

Then, in the steady state, we have

$$s\left(1 - \frac{U}{L}\right) = f\frac{U}{L},$$

which yields

$$\frac{U}{L} = \frac{1}{1 + f/s}.$$

As long as $s > 0$, which means that some of the unemployed cannot immediately find jobs, the unemployment rate will be positive.

Any policy aiming to lower the unemployment rate must make it easier to find jobs. The policies that would make it more difficult to fire workers, however, can easily backfire. Such policies would make employers reluctant to employ workers in the first place.

3.3.2   Frictional Unemployment

If $s = 0$ and $f > 0$, the unemployment rate in the preceding model is zero. We may describe such a labor market as *frictionless*. And the unemployment due to the fact that it takes time to find new jobs is called *frictional unemployment*.

The fundamental reason for the friction is the *heterogeneity* of jobs and workers, meaning that each worker, and also each vacancy, is different. And the problems of asymmetric information, imperfect labor mobility, and so on, would make the job matching even more difficult and time consuming.

Furthermore, there may be industrial or sectoral shifts happening in the economy. When the horse-wagon industry was declining, for example, workers in this industry would find their skills obsolete. To find a new job, say in the automobile industry, it takes time to learn new skills.

To reduce frictional unemployment, the government can help disseminate information about jobs and even provide training programs. The private sector can do at least equally well on information dissemination, especially in the current Internet age. But the government may be especially helpful in supporting training programs, since training has a positive *externality*: If a company trains a group of

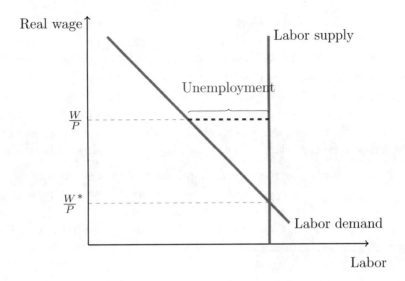

Figure 3.4 Structural unemployment.

workers, the company incurs the full cost of training, but cannot realize all of the benefits since some of the workers may go to other companies after training.

A prevalent policy regarding the job market is *unemployment insurance*, which helps to soften the economic hardship of the unemployed. As a result, especially when the unemployment insurance is overgenerous, workers may have less incentive to look for jobs urgently, and hence it may contribute to higher natural unemployment. However, unemployment insurance may help to achieve better matching between workers and jobs, hence enhancing the efficiency of the labor market.

3.3.3 Structural Unemployment

In the real world, the estimated natural rate of unemployment also includes the unemployment arising from wage rigidity, which we call *structural unemployment*. As shown in Figure 3.4, structural unemployment occurs when wages are higher than the market-clearing level and remain rigid.

Wage rigidity may come from the law of minimum wage. Minimum wage may increase structural unemployment among individuals with low or impaired skills (e.g., young or disabled people), whose market-clearing wage may be lower than the law of minimum wage dictates. Empirically, however, economists find that increasing the minimum wage does not necessarily lead to fewer jobs.[2]

Wage rigidity may also be due to strong labor unions. In industries with a strong union presence, union members ("insiders") may, through collective bargaining, manage to keep their wages artificially high. As a result, firms in the industry may tend to reduce employment.

Wage rigidity may also come from the practice of *efficiency wage*. Efficiency wage refers to the practice to pay employees more than equilibrium wage to increase the productivity of workers or reduce costs associated with turnover. High wage mitigates the problem of adverse selection since higher wage attracts and retains able employees. High wages also mitigate the problem of moral hazards since high wage increases the monetary loss of workers getting fired for shirking. If a large number of firms practice efficiency wage, however, the overall wage level of the economy would be higher than the market-clearing level, causing structural unemployment.

Like frictional unemployment, structural unemployment presumably does not fluctuate with economic cycles. And the actual unemployment rate is composed of the nonfluctuating natural rate of unemployment and a fluctuating component that we call *cyclical unemployment*. The relationship among these definitions of unemployment may be summarized as follows:

$$
\begin{aligned}
\text{natural unemployment} \quad &= \quad \text{frictional unemployment} + \text{structural unemployment} \\
&= \quad \text{actual unemployment} - \text{cyclical unemployment}
\end{aligned}
$$

Note that only the actual unemployment rate is observable. We need to estimate the natural rate of unemployment to obtain the cyclical component. Cyclical unemployment will be studied in Chapter 5.

3.4   Income Distribution

As previously discussed, the total output and total income must equal the output potential $\bar{Y}$ under classical assumptions. The remaining question is how the income would be distributed among owners of factor inputs, that is, those who provide capital and those who provide labor. As we can imagine, factor prices (real wage and real rental price of capital) would be crucial for the determination of the distribution.

The real wage is the payment to labor measured in units of output, W/P, where W is nominal wage and P is the price of output. (In empirical studies, P would be CPI or the GDP deflator).

The real rental price of capital is the rental price paid to the owner of capital in units of output, R/P, where R is the nominal rent. In most cases, firm owners also own the capital stock. But we can imagine that the firm rents capital from the owner of capital and pays rent, just like paying wages to the owner of labor (i.e., workers).

To study how the factor prices are determined, we introduce a representative-firm model.

3.4.1   A Representative-Firm Model

We assume that the markets for goods and services are competitive and that the markets for factors of production (labor and capital) are also competitive. Note that a market is competitive if no participant is large enough to affect prices. In other words, all market participants are price takers.

To determine the real wage and real rental price of capital, we look at the decision of a *representative firm*. We may imagine that the economy is composed of many small firms with the same technology $F(K_i, L_i)$, where K_i and L_i are capital and labor inputs to the ith firm, respectively. These firms produce the same product consumed by consumers with the same taste (utility function). As a result, the total production of the economy can be characterized by a representative firm with the production function $F(K, L)$, where K and L are the total capital and labor of the economy, respectively. Here, the constant-return-to-scale assumption on F is crucial, making possible the aggregation of firm-level technology into a macroeconomic production function.

The representative firm takes as given the price of its output (P), wage (W), and real rental price of capital (R), and solves the following problem:

$$\max_{K,L} P \cdot F(K, L) - W \cdot L - R \cdot K.$$

That is, the representative firm tries to maximize *economic profit* by choosing an optimal combination of capital and labor.

Concepts: Economic Profit and Accounting Profit

Consider a firm with two factor inputs: labor and capital. Economic profit is defined as income (revenue) minus costs of labor and capital. In the preceding problem for the representative firm, $P \cdot F(K, L)$ is revenue, $W \cdot L$ is the cost of labor, and $R \cdot K$ is the cost of capital (or return to capital).

Accounting profit is defined by the sum of economic profit and the return to capital. Since most firms own capital rather than rent them, return to capital is part of the accounting profit.

The first-order condition for the maximization problem with respect to K is as follows:

$$F_1(K, L) = \frac{R}{P}, \tag{3.3}$$

where $F_1 \equiv \partial F / \partial K$ denotes the partial derivative of F with respect to the first argument, K. Equation (3.3) says that the firm would employ capital up to the point where the MPK equals the real rental price of capital.

And the first-order condition for the maximization problem with respect to L is:

$$F_2(K, L) = \frac{W}{P}, \tag{3.4}$$

where $F_2 \equiv \partial F / \partial L$ denotes the partial derivative of F with respect to the second argument, L. Equation (3.4) says that the firm would employ labor up to the point where the marginal product of labor (MPL) equals the real wage.

Note that if we fix $K = \bar{K}$, the first-order condition for L gives us the *demand curve for labor*, i.e., the relationship between real wage (W/P) and the labor demanded (L): $F_2(\bar{K}, L) = W/P$. We can check that, since we assume a *decreasing* marginal product of labor, a lower real wage corresponds to a higher demand for labor.

3.4.2   Classical Theory of Income Distribution

Recall that the classical economy fully employs the total capital $\bar{K}$ and labor supply $\bar{L}$ (omitting the natural rate of unemployment), which implies that $\bar{K}$ and $\bar{L}$ must solve (3.3) and (3.4). That is to say, the representative firm maximizes its profit when $K = \bar{K}$ and $L = \bar{L}$. As a result, the owner of labor receives $F_2(\bar{K}, \bar{L}) \cdot \bar{L}$, and the owner of capital receives $F_1(\bar{K}, \bar{L}) \cdot \bar{K}$.

Interestingly, there is no economic profit left for the whole economy. To see this, note that under the constant-return-to-scale assumption on the production function, we have $F(zK, zL) = zF(K, L)$ for any $z > 0$. Then it follows from $\frac{dF(zK,zL)}{dz} = \frac{d(zF(K,L))}{dz}$ that

$$F_1(zK, zL)K + F_2(zK, zL)L = F(K, L).$$

Now let $z = 1$ and use the fact that $K = \bar{K}$ and $L = \bar{L}$, and we have

$$F_1(\bar{K}, \bar{L}) \cdot \bar{K} + F_2(\bar{K}, \bar{L}) \cdot \bar{L} = \bar{Y}.$$

To understand this intuitively, imagine an economy with many small firms with the same technology. Since the technology has constant return to scale, tiny would-be firms (say, workshops) can enter the market and compete with existing ones. As a result, we may deduce that there would be no economic profit for the existing firms.

Income Distribution in the Cobb–Douglas Economy

Suppose that a classical economy is characterized by the Cobb–Douglas production function, $F(K, L) = AK^\alpha L^{1-\alpha}$, we have

$$
\begin{aligned}
\text{MPK} &= F_1(K, L) = \alpha \frac{AK^\alpha L^{1-\alpha}}{K} = \alpha \frac{F(K, L)}{K} \\
\text{MPL} &= F_2(K, L) = (1-\alpha) \frac{AK^\alpha L^{1-\alpha}}{L} = (1-\alpha) \frac{F(K, L)}{L}.
\end{aligned}
$$

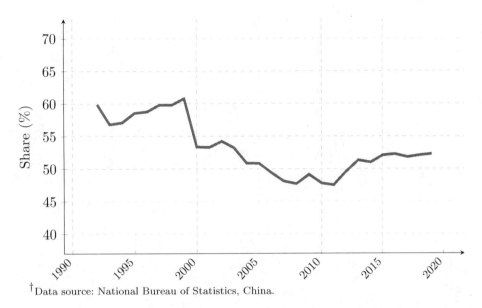

†Data source: National Bureau of Statistics, China.

Figure 3.5 Labor share of income in China.

The capital share of income is

$$F_1(\bar{K}, \bar{L}) \cdot \bar{K} = \alpha \bar{Y}$$

and the labor share of income is

$$F_2(\bar{K}, \bar{L}) \cdot \bar{L} = (1 - \alpha)\bar{Y}.$$

It would be an interesting empirical exercise to check whether the shares of capital and labor are constant. Figure 3.5 shows, however, that the labor share of income in China changes substantially over time.[3] During the 1990s, the labor share fluctuates around 60%. It dropped substantially in the first half of 2000s. The labor share reached the lowest point (47.5%) in 2011, after which we see a slow rebound. In 2019, the labor share of income in China stood at 52.3%.

The United States has a much longer data set on labor's share of income. Figure 3.6 shows the ratio of employee compensation in the national income. From 1929 to 1970, we can see a trend of increasing labor's share of income. From 1970 to recent years, we can see a downward trend.

In addition to trends, we can also see cycles in labor's share of income, which often peaks in the depth of recessions. To understand this, note that the return to capital often declines faster than the return to labor during recessions.

†The labor's share of income is measured by the ratio of total employee compensation to GDI. Data source: Wind Data Service (WIND).

Figure 3.6 Labor's share of income in the United States.

3.4.3   Labor Productivity and Real Wage

The *average labor productivity* (or simply labor productivity) of an economy is defined by the average output, Y/L. In the Cobb–Douglas economy, we have

$$\text{MPL} = F_2(K, L) = (1 - \alpha)\frac{AK^\alpha L^{1-\alpha}}{L} = (1 - \alpha)\frac{Y}{L}.$$

Hence the MPL is proportional to the average labor productivity in the Cobb–Douglas economy. Once again, it would be interesting to investigate whether this is the case in the real economy. Table 3.1 shows that, in the United States where long data are available, the growth rates of labor productivity and real wage are positively correlated. At the same time, however, the growth of real wage lags behind that of labor productivity. This observation is consistent with the fact that the labor's share of income has been declining in the United States during the sample period.

3.5   Interest Rate

Interest is payment from a borrower to the lender for the price of using borrowed money. The interest rate (or rate of interest) is interest per amount due *per period*, which is often a year. Even if the borrowing is for a shorter term, say a month, we still quote the interest rate in annual percentages. For example, if the interest payment on a one-month loan of 100 is 1, then the interest rate is 1% per month, or an annualized 12.68%.[4] It is convenient to use annualized rates to compare interest rates on loans with different maturities.

Table 3.1 Growth in labor productivity and real wage in the United States.

Period	Average growth in labor productivity	Average growth in real nonfarm compensation
1959–2019	2.1	1.3
1959–1972	2.8	2.3
1973–1994	1.6	0.7
1995–2007	2.7	1.6
2008–2019	1.3	0.8

[†]Data source: Federal Reserve Economic Data (FRED).

Without explicit qualifications, interest rate in macroeconomics refers to *risk-free* interest rate, the interest rate on loans or bonds without credit risk. For example, the interest rate on China's government bonds is a risk-free rate for savers who do not worry about the exchange rate risk.[5]

Note that interest is a different concept from rental price of capital. Roughly speaking, interest is return to money, while rental price of capital is return to capital.[6] A dramatic macroeconomic phenomenon in the past four decades is that interest rates in the Western world have declined to zero or even negative values, while the return to capital remains stable.[7]

3.5.1 Real Interest Rate

Interest rate quotes in the practical world are nominal interest rates, which do not account for inflation. The real interest rate is the interest rate a lender receives (or expects to receive) after accounting for the effect of inflation. Given a nominal interest rate, if inflation is high (or is expected to be high), then the real interest rate is low. In economics, we often assume that people care about the real interest rate, which is the "real" opportunity cost of money.

The concept of the real interest rate is best understood in the context of "real" borrowing. For example, if I borrow 100 kg of rice from my neighbor and I have to pay a debt of 110 kg of the same rice, then the real interest rate of my borrowing is 10%.

If I borrow money (and then use money to buy rice), however, then the problem of calculating the real interest rate becomes more difficult. The difficulty lies in how to account for inflation. For example, suppose that I borrow 1,000 CNY from my neighbor and buy 100 kg of rice (the rice price is 10 CNY/kg). If I pay a debt of 1,100 CNY next year, then the nominal interest rate is 10%. If the rice price does not change, then the real interest rate is also 10%. But if the rice price rises to 11 CNY/kg, then the real interest rate is zero. A zero real interest rate means that the borrowed money has the same purchasing power as the money paid back.

Unlike nominal interest rate, which we can directly observe, the real interest rate needs to be estimated. There are two ways to define real interest rates. One is called the *ex post* real interest rate or *realized* real interest rate,

$$r = i - \pi, \tag{3.5}$$

where i is the nominal interest rate, r is the real interest rate, and π is the inflation rate. For example, if the nominal interest rate on a loan is 5% and the inflation rate turns out to be 3%, then the ex post real interest rate is 2%.

The other definition gives the *ex ante* real interest rate,

$$r = i - E\pi, \tag{3.6}$$

where $E\pi$ is the expectation of inflation. The ex ante real interest rate is useful when loaners and debtors negotiate a (nominal) interest rate and they need to form an expectation about the future inflation. For example, if a loaner and a debtor agree on a nominal interest rate of 5% on a one-year loan and they expect that there will be an inflation of 3% over the next year, then the ex ante real interest rate is 2%.

Note that (3.5) is called the Fisher equation (named after Irving Fisher) and (3.6) is called the modified Fisher equation.

3.5.2   A Classical Model of Interest Rate

In the modern world, central banks determine one or more key interest rates such as the federal funds rate of the US Federal Reserve, the main refinancing operations (MRO) rate of the European Central Bank, and so on. Although other interest rates (long-term government bonds, corporate bonds, bank loans, etc.) are mostly equilibrium outcomes of the market demand and supply, they are immensely influenced by the policy rates that the central banks control.

Classical economists, however, live in the era of small government with very limited central banking. They generally view the interest rate as a price that brings demand and supply of funds into equilibrium, without much influence from any monetary authority. In this section, we present a model that captures such a view. The model specifies a set of behavioral assumptions and imposes an equilibrium condition. We will use the model to examine the effects of external shocks (e.g., change in fiscal policy).

For simplicity, we assume that the net export equals zero, $X = 0$. This implies either a closed economy or an open economy with balanced trade. Then the national income accounts identity becomes

$$Y = C + I + G, \tag{3.7}$$

where Y represents GDP, C represents consumption expenditure, I represents investment expenditure, and G represents government expenditure. To define national saving $S = Y - C - G$, we may rewrite (3.7) as

$$S = I.$$

This equation states that "saving must equal investment." If we regard saving as the supplier of funds and investment as the demander of funds, then the equation may be interpreted as an equilibrium condition in a financial market. We will build a model on this equilibrium condition.

In the following, we make a set of behavioral assumptions on the consumption expenditure (C) and investment expenditure (I). Specifically, we introduce a consumption function and an investment function to characterize consumption and investment in the economy, respectively. And we regard the government expenditure (G) and tax (T) as exogenous variables, whose values are given outside the model. After building the model, we may change exogenous variables and see what happens to endogenous variables (in this case, the real interest rate). We may call such analysis a *virtual experiment*.

Consumption Function

Assume that the tax T is levied on household income. The disposable income is then $Y - T$, the total income minus tax. The *consumption function* characterizes the total consumption expenditure (C) by a function of the disposable income, $C = C(Y - T)$. We assume that $C(\cdot)$ is an increasing function. That is, more disposable income leads to more consumption.

We define the *marginal propensity to consume* (MPC) as the amount of additional consumption given unit increase in disposable income. Mathematically, MPC is the first derivative of the consumption function with respect to Y:

$$MPC = \frac{dC(Y)}{dY}.$$

For example, if $C(\cdot)$ is a linear function, e.g.,

$$C(Y - T) = 100 + 0.7(Y - T),$$

then MPC is a constant and MPC $= 0.7$.

Investment Function

Since higher real interest rates discourage borrowing and hence investment, we assume that the investment expenditure of the economy is a decreasing function of the real interest rate, $I = I(r)$ with $I'(r) < 0$.

Fiscal Policy

The fiscal policy determines how much the government will tax and spend. In this model, we capture the fiscal policy by two exogenous variables: the tax revenue of the government (T), and the government expenditure (G). If $G = T$, we have a *balanced budget*; if $G > T$, we have a *budget deficit*; and if $G < T$, we have a *budget surplus*.

The budget surplus $(T - G)$ is also called the *public saving*. A negative public saving means budget deficit. And we may define the private (nongovernment) saving as follows:
$$S_{ng} = Y - C - T.$$
By adding the public saving and private saving together, we obtain national saving: $S = Y - C - G$.

Equilibrium in the Financial Market

We assume there exists a simple financial market for loanable funds. Those with savings would lend their savings to borrowers (investors) in the financial market. We assume that the national savings, $Y - C - G$, is the supply of loanable funds in the financial market. On the other hand, the demand for loanable funds comes from the investment need, $I(r)$.

In equilibrium, the real interest rate (r) must adjust so that savings (supply of loanable funds) equals investment (demand for loanable funds):

$$\bar{Y} - C(\bar{Y} - T) - G = I(r). \tag{3.8}$$

Note that the left-hand side is the saving (S). The unknown real interest rate is the only endogenous variable in the model. All the remaining variables, T, G, and $\bar{Y}$, are exogenous variables. Recall that $\bar{Y}$ is the output potential of the economy and that, under the classical assumptions, the total output of the economy equals the output potential. The solution of the preceding equilibrium equation is illustrated in Figure 3.7. Note that in the model, saving does not depend on the interest rate, hence a vertical supply (or saving) curve.

3.5.3   Virtual Experiment

Models allow us to conduct virtual experiments on the economy without actually fiddling with it. We now use the previous model to study how exogenous shocks would affect the equilibrium real interest rate.

From a mathematical point of view, the equilibrium condition in (3.8) defines an *implicit function* of r, the only endogenous variable. When exogenous variables change $(\bar{Y}, T, G)$, the equilibrium r changes. The implicit function characterizes the

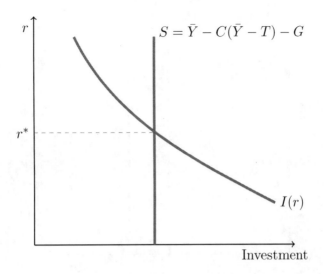

Figure 3.7 Determination of real interest rate.

dependence of the equilibrium r on exogenous variables, which we may denote by $r(\bar{Y}, T, G)$.

A virtual experiment is thus a study of the implicit function. For example, we may be interested in the question of how r would change if G increases, holding $\bar{Y}$ and T fixed. Assuming that the implicit function $r(\bar{Y}, T, G)$ is differentiable,[8] we just need to study the partial derivative of r with respect to G:

$$\frac{\partial r(\bar{Y}, T, G)}{\partial G} \equiv \lim_{\Delta \to 0} \frac{r(\bar{Y}, T, G + \Delta) - r(\bar{Y}, T, G)}{\Delta}.$$

The *implicit function theorem* (see Section A.2 for a review) can be employed to study the preceding partial derivative. For example, we may apply the implicit function theorem to (3.8) and obtain the following:

$$\frac{\partial r(\bar{Y}, T, G)}{\partial G} = -\frac{-1}{-I'(r)} > 0.$$

That is, if the government increases spending, then the real interest rate would rise.

Graphically, the increased government spending shifts the saving curve to the left (Figure 3.8), resulting in a higher equilibrium real interest rate. The same would be true if there is a tax cut ($T \downarrow$). Both the increase in G and the decrease in T would reduce national savings. The former reduces national savings by reducing public savings ($T - G$), and the latter reduces national savings by increasing private consumption.

A higher real interest rate corresponds to lower investment. Economists would say that fiscal stimulus ($G \uparrow$ or $T \downarrow$) *crowds out* the private investment. And under

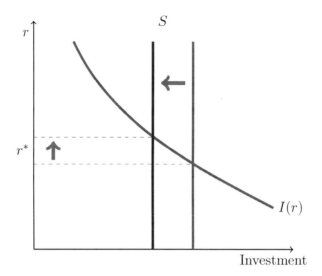

Figure 3.8 The effect of fiscal stimulus.

classical assumptions, the crowding out is complete, meaning that the stimulus would fail to increase total output or employment.

3.5.4   Explain the Decline of Real Interest Rate

We can use this model for economic explanation. For example, the real interest rate in the Western world has been declining for almost forty years (see Figure 3.9 for the US case). We may conjecture that the lack of investment enthusiasm, which itself may be due to the lack of investment opportunities, may be to blame. We now check whether the model prediction is consistent with the conjecture.

We introduce an exogenous variable, d, that enters the investment function, $I = I(r, d)$. We assume that d measures investment enthusiasm and that $\partial I / \partial d > 0$. The model in (3.8) becomes

$$\bar{Y} - C(\bar{Y} - T) - G = I(r, d).$$

We need to check whether a declining d leads to a declining r, holding other exogenous variables fixed. Since the left-hand side is fixed and I is increasing in d and decreasing in r, r must decline as d declines in order for the equation to hold. Applying the implicit function theorem, we obtain

$$\frac{\partial r(\bar{Y}, T, G, d)}{\partial d} = -\frac{-I_2(r, d)}{-I_1(r, d)} > 0,$$

where $I_1 \equiv \partial I / \partial r < 0$ and $I_2 \equiv \partial I / \partial d > 0$. Hence r must decline when d declines.

Graphically, the decline of d corresponds to the shift the investment curve to the left (Figure 3.10), meaning that the investment demand decreases at every r. This results in a lower equilibrium real interest rate.

†Data source: FRED. The real interest rate is measured by interest rate on ten-year Treasury minus CPI YoY inflation.

Figure 3.9 The US real interest rate (1981–2021).

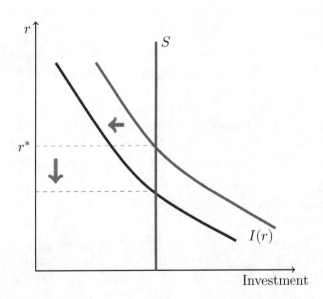

Figure 3.10 The effect of declining investment enthusiasm.

3.6   Money and Inflation

3.6.1   Money

Money is the stock of assets that can be readily used to make transactions. Functions of money include store of value, unit of account, and medium of exchange. The last function, to intermediate the exchange of goods and services, is especially important for classical thinkers. If there is no money and people barter goods and services with each other, trading opportunities would be much reduced, since it is highly unlikely to find "double coincidence of wants." The introduction of money, which is acceptable by everybody for everything, solves this problem.

Furthermore, money makes pricing simple. Imagine a market with N different goods; without money, we need $N(N-1)/2$ pairs of price quotes. But if money is used to intermediate exchanges, only N price quotes are needed.

Given such convenience afforded by money, it is not surprising that human society has used money, in one form or another, from very early history. At first, people use commodity money such as shells, gold, silver, and so on. But transactions using commodity money (say gold) is costly since the purity and weight of a piece of gold have to be examined in every transaction. To reduce transaction costs, a bank (possibly with authorization from the government) may mint gold coins of known purity and weight. To further reduce cost, the bank may issue gold certificates, which can be redeemed for gold. The gold certificate eventually becomes gold-backed paper money.

In modern times, especially after the industrial revolution, economic growth sped up, outpacing the growth of the gold supply. Hence the limited supply of gold has a deflationary effect on the economy if a country keeps using gold as money. Eventually, it is realized that if people do not care about the option of redeeming gold, the bank can issue certificates that are not backed by gold in the vault. The modern central bank does exactly this, and these certificates become fiat money. Fiat money is valued because people expect it to be valued by everyone else.

In the traditional sense, money includes cash, central bank reserves, and bank deposits. As financial markets evolve, more financial assets take on "moneyness" and become money (e.g., government bonds). The supply of cash and reserves is controlled by the monetary authority (the central bank), which deliberate and implement monetary policies. The supply of bank deposits is determined by bank lending, which is in turn determined by prevailing interest rates, risk appetite, investment opportunities, and so on.

The monetary authority in China is the People's Bank of China (PBC). In the United States, the monetary authority is the Federal Reserve (the Fed). A monetary authority may serve more than one sovereign nation. The European Central Bank

(ECB), for example, serves as the monetary authority for the entire eurozone, a group of sovereign European countries.

3.6.2 Inflation

Inflation is sustained increase in the general price level of goods and services. Temporary fluctuations in price level do not constitute inflation. For example, seasonal increase in price before and during the Spring Festival in China may not be inflation, since the price would often decline after the holiday, as demand wanes and supply recovers. Price increases in some particular goods or services are also not regarded as inflation unless they are accompanied by the rise in the general price level.

If there is a sustained decrease in the general price level, we call it *deflation*. A related concept is *disinflation*, which refers to the case where the inflation rate declines. As discussed in the previous chapter, we use CPI or the GDP deflator to measure inflation.

When there is inflation, the purchasing power of the money declines. And there are losers and winners from inflation. Losers include people who save, people who hold bonds, and, generally, people who receive fixed incomes. Retired pensioners are especially vulnerable. Unexpected inflation is equivalent to redistribution of wealth from savers to borrowers, who are winners of inflation. Unexpected inflation also increases a sense of uncertainty in the economy, discouraging investment.

Even expected inflation has costs. First, high inflation leads to a high frequency of price changes, which are costly because sellers and buyers have to renegotiate prices, and new menus have to be printed (metaphorically, menu costs). Second, high inflation leads to high opportunity cost of holding cash, causing inconveniences of insufficient cash holding. It can be metaphorically called "shoe-leather cost," meaning that more frequent visits to banks would cause one's shoes to wear out more quickly. Third, high inflation makes price signal noisy, affecting the ability of the "invisible hand" to allocate resources. Fourth, tax brackets are often in nominal terms (e.g., the minimum taxable monthly salary is 3,500 CNY in China), and high inflation would make tax burden heavier than intended.

When prices lose control and inflation skyrockets, the economy may fall into a full crisis. According to a loose definition, if inflation exceeds 50% per month, we call it *hyperinflation*. All the costs of moderate inflation previously described become prohibitive under hyperinflation. Money may cease to function as a store of value, and may not serve its other functions (unit of account, medium of exchange). People may have to barter or use a stable foreign currency.

What causes hyperinflation? An easy and classical answer is that hyperinflation is caused by excessive money supply growth. When the central bank prints money, the price level rises. If it prints money rapidly enough, the result is hyperinflation. But why would a central bank print money like crazy? In most cases, it would be due to fiscal problems. When a government experiences fiscal crisis due to either extraordinary expenditure (war, indemnity, etc.) or impaired tax power or both, the government may resort to excessive money printing.

However, there is one benefit of moderate inflation that proves important for the health of macroeconomy. It is a well-supported fact that nominal wages are rigid, even during recessions. Inflation allows real wages to reach equilibrium levels without cutting the nominal wage. Therefore, moderate inflation makes the labor market less frictional.

On the other hand, deflation may look good, since it implies increased purchasing power of money. But deflation is almost intolerable in a modern economy, as it makes debts more difficult to service, discourages investment, and thus aggravates unemployment. This is why, recently, central banks around the world have been conducting aggressive monetary policies (quantitative easing, negative interest rates, etc.) to maintain positive inflation.

3.6.3   Quantity Theory of Money

The quantity theory of money is the most important classical theory about money and inflation.

Suppose there is only one good in the economy with price P. Let T be the total number of transactions during a period and M the money in circulation. We may define the transaction velocity of money in this simple economy by

$$V \equiv PT/M.$$

The quantity theory of money is thus stated as an identity,

$$MV = PT.$$

In reality, there is an almost infinite number of goods and services with different prices. It is obviously not appropriate to count the transactions of different goods equally. For example, the purchase of a car uses a lot more money than that of a cell phone. A natural way to count transactions of heterogenous goods and services is to *weight* each transaction with constant prices, just like the calculation of real GDP. This gives us a more practical quantity theory of money:

$$MV = PY, \tag{3.9}$$

where Y denotes real GDP. Note that the new version of quantity theory is nothing but an alternative definition of the velocity of money.

We may also interpret the equation in (3.9) as an equilibrium condition in the money market. Rewrite (3.9) as

$$M/P = kY, \tag{3.10}$$

where $k \equiv 1/V$. If V is, as usual, assumed to be a constant, so is k. We may interpret the left-hand side as the real money supply and the right-hand side as money demand, which is assumed to depend on the total income only. We can read the equilibrium condition as follows:

$$\text{``real money supply''} = \text{``money demand.''}$$

Note that k characterizes how much money people wish to hold for each unit of income. It is by definition inversely proportional to V: When people hold lots of money relative to their incomes, money changes hands infrequently.

Money and Output

According to the classical AD-AS model, the output of a classical economy always matches the output potential, $Y = \bar{Y}$. Thus, money does not affect output, and monetary policy is ineffective.

For this to be compatible with the quantity theory of money, the general price level should be perfectly flexible. When the money supply rises, price should rise proportionally so that M/P remain constant. If P rises slower than M, the quantity theory of money would predict a rise in Y since k is assumed to be a constant.

Of course, the flexibility of the general price level is implied by the classical assumption of flexible prices.

Money and Inflation

We take total differentiation of (3.9) and obtain

$$\frac{dM}{M} + \frac{dV}{V} = \frac{dP}{P} + \frac{dY}{Y}.$$

Note that dM/M and dY/Y are growth rates of money supply and real GDP, respectively, and that dP/P is the inflation rate. If we assume that the velocity V is constant, then $dV/V = 0$. The quantity theory of money implies that, given the real GDP growth rate, a higher growth rate of the money supply leads to higher inflation.

In the real world, inflation does not necessarily co-move with the growth in the money supply. Figure 3.11 shows the annual inflation and growth of money supply in China. Although there are periods when the two move roughly in tandem, there are also periods when they move in opposite directions. For example, M2 grew rapidly in 2009 thanks to the Four-Trillion-Stimulus program. But inflation declined to negative territory amid the global recession.

However, when money supply is excessive, as would happen during episodes of hyperinflation (e.g., China in the late 1940s, Germany in 1923), the co-movement between the growth of money supply and inflation is clear.

†Data source: National Bureau of Statistics, China.

Figure 3.11 China's annual inflation and M2 growth.

3.6.4   China's Hyperinflation in the 1940s

In the following, we document the Chinese hyperinflation in the 1940s. The hyperinflation had a long-lasting impact on the Chinese economy, especially on the weight of price stability among policy priorities.

Background

In 1935, China's Nationalist government carried out a currency reform with two major tasks. First, the reform centralized the bank-note issuance to four major national banks and started to issue a unified currency: Fabi ("legal note"). Second, the reform gave up the former silver-based currency and started to peg Fabi to the British pound, which served as the reserve currency. In 1936, the US dollar became another reserve currency for Fabi. However, the Nationalist government soon found it was unable to maintain the link to pound or dollar, with its fiscal capacity much impaired by the full-scale Japanese invasion starting from 1937.

Hyperinflation: Stage One

The currency reform was to tackle the problem of deflation due to the outflow of silver, which was, in turn, caused by the US effort to increase its silver reserve. For this objective, the reform was a success. Soon enough, inflation picked up. And as World War II started and the fiscal condition became desperate, seigniorage became the major fiscal revenue for the Nationalist government. As a result, inflation turned

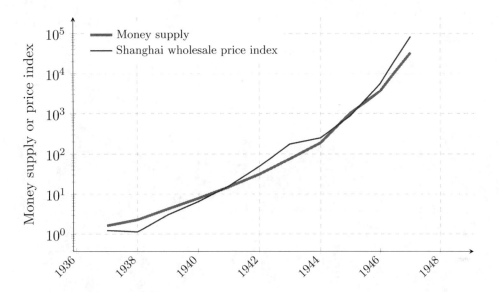

[†]Data source: Liu (1999), *Research on China's Central Banking.*

Figure 3.12 China's hyperinflation in the 1940s (1937–1948).

from moderate to extreme. From 1937 to 1945, the year when the war with Japan ended, the money supply grew from 1.6 billion to 1 trillion Yuan (unit of Fabi), and the price level in Shanghai (measured by the wholesale price index) increased from 1.2 to 885 (Figure 3.12).

Hyperinflation: Stage Two

And this was not the end of the story. China's civil war soon broke out. Since the Nationalist government was unable to support its war with tax revenue, it continued to rely on seigniorage. By the end of 1947, the money supply already multiplied to 33.2 trillion Yuan. In the meantime, inflation accelerated. By August 1948, the money supply reached 604.5 trillion, and inflation in Shanghai more than doubled in eight months (Figure 3.12).

At this point, the Nationalist government conducted another currency reform: issuing a new currency to replace Fabi. This new currency, called the Gold-Yuan Coupon (GYC),[9] was designed to be backed by the gold reserve. But the Nationalists did not have enough gold reserve. Nor were they able to stabilize, let alone expand, fiscal revenue. It was a monetary reform without the companion of a fiscal reform. And making matters worse, the Nationalist army was losing on almost all of the battlefields. The reform was doomed.

From August 1948 to the end of the year, the supply of GYC ballooned from 0.5 billion to 8.3 billion, and the price level in Shanghai went up from 1.9 (a different index from that mentioned previously) to 35.5. By April 1949, the GYC supply

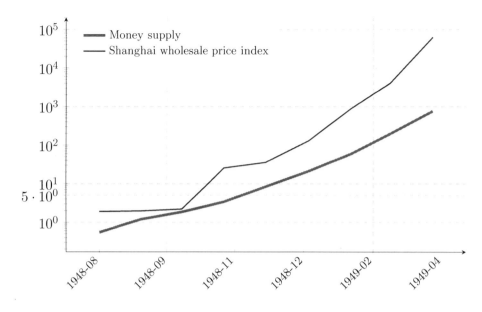

†Data source: Liu (1999).

Figure 3.13 China's hyperinflation in the 1940s (August 1948–April 1949).

multiplied to 760 billion, and inflation averaged 130% every month (Figure 3.13). The economy was in full collapse.

Legacies

It is widely believed that the hyperinflation contributed to the end of the Nationalist regime on the mainland. But hyperinflation itself reflected deep problems in the Nationalists' rule. For one thing, the central government did not have effective control over all of China, even before the Japanese invasion. Given the limited fiscal capacity, the excessive extraction of seigniorage revenue became a necessity for defending the country against the Japanese.

After the Japanese surrendered, the Nationalists had the opportunity to consolidate its fiscal position. But its paramount leader, Chiang Kai Shek, continued to rely on seigniorage to wage an unpopular civil war, believing in an easy victory. The hyperinflation in 1947 and onward reflected the failure of the Nationalists' economic management as well as their military failure.

After the Communists won the civil war and established the People's Republic of China, they introduced a new monetary regime, and the price soon stabilized. Knowing that its dramatic success was partly due to the hyperinflation during the Nationalists' reign, the new rulers of China made maintaining price stability one of their highest policy priorities.

3.6.5   Classical Dichotomy

We can combine the classical AD-AS model in (3.2), the classical model of real interest rate in (3.8), the quantity theory of money in (3.10), and the Fisher equation in (3.5):

$$
\begin{aligned}
Y &= \bar{Y}, \\
I(r) &= Y - C(Y - T) - G, \\
\frac{M}{P} &= kY, \\
i &= r + \pi.
\end{aligned}
$$

Note that in this integrated model, real variables (e.g., Y and r) are determined without considering money. Money supply only influences the general price level, which in turn determines the nominal values such as nominal GDP, nominal interest rate (i), and so on. The idea of separating "real" from "nominal" analysis is called the *classical dichotomy*. If the classical dichotomy holds, we also say that money is *neutral*.

Naturally, monetary policy is irrelevant if money is neutral. The expansion of the money supply, according to the classical theory, only drives up the price level and the nominal interest rate. It does not reduce the real interest rate or influence the output or employment. In the real world, however, evidence abounds that monetary policy has real effects.

3.7   Exchange Rate

The exchange rate (also known as the foreign-exchange rate, or forex rate) between two currencies is the rate at which one currency exchanges for another.

In this course, we adopt the convention that the exchange rate is in units of foreign currency per domestic currency. Under this convention, a rise in the exchange rate is called *appreciation*; a fall in the exchange rate is called *depreciation*. Appreciation is also called *strengthening*, while depreciation is also called *weakening*.

Because a country trades with many countries, it is often useful to calculate the effective exchange rate, an index measuring the value of the domestic currency against a basket of foreign currencies. Figure 3.14 shows the exchange rate of the Chinese Yuan (CNY) with respect to the US dollar (USD) and the nominal effective exchange rate (NEER) of CNY. Note that USDCNY represents the amount of CNY a USD can exchange. When USDCNY declines, it means that CNY appreciates against USD.

It is interesting to note that during 2015, CNY depreciated about 8% against USD. But in terms of effective exchange rates, CNY appreciated approximately

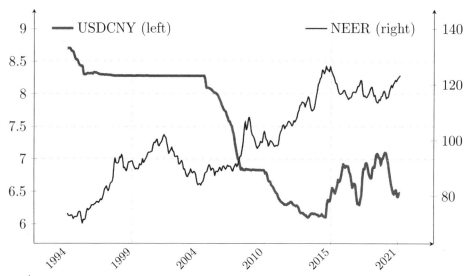

†Data source: WIND. USDCNY represents the amount of CNY a USD can exchange. NEER represents the nominal effective exchange rate of CNY.

Figure 3.14 The exchange rates of Chinese Yuan (CNY).

10% relative to its trading partners. So looking at only one bilateral exchange rate, however important it is, may make us miss the big picture of a currency's exchange rate movement.

3.7.1   Real Exchange Rate

The real exchange rate is the purchasing power of a currency relative to another currency at current nominal exchange rates and prices. Let e be the nominal exchange rate, P the domestic price in domestic currency, and P^* the foreign price in foreign currency. Since e is in units of foreign currency per domestic currency, the domestic price in foreign currency is eP. (Here we may imagine that there is only one good in the world. Thus the price level is just the price for the good, making price levels in two countries comparable.) Then the real exchange rate (ε) is defined by the ratio of the domestic price in foreign currency to the foreign price in foreign currency:

$$\varepsilon = \frac{eP}{P^*}. \tag{3.11}$$

The lower the real exchange rate, the less expensive domestic goods and services are relative to foreign ones.

Example: Real Exchange Rate

Suppose both China and the United States produce and consume one good, the Big Mac. And suppose that the Big Mac costs 20 CNY in China and 4 USD in the United States and that the nominal exchange rate is 6 USDCNY.

Then the real exchange rate between China and the United States is

$$\varepsilon = \frac{\frac{1}{6} \cdot 20}{4} = \frac{5}{6}.$$

Since the real exchange rate is less than 1, we say that PPP does not hold, and CNY is undervalued: It is profitable to buy Big Macs in China, sell them in the United States, and convert the USD proceeds back to CNY.

3.7.2 Purchasing Power Parity

Examining the definition of the real exchange rate in (3.11), we can see that if domestic and foreign currencies have identical purchasing power, then the real exchange rate (ε) should be exactly one. Indeed, if $\varepsilon = 1$, we say that the exchange rates are at *purchasing power parity* (PPP). Theoretically, PPP is implied by the *law of one price*, which states that the same good should have the same price. If $\varepsilon > 1$, the domestic currency is overvalued in terms of purchasing power, meaning that domestic prices are higher than foreign prices in general. If $\varepsilon < 1$, the domestic currency is undervalued in terms of purchasing power.

If PPP holds, we have

$$e_t = P_t^*/P_t. \tag{3.12}$$

In practice, since P_t and P_t^* are measured by price indices, they are not comparable. Thus (3.12) is not useful for empirically testing whether PPP holds. Instead, we may take log difference of (3.12). Since $\pi_t = \log(P_t/P_{t-1})$, we have

$$\log\left(\frac{e_t}{e_{t-1}}\right) = \pi_t^* - \pi_t, \tag{3.13}$$

where π_t^* and π_t are foreign and domestic inflations, respectively. Note that $\log(e_t/e_{t-1})$ represents the rate of appreciation of the domestic currency from time $t - 1$ to t. Equation (3.13) says that, under PPP, if foreign inflation is higher than domestic inflation, the domestic currency would appreciate by the inflation gap $(\pi_t^* - \pi_t)$.

If we further assume a common real interest rate in the two economies, then we have

$$\log\left(\frac{e_t}{e_{t-1}}\right) = i_t^* - i_t, \tag{3.14}$$

where i_t^* and i_t are foreign and domestic nominal interest rates, respectively. Equation (3.14) says that if the foreign nominal interest rate is higher than the domestic one, the domestic currency tends to appreciate. The equation in (3.14) is often called *uncovered interest rate parity*, which characterizes an equilibrium where investors of the weak currency have to be compensated with a higher interest rate.

PPP does not generally hold in practice, especially in the short term. First, not all goods are tradable. Second, there are trading barriers and trading costs. These make cross-country arbitrage of price differences incomplete and costly. As a result, researchers find little empirical support for PPP if they use short-term data to test implications of PPP, such as (3.13). However, more support of PPP can be found in long-term data.

3.7.3 Trade Balance and Capital Flow

In an open economy, domestic spending need not equal its output. The difference is the net export, which is the total value of export minus that of import. According to the national income identity,

$$Y - (C + I + G) = X = EX - IM,$$

where Y is output, $(C + I + G)$ represents domestic spending, X stands for net export, EX stands for export, and IM stands for import. All these variables are in the *real* sense.

If domestic spending is less than the output, then $X > 0$ and the surplus of goods and services is lent to foreigners. If domestic spending exceeds the output, then $X < 0$ and the country borrows goods and services worth $(-X)$ from abroad. The net export is also called the trade balance.

The flow of goods and services is mirrored by capital flow. If $S = Y - (C + G)$ is the national saving, we have

$$S - I = X. \tag{3.15}$$

The left-hand side is the difference between the national saving (S) and investment (I), which is the *excess saving* of the economy. Since the excess saving has to flow out of the country, we may also call $(S - I)$ the *net capital outflow*.

Equation (3.15) says that the net capital outflow always equals the net export. If $S - I = X > 0$, the country lends its excess saving $(S - I)$ to foreigners. And if $S - I = X < 0$, then the country borrows $(I - S)$ from abroad.

To understand this identity more intuitively, we examine an imagined example. If BYD (a Chinese auto company) sells an electric car to a US consumer for 10,000

USD, how does the sale change China's trade and capital flow? On trade, the Chinese export rises by 10,000 USD. On capital flow, if BYD invests the 10,000 USD in the US securities (e.g., stocks or bonds), then Chinese capital outflow rises by 10,000 USD. The same is true even if BYD keeps the cash, which is the most liquid US "security" issued by the US government. If BYD converts the 10,000 USD into CNY at a local Chinese bank, then the bank also has to do something about it. If the bank chooses to purchase the US securities or to keep the dollar cash, then Chinese capital outflow again rises by 10,000 USD. If the bank sells the dollar to the central bank, which uses the 10,000 USD to purchase US treasury bills, we would still see a 10,000 USD rise in capital outflow.

3.7.4 A Model of a Small Open Economy

Now we introduce a model that characterizes the determination of the real exchange rate, which further determines net export or net capital outflow. The model is classical in the sense that output is given (exogenous) under classical assumptions and that the real exchange rate, the only endogenous variable, is assumed to be flexible.

The Model

We consider a small open economy and make the following assumptions:

(i) There is a common real interest rate (r^*) in the world.

(ii) The capital flow of the small economy does not affect the world interest rate.

(iii) The net export is a decreasing function of the real exchange rate, $X(\varepsilon)$, with $X'(\varepsilon) < 0$.

To justify (i), we may assume that capital is perfectly mobile across borders. As a result, global arbitragers would make sure the real interest rate is the same across the world. The assumption (ii) is a key characteristic of a small economy. The excess saving of the small economy does not affect the world interest rate. In other words, the small economy is a "price taker" of the world interest rate r^*. The combination of (i) and (ii) makes the real interest rate *exogenous* in the model. Finally, (iii) is a reasonable assumption since a higher real exchange rate encourages imports and makes the export sector less competitive.

Building on (3.15), we have

$$S - I(r^*) = X(\varepsilon), \tag{3.16}$$

where $S = \bar{Y} - C(\bar{Y} - T) - G$. We may interpret the net capital outflow, which is the left-hand side of (3.16), as the demand for foreign currency. The net export, on

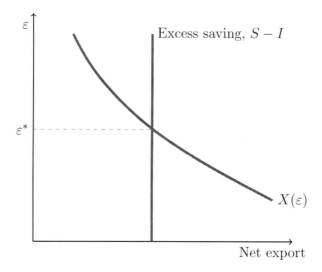

Figure 3.15 A model of small open economy.

the other hand, represents the supply of foreign currency. Then we may interpret (3.16) as an equilibrium condition on the foreign exchange market, where exporters would sell their foreign currency to those who want to hold foreign financial assets.

Note that both S and I are exogenous, since they are functions of exogenous variables. Consequently, the demand side of the foreign exchange market (the left-hand side of (3.16)) is given. The real exchange rate adjusts the right-hand side to make supply equal to demand. We assume that the real exchange rate is flexible so that the foreign exchange market always clears. Figure 3.15 illustrates the solution of the model graphically.

Next we conduct three virtual experiments on the model: a fiscal stimulus, a rise in the world interest rate, and implementation of protectionist trade policy. We use graphical analysis and leave algebraic analysis (using the implicit function theorem) for exercises.

Fiscal Stimulus

Fiscal stimulus may take two forms, cutting taxes ($T \downarrow$) or increasing government spending ($G \uparrow$). Both would reduce national saving (S), thus reducing the excess saving ($S - I$), which constitutes demand for foreign currency. As a result, the real exchange rate must appreciate (the foreign currency becomes cheaper) so that the foreign exchange market can get back to equilibrium.

Graphically, the reduction of national savings would shift the excess-saving curve (Figure 3.15) to the left, resulting in a higher equilibrium real exchange rate. That is, the domestic currency would appreciate.

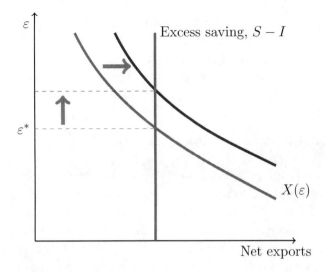

Figure 3.16 The effect of a protectionist shock.

The appreciation of the domestic currency would depress exports and stimulate imports. As the total output remains at the level of output potential, the reduction of net exports must be such that the fiscal stimulus would fail to stimulate the total output. This prediction is similar to the complete "crowding out" of the investment by a fiscal stimulus in the closed economy.

A Rise in the World Interest Rate

If the world interest rate rises $(r^* \uparrow)$, the investment expenditure would decline and the excess savings $(S - I)$ would increase. This would shift the excess-saving curve (Figure 3.15) to the right, resulting in a lower equilibrium real exchange rate.

The depreciation of the domestic currency would stimulate the net exports. Since the total output remains at the potential level when a rising world interest rate depresses the investment demand, a rising foreign demand fully compensates for the loss of aggregate demand.

Protectionist Policy Shock

Suppose that the government implements a protectionist policy that discourages imports and encourages exports. At every real exchange rate (ε), the policy would make the net export $X(\varepsilon)$ bigger. As a result, the $X(\varepsilon)$ curve would shift to the right (Figure 3.16), and the equilibrium real exchange rate will rise. Thus the classical model predicts that the protectionist policy would fail to lift the net export. The only effect of the policy is the appreciation of the domestic currency.

The reason why we reach such a dramatic conclusion is that we assume the excess savings $(S - I)$ does not depend on the exchange rate. And the excess savings alone determine the net export in our model. To increase net export or decrease the trade deficit, classical economists would argue that the government should increase national savings by, for example, cutting government expenditure.

3.7.5   A Model of a Large Open Economy

In the small open economy model, we assume that the economy is a price taker of the world interest rate. That is, the excess saving of the economy does not affect the world interest rate. This makes the world interest rate an exogenous variable in the small open economy model. If this condition does not hold, meaning that the capital outflow of the economy does affect the world interest rate, then we have to develop a model with two endogenous variables: the world (real) interest rate and the real exchange rate. We call it the model of a large open economy. Presumably, the savings and investment behavior of a large economy would have an impact on the world interest rate.

The Model

For the large open economy model, we make the following assumptions:

(i)   There is a common real interest rate (r) in the world.

(ii) The world interest rate declines when the net capital outflow from the economy increases. Equivalently, the net capital outflow is a decreasing function of the world interest rate, $F(r)$, with $F'(r) < 0$.

(iii) The net export is a decreasing function of the real exchange rate, $X(\varepsilon)$, with $X'(\varepsilon) < 0$.

Assumptions (i) and (iii) are the same as in the small open economy model. The second assumption speaks to the "largeness" of the large open economy. To see why it is reasonable, note that an increase in the net capital outflow of a large economy would make capital more abundant in the world capital market, depressing the world (real) interest rate.

By definition, the net capital outflow equals the excess saving, $F = S - I$. Rearranging the terms, we have

$$S = I + F.$$

We may interpret S as the supply side of loanable funds in the (domestic) financial market. The demand side has two components: the investment demand and the capital-outflow demand. We may imagine that savers supply loanable funds to the financial market, entrepreneurs borrow funds to invest in the economy, and the excess saving goes to people who want to hold foreign financial assets. Note that F can be negative. In this case, entrepreneurs borrow funds from abroad to invest in the economy. The identity $S = I + F$ gives us the first equilibrium condition.

Recall that the net exports always equals the net capital outflow:

$$X = F.$$

We may interpret X as the supply side in the foreign exchange market and F as the demand side. In the foreign exchange market, exporters would sell their foreign currency (obtained from the sale of goods to foreigners) to those who want to hold foreign financial assets. The identity $X = F$ gives us the second equilibrium condition.

Building on the preceding two equilibrium conditions, we have the following model for a large open economy:

$$
\begin{aligned}
S &= I(r) + F(r). & (3.17) \\
X(\varepsilon) &= F(r). & (3.18)
\end{aligned}
$$

We have two endogenous variables in the model of two equations: the world real interest rate (r) and the real exchange rate (ε). But the analysis of the model is straightforward. Note that there is only one endogenous variable (r) in (3.17), which solely determines the equilibrium real interest rate r^*. Next, we can analyze the equilibrium exchange rate ε, treating r^* as given.

Graphically, (3.17) corresponds to the vertical line on the two-dimensional diagram in Figure 3.17. On the other hand, (3.18) dictates that a bigger r must accompany a bigger ε. Thus the curve corresponding to (3.18) must be upward-sloping.

Using the model, we can conduct virtual experiments on a large open economy. We first analyze the impact of a fiscal stimulus on the economy. Then we analyze what would happen if the government implements a protectionist policy.

Fiscal Stimulus

The fiscal stimulus, whether in the form of increased government expenditure or tax cuts, is a negative shock to the national savings (S). We first analyze the impact of the shock on the equilibrium interest rate r^* by inspecting (3.17). Then we analyze the impact on ε^*, treating the change in r^* as given.

Since both $I(r)$ and $F(r)$ are decreasing functions of r, r^* must rise when S declines. Graphically, the vertical line in Figure 3.17 shifts to the right. As a result, the equilibrium exchange rate also rises.

We may verify the second prediction by inspecting (3.18). Since $F(r^*)$ has declined after the negative shock to S, $X(\varepsilon^*)$ should also decline. Since $X(\varepsilon)$ is

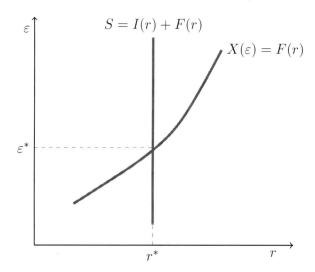

Figure 3.17 A model of large open economy.

decreasing in ε, the equilibrium exchange rate ε^* must rise (appreciate). In conclusion, a negative shock to national savings would result in a higher real interest rate and an appreciation of the domestic currency.

Protectionist Shock

The protectionist shock would have an impact on the net export function $X(\cdot)$, which appears only in the second equation (3.18). The vertical curve corresponding to the first equation does not shift. We now analyze how the upward-sloping curve $(X(\varepsilon) = F(r))$ shifts under the shock.

If we fix any ε, $X(\varepsilon)$ would increase as the protectionist shock takes place. To make $F(r)$ increase as well, r must decline. As this is true for every ε, we conclude that the curve $(X(\varepsilon) = F(r))$ must shift to the left (Figure 3.18). Hence a protectionist shock (e.g., raising import tariffs) would result in the appreciation of the domestic currency.

3.8   Concluding Remarks

The classical models in this chapter deal with the long-run equilibrium, assuming that the productive capacity of the economy does not grow. Although the theories are intellectually satisfying and the arguments are sometimes convincing, they do not directly deal with two of the most important questions in macroeconomics, economic growth and fluctuations. On the need for thinking about short-term fluctuations, Keynes famously made the following remark:

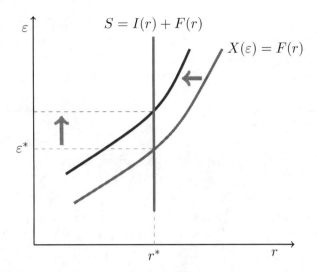

Figure 3.18 The effect of a protectionist shock.

In the long run we are all dead. Economists set themselves too easy, too useless a task if in tempestuous seasons they can only tell us that when the storm is long past the ocean is flat again.

Nonetheless, understanding classical models is still useful. First, they may serve as the benchmark, the starting point from which we may conduct further research. Second, when prices are flexible (i.e., during periods of high inflation), the long-term equilibrium analysis may shed light on the short-term trends. Finally, thanks to its simplicity, the classical theories are often influential. For example, the quantity theory of money almost dominates in the popular media. To have productive dialoguess with nonprofessionals, economists should understand classical theories, both their strengths and weaknesses.

Exercises

(1) Suppose that the output of an economy can be characterized by the Cobb–Douglas function,
$$F(K, L) = EK^\alpha L^{1-\alpha}, 0 < \alpha < 1.$$

- (a) Calculate the marginal product of labor (MPL) and the marginal product of capital (MPK). Check whether they are positive.

- (b) Calculate the second derivatives. Check that MPL is decreasing as L increases and that MPK is decreasing as K increases.

- (c) Verify that the Cobb–Douglas function satisfies constant return to scale.

(2) Suppose that every year in Shanghai, 2% of married couples get divorced and 3% of single adults get married. Define a steady state, and what would be the steady-state percentage of single people in the adult population?

(3) Suppose that an economy has two sectors: manufacturing and services. The labor demand curve in these two sectors are different, as follows

$$
\begin{aligned}
L_m &= 200 - 6W_m \\
L_s &= 100 - 4W_s,
\end{aligned}
$$

where L and W denote labor (number of workers) and wage, respectively, and the subscripts denote the sectors. The economy has a labor force of 100.

(a) If workers are free to move between sectors and there is no skill barrier, then calculate wage and employment in each sector.

(b) Now suppose that the manufacturing union manages to raise the wage in the manufacturing sector to 25 and that all workers who cannot get manufacturing jobs move to the service sector. Calculate the wage and employment in each sector.

(c) Now suppose that all workers have a reservation wage of 15. We may assume that a worker with a wage below 15 cannot afford to live in the city. He would rather go back to the countryside, where living cost is minimal, to wait for a union job (with wage 25) to open up. What is the economy's unemployment rate?

(4) Apply the classical theory of income distribution to predict the effect on the real wage and the real rental price of capital if the following events happen:

(a) An earthquake damages part of the capital stock.

(b) The government raises the retirement age.

(c) Inflation raises all prices (output price and factor-input prices) by 10%.

(d) A technological breakthrough improves the production function (suppose the production function is labor augmenting).

(e) Following (d), what if the production function is capital augmenting?

(5) Consider a closed economy characterized by the following equilibrium condition and specifications:

$$Y = C(Y - T) + I(r) + G,$$
$$Y = 8,000,\ G = 1,000,\ T = 800,$$
$$C(Y - T) = 1,000 + 3/4(Y - T),$$
$$I(r) = 1,200 - 100r.$$

(a) Calculate private saving, public saving, and national saving.

(b) Calculate the equilibrium real interest rate.

(c) Suppose that the government reduces its expenditure to achieve a balanced budget. Calculate private saving, public saving, and national saving. Then calculate the new equilibrium real interest rate.

(6) Consider the following equilibrium condition in the financial market:

$$Y - C(Y - T, r) - G = I(r),$$
$$C_1 \equiv \frac{\partial C}{\partial Y} > 0,\ C_2 \equiv \frac{\partial C}{\partial r} < 0,\ I'(r) < 0.$$

(a) Apply the implicit function theorem and obtain $\frac{\partial r}{\partial G}$. Is it positive or negative?

(b) If the government increases spending, what would happen to the real interest rate? What would happen to national saving, government saving, and private saving?

(7) The following table lists some exchange rates and Big Mac prices. Use the theory of purchasing power parity to fill in the blanks with a number or "?" if the figure cannot be inferred from the information.

Country	Currency	Big Mac price	Exchange rate (per dollar) Predicted (PPP)	Actural
USA	USD	5		
China	CNY	20		7
Japan	JPY		75	100
UK	GBP	4	0.8	

(8) Consider a small open economy characterized by the following equilibrium condition and specifications:

$$Y = C(Y - T) + I(r) + G + X(\varepsilon),$$
$$Y = 8,000,\ G = 1,000,\ T = 800,$$
$$C(Y - T) = 1,000 + 3/4(Y - T),$$
$$I(r) = 1,200 - 100r,$$
$$X(\varepsilon) = 500 - 200\varepsilon,$$
$$r = r^* = 5.$$

(a) Calculate the national savings, excess savings, and net capital outflow.

(b) Calculate the equilibrium real exchange rate.

(c) Suppose that the government increases its expenditure by 200 and leaves tax unchanged (in effect, the budget deficit increases by 200). Calculate the private savings, national savings, excess savings, and net capital outflow. Then calculate the new equilibrium real exchange rate.

(9) Apply the implicit function theorem to (3.16).

(a) Obtain $\frac{\partial \varepsilon}{\partial G}$ and $\frac{\partial \varepsilon}{\partial T}$. Are they positive or negative?

(b) Obtain $\frac{\partial \varepsilon}{\partial r^*}$. Is it positive or negative?

(c) Introduce an exogenous variable τ (say, a duty on imported goods) and make the net export a function of both ε and τ: $X(\varepsilon, \tau)$ with $X_2 \equiv \frac{\partial X}{\partial \tau} > 0$. Apply the implicit function theorem to

$$\bar{Y} - C(\bar{Y} - T) - G - I(r^*) = X(\varepsilon, \tau),$$

and obtain $\frac{\partial \varepsilon}{\partial \tau}$. Is it positive or negative?

(10) Consider a large open economy with flexible prices. What would happen to the interest rate and exchange rate if the following events occur?

(a) A business-friendly party wins the election and takes control of the government.

(b) In the name of "national security," the government increases tariffs on goods from a major trading partner.

(c) After a terrorist attack, the country goes to war in the Middle East.

Notes

.

[1] This result is known as Schwarz's theorem, Clairaut's theorem, and Young's theorem.

[2] For a famous empirical study of the minimum wage, read Card and Krueger, 1994, Minimum Wages and Employment: A Case Study of the Fast-Food Industry in New Jersey and Pennsylvania. *American Economic Review*, September, 84(4), 772–793.

[3] We calculate the labor share of income using the income to the household sector in the flow-of-funds table (nonfinancial transactions).

[4] This is obtained by $(1 + 0.01)^{12} - 1$.

[5] In China, market participants call risk-free bonds "interest-rate bonds" (利率债). And bonds with credit risk are called "credit bonds" (信用债)

[6] Classical economists may use the word "capital" in place of money. Alfred Marshall, for example, define interest as the price paid for the use of capital in any market. Here the word capital means money.

[7] Paul Gomme, B. Ravikumar, and Peter Rupert, 2015, Secular Stagnation and Returns on Capital, *Economic Synopses*, 19 Federal Reserve Bank of St. Louis.

[8] The implicit function is differentiable if both sides of the equation are differentiable. In this case, we need to assume that both $C(\cdot)$ and $I(\cdot)$ are differentiable.

[9] 金圆券

4

Economic Growth

Poverty is not socialism. – Deng Xiaoping[1]

4.1 Introduction

Economic growth, or economic development, is no doubt one of the most important topics in macroeconomics. For poor countries, a stagnant economy means persistent absolute poverty. In absolute poverty, the need for survival dominates all other desires of human beings. Human lives in absolute poverty can be extremely miserable and dangerous.

In relative terms, a slight but persistent difference in growth rate would result in huge income gaps among nations. The following table illustrates how three different growth rates of income per capita (from the same level, say 100) lead to starkly different outcomes many (10, 30, 100) years later.

Growth rates/Years	0	10	30	100
1%	100	110.5	134.8	270.5
3%	100	134.4	242.7	1,921.9
8%	100	215.9	1,006.3	219,976.1

Economic growth is important not only in terms of the outcome (that is, a wealthy society) but also the path that leads to the outcome. Economic growth is good in itself. People in a growing economy tend to be more optimistic about the future. They tend to be more open and tolerant because the economic pie is getting bigger. Even a wealthy nation, if it stops growing, can fall to the prey of intolerance and hostility because people are trapped in a zero-sum game.

To simplify the analysis of economic growth, we focus on the long-term trend of output potential $\bar{Y}_t$. Note that I add a time subscript to emphasize that, in

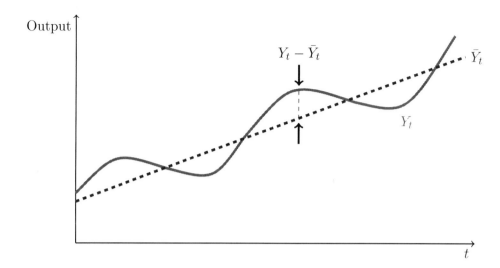

Figure 4.1 Long-term trend of output potential and output gap.

this chapter, the output potential may be growing over time. We may imagine that business cycles are short-term fluctuations around the long-term trend of the output potential. More precisely, we may write the following:

$$Y_t = \bar{Y}_t + \left(Y_t - \bar{Y}_t\right),$$

where $\bar{Y}_t$ represents the trend of *output potential* and $\left(Y_t - \bar{Y}_t\right)$ is the *output gap*. Figure 4.1 illustrates the relationship between the long-term trend of output potential $(\bar{Y}_t)$ and the output gap $\left(Y_t - \bar{Y}_t\right)$.

We may assume that short-term fluctuations in the output gap are independent of the long-term trend, meaning that the short-term fluctuation does not have an impact on the long-term trend, and vice versa. Under this assumption, we can safely disregard the fluctuations in the output gap in this chapter and focus on the long-term trend only. To justify the assumption, we may argue that the long-term trend reflects the supply-side changes, such as the accumulation of capital, technological progress, etc., while the short-term fluctuation reflects the short-term changes in the aggregate demand.

Note, however, the independence of the output gap from the trend is only an assumption. It may well be that the short-term fluctuation may interact with the change in the trend. A severe recession, for example, may permanently damage the growth potential if the recession brings mass unemployment, social unrest, political instability, and so on. On the bright side, a severe downturn may also strengthen political support for reforms in the government, hence paving the way for better growth in the future. Indeed, the reform of the Chinese state sector in the late 1990s happened during a severe downturn, when the state-owned enterprises were in deep trouble.

In the rest of the chapter, we ignore the fluctuations in the output gap and assume that $Y_t = \bar{Y}_t$ for all t. We first introduce two versions of Solow models that characterize the dynamics of economic growth. The first Solow model depicts a dismal picture of economic growth or, more precisely, nongrowth. This model is relevant to economies in the so-called poverty trap, or the agricultural economies before the Industrial Revolution. To model the lucky few countries that experienced sustained growth, we introduce the second Solow model that incorporates an exogenous *technological progress*, which helps to overcome the decreasing marginal product of capital, thus achieving sustained growth.

The exogenous "technological progress" includes all kinds of progress in the society that is conducive to economic prosperity. It includes not only progress in science and engineering but also the increasing capability of public-goods provision, resource allocation and mobilization, and so on. The sustained improvement in these capabilities is essential to sustainable economic growth. Assuming an exogenous "technological progress," as does the Solow model, is not very helpful for understanding the causes of economic growth.

To understand how "technological progress" comes about, we first introduce an endogenous growth model that does not require an exogenous process of technological progress. Then we introduce two important theories that explain technological progress: the theory of creative destruction proposed by Joseph Schumpeter and the two-sector Lewis model. Both models are very relevant for the study of Chinese economic growth.

Note that since economic growth is a long-term story, we will continue to work under the classical assumptions. As a result, the models in this chapter are all about the supply side of the economy. This chapter differs from the previous one in that we talk about a possibly expanding supply side.

4.2 Solow Model without Technological Progress

We now introduce the Solow model, named after Robert M. Solow. We first introduce a simple version, which characterizes the role of factor accumulation in economic growth.

4.2.1 The Model

We assume that all available factor resources (e.g., labor and capital) are fully employed in production. This is a reasonable assumption since we are studying the long-term growth of the output potential $Y_t = \bar{Y}_t$. Furthermore, we make the following assumptions.

Assumptions

(a) Closed economy ($X = 0$).

(b) No government spending ($G = 0$).

(c) Fixed constant-return-to-scale technology, $F(K, L)$.

(d) The saving rate s is a constant and $0 \leq s \leq 1$.

(e) Population grows at a constant rate n.

(f) Capital depreciates at a constant rate δ.

The assumptions (a) and (b) are for the simplification of analysis. Assumption (c) says that there is no technological progress. Assumption (d), together with (a) and (b), implies that both investment and consumption expenditures are fixed fractions of the total income:

$$I_t = sY_t, \quad C_t = (1 - s)Y_t.$$

Note that $Y_t = C_t + I_t$ for all t is a rather strong statement. It says that the aggregate demand ($C_t + I_t$) automatically accommodates the aggregate supply, Y_t.

Assumption (e) says that the population grows by $n \times 100\%$ per unit of time (say, a year). If the population starts with L_0 at time 0, the population at time t would be $L_t = L_0 e^{nt}$. We can also characterize population growth using a differential equation:

$$\dot{L}_t = nL_t, \tag{4.1}$$

where $\dot{L}_t$ represents $\frac{dL_t}{dt}$. We may easily check that $L_t = L_0 e^{nt}$ solves (4.1).

Dot Notation and Differential Equation

Note that L_t is a simplified notation for $L(t)$, a function of continuous time t. And $\dot{L}_t$ represents the derivative of L with respect to t:

$$\dot{L}_t \equiv \frac{dL_t}{dt}.$$

Using differential equations to characterize L_t, K_t, and so on, we make an implicit assumption that these variables are smooth functions of t, so smooth that they are differentiable with respect to t.

Assumption (f) says that per unit of time (say, a year), the capital stock declines by $\delta \times 100\%$. If we have an initial capital stock K_0 and there is no new investment, then

$$K_t = K_0 e^{-\delta t}.$$

That is, the capital stock wears out exponentially. We may easily check that this exponential function solves the following differential equation:

$$\dot{K}_t = -\delta K_t.$$

Since, at the same time, investment increases the capital stock, we can characterize capital accumulation by the following differential equation:

$$\dot{K}_t = sY_t - \delta K_t. \tag{4.2}$$

The left-hand side of (4.2) is the change in the capital stock per unit of time. The right-hand side is the additional capital stock brought by new investment (sY_t), minus the depreciation of the capital stock (δK_t).

We may also represent (4.1) and (4.2) in discrete-time form (difference equation):

$$
\begin{aligned}
L_t - L_{t-1} &= nL_{t-1}, \\
K_t - K_{t-1} &= sY_{t-1} - \delta K_{t-1}, \\
t &= 1, 2, 3, \ldots
\end{aligned}
$$

This formulation is useful in conducting simulations using spreadsheets.

Per Capita Production Function

Let $y_t = Y_t/L_t$ and $k_t = K_t/L_t$. Obviously, y_t is the average output, or per capita output, and k_t is the average capital, or per capita capital. Using the constant-return-to-scale property of F, we have

$$y_t = \frac{Y_t}{L_t} = \frac{F(K_t, L_t)}{L_t} = F(k_t, 1).$$

We define a *per capita production function*, $f(k_t) \equiv F(k_t, 1)$. Then we have

$$y_t = f(k_t).$$

We may also call $f(\cdot)$ the *individual production function*. We assume that

$$f(0) = 0, f'(k) > 0, f''(k) < 0. \tag{4.3}$$

That is, zero capital produces zero output, and the marginal product of capital (MPK) is positive and declining as k increases. Sometimes we may also assume that

$$\lim_{k \to 0} f'(k) = \infty, \quad \text{and} \quad \lim_{k \to \infty} f'(k) = 0. \tag{4.4}$$

This assumption says that MPK is very large when capital stock is very low, and that MPK is close to zero when capital stock is very large.

Without government spending and net export, the aggregate demand for goods and services comes from consumption (C) and investment (I) only. In per capita terms, we have

$$y_t = c_t + i_t,$$

where $c_t = C_t/L_t$ and $i_t = I_t/L_t$. The per cap investment is a constant fraction of the per capita output:

$$i_t = y_t - c_t = sy_t = sf(k_t).$$

4.2.2 Steady State

To characterize the accumulation of the per capita capital, we first calculate

$$\dot{k}_t = \frac{d}{dt}\left(\frac{K_t}{L_t}\right) = \frac{\dot{K}_t}{L_t} - \frac{K_t \dot{L}_t}{L_t^2}.$$

If we plug in (4.1) and (4.2), we obtain

$$\dot{k}_t = sf(k_t) - (\delta + n)k_t. \qquad (4.5)$$

The per capita investment $(sf(k_t))$ increases the per cap capital (k_t), while depreciation and population growth make k_t decline.

The assumptions (4.3) and (4.4) ensure that the differential equation in (4.5) has a *steady state*. It means that, as capital accumulates from a low level, it will reach a point where new investment equals depreciation and dilution by population growth:

$$sf(k^*) = (\delta + n)k^*. \qquad (4.6)$$

At this level of capital, k^*, the economy reaches a steady state, where capital per capita does not increase or decrease. We call k^* the steady-state level of capital. Note that the population growth rate (n) has a similar effect on steady-state capital stock with the depreciation rate (δ) since both population growth and depreciation reduce per capita capital stock.

Figure 4.2 graphically characterizes the steady-state of the model. Since $f'(k)$ is very large when k is very small, $sf(k)$ will be initially above $(\delta + n)k$ as k increases from 0. As k gets larger and larger, $f'(k)$ keeps declining and eventually goes to zero. This makes sure that $sf(k)$ (the solid line) will cross $(\delta + n)k$ (the dashed line) somewhere. Hence the existence of a steady state.

Note that the steady-state level of capital k^* is a *stable* steady state, meaning that k_t would get back to k^* after a perturbation. Suppose, for example, a shock pushes k_t below k^*. Since the new investment $(sf(k_t)$, the solid line) is higher than the depreciation and the dilution due to population growth $((\delta + n)k_t$, blue line), k_t would rise until it reaches k^*.

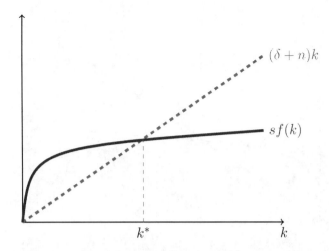

Figure 4.2 The Solow model without technological progress.

Similarly, if k_t is pushed above k^*, then the new investment would be lower than the depreciation and the dilution (due to population growth). As a result, the capital stock per capita would decline until it reaches k^*.

The Solow model without technological progress allows only one type of growth, the growth from a nonsteady state with a k_t lower than k^*. If the initial level of capital is well below the steady-state level (say, due to war damage), then the new investment may be much higher than the depreciation and the dilution due to population growth, resulting in the fast accumulation of capital and fast economic recovery. We may call this *catch-up growth*. Germany and Japan, after World War II, arguably experienced such growth.

Numerical Experiment: How to Reach a Steady State

Suppose that $F(K, L) = K^{0.5}L^{0.5}$. Then we have

$$y = k^{0.5}.$$

Let $n = 0$, $s = 0.3$, $\delta = 0.1$, $k_0 = 4$. Using the discrete-time formulation,

$$k_t - k_{t-1} = 0.3k_{t-1}^{0.5} - 0.1k_{t-1}, \quad t = 1, 2, \ldots,$$

we can calculate k_1, k_2, ..., iteratively. The Excel spreadsheet Solow1.xlsx, available at `http://jhqian.org/macrobook`, conducts a numerical simulation. We can check how the economy, from the initial point $k_0 = 4$, reaches the steady-state $k^* = 9$, the solution to $0.3\left(k^*\right)^{0.5} = 0.1k^*$.

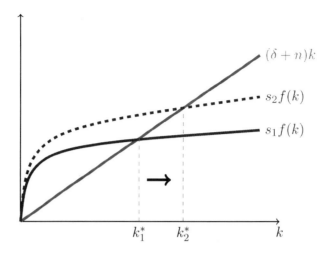

Figure 4.3 The effect of a higher saving rate.

If the economy is already at a steady state, however, then the per capita capital stock would cease to grow. The Solow model without technological progress thus paints a rather dismal picture of the economy. As the per capita capital stock stops growing, the per capita output and income also stagnates at $y^* = f(k^*)$. Although the total income continues to grow as the population grows, $Y_t = y^* L_t = y^* L_0 e^{nt}$, the average life quality, which is largely a function of average income, cannot improve.

4.2.3   The Effect of the Saving Rate

To see the effect of a change in the saving rate, s, we examine the equation characterizing the steady state in (4.6), which defines an implicit function $k^*(s, \delta, n)$. Applying the implicit function theorem, we have

$$\frac{\partial k^*}{\partial s} = -\frac{f(k^*)}{s f'(k^*) - (\delta + n)}.$$

We must have $s f'(k^*) < \delta + n$, otherwise the curve $sf(k)$ cannot cross with the line $(\delta + n)k$ at k^*. Hence $\frac{\partial k^*}{\partial s}$ must be positive, meaning that an increase in saving rate would lead to a higher level of steady-state capital and income (see Figure 4.3). However, once the economy reaches the new steady state, the income per capita stagnates once again.

4.2.4   Golden-Rule Level of Capital

If the saving rate is zero, the corresponding steady-state capital, income, and consumption would all be zero. And if the saving rate is one, then there would be nothing left for consumption. Hence neither too little saving nor too much saving would be desirable. And we might guess that there should be an optimal saving rate that achieves a maximum level of consumption in the steady state.

At steady state, the consumption is given by

$$c^* = f(k^*) - sf(k^*) = f(k^*) - (\delta + n)k^*.$$

We call the level of steady-state capital that corresponds to the maximum consumption the *golden-rule level of capital*. We may denote the golden-rule level of steady-state capital by k_g^*, which solves the following maximization problem:

$$\max_{k^*} c(k^*) = \max_{k^*} f(k^*) - (\delta + n)k^*.$$

To maximize $c(k^*)$, k_g^* must satisfy the following first-order condition:

$$f'\left(k_g^*\right) = \delta + n. \tag{4.7}$$

The first-order condition says that, when $k^* = k_g^*$, the marginal product of capital (MPK) equals the depreciation rate plus the population growth rate.

Recall that the steady-state level of capital is an increasing function of the saving rate, $\partial k^*/\partial s > 0$. We might adjust s to achieve the golden-rule level of capital. If the initial level of capital is lower than the golden-rule level, we might increase the saving rate to achieve the golden-rule level. If the initial level of capital is higher than the golden-rule level, then we might decrease the saving rate to achieve the golden-rule level.

Numerical Experiment: Approaching the Golden Rule of Capital

Following the previous numerical experiment, we solve the steady-state condition:

$$s\left(k^*\right)^{1/2} = 0.1k^*,$$

which yields $k^*(s) = 100s^2$. Since $s = 0.3$, we obtain the steady-state level of capital in this economy, $k^* = 9$.

The golden-rule steady-state capital is obtained from

$$1/2 \left(k_g^*\right)^{-1/2} = 0.1,$$

which gives $k_g^* = 25$. Hence the steady-state level of capital is too low. We might increase the saving rate to achieve the golden rule. Which saving rate corresponds to the golden rule? We solve $100s^2 = 25$ and obtain $s_g^* = 0.5$.

The Excel spreadsheet Solow1.xlsx, available at `http://jhqian.org/macrobook`, shows how the economy dynamically adjusts to the increase of saving rate from 0.3 to 0.5.

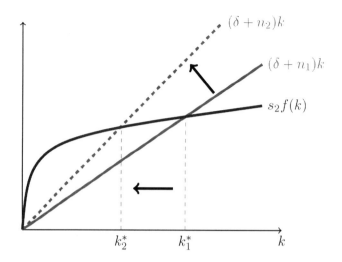

Figure 4.4 The effect of higher population growth.

4.2.5   The Effect of Population Growth

To see how population growth affects steady-state income, we once again apply the implicit function theorem to (4.6), and we have

$$\frac{\partial k^*}{\partial n} = -\frac{-k^*}{sf'(k^*) - (\delta + n)} < 0.$$

Hence higher population growth leads to lower per cap capital, output, and income in steady state. Graphically, Figure 4.4 shows how an increase in the population growth rate reduces the steady-state per capita capital.

Empirically, we do see a negative correlation between population growth and income per capita. However, this correlation does not prove that higher population growth causes lower economic growth. In fact, population growth may well be endogenous. In wealthy societies, for example, costs of raising and educating children are high, making people reluctant to have more children.

4.3   Solow Model with Technological Progress

The Solow model without technological progress predicts that there is no sustainable growth in income per capita. The dismal prediction may be true for many poor countries in the world, or the world as a whole before the industrial revolution. But after the industrial revolution, there are a number of countries that have experienced sustained growth in the span of several decades or centuries (e.g., the United Kingdom and the United States). The existence of such countries refutes the Solow model without technological progress as a general characterization of all economies. To accommodate such successful stories, we introduce technological progress into our model.

4.3.1 The Model

We assume that the economy has an expanding production function. Specifically, in this section, we assume that the economy is endowed with the following production function:

$$Y_t = F(K_t, A_t L_t),$$

where A_t represents the level of efficiency in the economy as a whole. The way A_t enters the production function is called *labor augmenting*. If A_t increases over time, we say that the economy is experiencing *technological progress* that makes labor more productive. We assume that A_t is exogenous and satisfies

$$A_t = A_0 e^{gt}.$$

That is, the technology grows exponentially at a constant rate, g. The exponential technological progress has an equivalent differential-equation form:

$$\dot{A}_t = g A_t. \tag{4.8}$$

And we make the following assumptions:

(a) Closed economy $(X = 0)$.

(b) No government spending $(G = 0)$.

(c) The function $F(\cdot, \cdot)$ has constant return to scale.

(d) The saving rate s is a constant and $0 \leq s \leq 1$.

(e) Population grows at a constant rate n.

(f) Capital depreciates at a constant rate δ.

We let $y_t = Y_t/(A_t L_t)$ and $k_t = K_t/(A_t L_t)$. We call y_t the *output per effective worker* (p.e.w.), and k_t the p.e.w. capital stock. We have

$$y_t = \frac{F(K_t, A_t L_t)}{A_t L_t} = F(k_t, 1).$$

As in the Solow model without technological progress, we define $f(k_t) \equiv F(k_t, 1)$, and write

$$y_t = f(k_t).$$

We may call $f(\cdot)$ the *p.e.w. production function*. As in the first Solow model without technological progress, we assume (4.3) and (4.4).

4.3.2   Steady State

Using $\dot{A}_t = gA_t$, $\dot{L}_t = nL_t$, and $\dot{K}_t = sF(K_t, A_tL_t) - \delta K_t$, we can work out the dynamics of p.e.w. capital accumulation:

$$
\begin{aligned}
\dot{k}_t &= \frac{d}{dt}\left(\frac{K_t}{A_tL_t}\right) = \frac{\dot{K}_t}{A_tL_t} - \frac{K_t\dot{L}_t}{A_tL_t^2} - \frac{K_t\dot{A}_t}{L_tA_t^2}\\
&= sf(k_t) - (\delta + n + g)k_t.
\end{aligned} \tag{4.9}
$$

Note that the preceding differential equation has the same form with (4.5). The assumptions (4.3) and (4.4), once again, ensure that k_t has a steady state.

The steady-state capital p.e.w., k^*, is characterized by the following equation:

$$
sf(k^*) - (\delta + n + g)k^* = 0. \tag{4.10}
$$

At steady state, the p.e.w capital stock is a constant:

$$
\frac{K_t}{A_tL_t} = k^*.
$$

This implies that the total output, $Y_t = A_tL_tf(k^*)$, grows at the constant rate $n + g$ and that the per capita output, $Y_t/L_t = A_tf(k^*)$, grows at the constant rate g. Thus the Solow model with technological progress can explain sustained growth in per capita output or income.

The steady-state condition in (4.10) defines an implicit function $k^*(s, \delta, n, g)$. Using the same technique as in the previous section, we may analyze the effect of saving rate (s) on the steady-state p.e.w. capital stock (k^*). There is also an optimal saving rate that corresponds to the golden rule of capital, which results in maximum consumption. We leave these analyses to exercises.

4.3.3   Balanced-Growth Path

The steady state of the Solow model describes a balanced-growth path, where income, capital stock, consumption, and investment grow at the same speed. On the balanced-growth path, many important ratios remain constant or grow at the same speed. For example, the ratio of total consumption to total income is by assumption a constant, $(1-s)$. For another example, the capital output ratio K_t/Y_t is a constant at the steady state:

$$
\frac{K_t}{Y_t} = k^*/f(k^*).
$$

The capital output ratio is a measure of the amount of capital needed for producing a unit of output. Note that the capital output ratio is nothing but the inverse of *capital productivity* Y_t/K_t.

On the other hand, the capital per capita K_t/L_t and the labor productivity (or the per capita income) Y_t/L_t grow at the same speed as technological progress since

$$\frac{K_t}{L_t} = k^* A_t \quad \text{and} \quad \frac{Y_t}{L_t} = f(k^*) A_t.$$

We may infer that the real wage should also grow at the same speed as labor productivity and that the real rental price of capital should be constant since capital productivity is constant. Recall that in a competitive economy, the real wage equals the marginal product of labor (MPL), and the real rental price of capital equals the marginal product of capital (MPK). At the steady state, we have

$$
\begin{aligned}
\text{MPL}_t &= \frac{\partial Y_t}{\partial L_t} = \frac{\partial}{\partial L_t}\left(A_t L_t f\left(\frac{K_t}{A_t L_t}\right)\right) = A_t\left(f(k^*) - k^* f'(k^*)\right), \\
\text{MPK}_t &= \frac{\partial Y_t}{\partial K_t} = \frac{\partial}{\partial K_t}\left(A_t L_t f\left(\frac{K_t}{A_t L_t}\right)\right) = f'\left(\frac{K_t}{A_t L_t}\right) = f'(k^*).
\end{aligned}
$$

Thus the Solow model with technological progress implies that the real wage grows at the same speed with labor productivity and that the real return to capital remains constant. It should be noted that we obtain these results because we assume a labor-augmenting technological progress. Interested readers may explore what might happen if the technological progress is capital-augmenting.

4.3.4   Optimism of Growth

In contrast to the Solow model without technological progress, the Solow model with technological progress paints a much more optimistic picture of economic growth. It implies that all countries, as long as they embrace the same "technology" in the world, would achieve sustainable growth.

Note that $k^* = 0$ is also a steady state in (4.10). We may call it the *subsistence steady state*. At the subsistence steady state, people can barely feed themselves, and nothing remains for investment. But the subsistence steady state is not stable. Any positive perturbation, which gives people some capital stock, would push the economy into a virtuous cycle: higher income, more investment, more capital stock, higher income, and so on. Eventually, the economy would settle into the balanced-growth steady state $(k^* > 0)$.

And, importantly, the steady-state capital and income have nothing to do with the initial level of capital and income. Note that the steady-state p.e.w. capital (k^*) is a function of saving rate, the rate of technological progress, the rate of population growth, and the depreciation rate. That is, $k^* = k^*(s, g, n, \delta)$, which is implicitly defined in (4.10). If a poor country has the same saving rate, the same growth rate of population, and the same depreciation rate and enjoys the same technology as an advanced high-income country, then the Solow model with technological progress predicts that the poor country would converge to the high-income country in terms of average living standards.

The prediction of convergence, however, has very limited empirical support. Many poor countries have remained poor in the past half-century. And only a few countries in East Asia, notably the Asian Tigers, have grown from low-income countries to achieve high-income status. It remains to be seen whether China, full of potential, can become a high-income country.

To reconcile theory and facts, recall that the "technology" in the Solow model encompasses not only science and engineering but also the quality of government and market institutions, transportation and communication infrastructures, social trust, and so on. And, accordingly, technological progress has multiple meanings. It means not only scientific or engineering advances but also improvement in infrastructure, and most importantly, the improvement of governance. While scientific and engineering know-how does not have national borders, all the other "technology" has national borders. To improve the "technology" within borders, the government should continuously reform itself. Most emerging countries, however, either do not have a strong government to implement reforms or have a strong government without incentives to reform themselves. Hence the lack of successful stories about economic development.

4.4   Endogenous Growth

A major criticism of the Solow model is on the assumption of an exogenous technological progress. And since technological progress is the most important variable that makes the Solow model predict sustainable growth, one must ask how nations can achieve technological progress, whatever it means. Assuming the existence of an essential element without further explanations may remind serious readers of the famous can-opener joke about economists.

The Can-Opener Joke

There is a story about a physicist, a chemist, and an economist who were stranded on a desert island. They were hungry and empty-handed, but they found a can of food. The physicist and the chemist each devised an ingenious mechanism for getting the can open; the economist merely said, "Assume we have a can opener!"

– in *Economics as a Science* (1970) by Kenneth E. Boulding.

Thus economists start to come up with models of *endogenous growth*, which either makes technological progress endogenous or discards it all together. In this section, we introduce the famous AK model that follows the latter approach. It generates sustainable growth without using the exogenous device of technological progress.

The AK model assumes that the population is constant and that the technology of the economy is linear. Specifically, we assume

$$Y_t = AK_t,$$

where Y_t is output, K_t is capital stock that includes "knowledge" or human capital, and $A > 0$ is a constant, representing both the *marginal product of capital* and the *average product of capital*. Capital accumulation follows

$$\dot{K}_t = sY_t - \delta K_t,$$

where s is saving rate, and δ is the depreciation rate. It is obvious that

$$\frac{\dot{Y}_t}{Y_t} = \frac{\dot{K}_t}{K_t} = sA - \delta. \tag{4.11}$$

As long as $sA > \delta$, the AK model produces sustained growth without making an exogenous assumption on technological progress. And the growth in the AK model is driven by investment or accumulation of capital. The linear technology, which has a constant return to capital, is the crucial assumption that makes investment-driven growth sustainable. In contrast, the Solow model without technological progress assumes diminishing return to capital, making investment-based growth unsustainable. To make a case for constant return to capital, we may understand that the capital stock in the AK model includes "knowledge." Here, knowledge includes scientific understanding, engineering know-how, managerial and marketing skills, the creativity of artistic design, and so on. Knowledge arguably has increasing returns: More knowledge makes better applications of knowledge. Physical capital, in contrast, generally has diminishing returns. If the total capital stock is composed of diminishing-return physical capital and increasing-return knowledge, then we may have a constant-return-to-capital technology for the whole economy.

According to (4.11), the growth rate of the AK economy at the steady state depends on the saving rate (s), the average product of capital (A), and the depreciation rate (δ). The more saving, the more investment, especially in "knowledge," the better chance of sustainable growth. And higher growth rate requires a higher saving rate and higher investment.

A higher average product of capital means better *quality* of the existing capital stock, which in turn depends on the quality of past investment. Thus the AK model indicates that economic growth relies on not only the quantity of investment but also the quality of investment.

Finally, a lower depreciation rate would be good for growth. "Knowledge" arguably has a lower depreciation rate than physical capital. The investment in knowledge increases the share of human capital in the capital stock, lowering the overall depreciation rate.

4.5   Growth Accounting

A nation can achieve economic growth, either by accumulating factor inputs (e.g., labor and capital) or by increasing efficiency ("technology" of the aggregate economy). The job of growth accounting is to assess the contribution of factor inputs and efficiency gain to economic growth. Note that since the marginal product of (physical) capital generally declines as the capital stock increases, the economic growth that relies on capital accumulation is unsustainable. And the growth that relies on population growth is not particularly attractive since it does not raise the average income. In contrast, if a substantial part of economic growth comes from efficiency gain, then the growth is sustainable and good for improving the average well-being.

For the simplicity of accounting for contributions to growth, we assume that the economy can be characterized by

$$Y_t = A_t F(K_t, L_t),$$

where $F(\cdot, \cdot)$ is a constant-return-to-scale production function and A_t is a positive process that measures the technological progress of the economy. Note that the technological progress here augments not only labor but also capital. In this sense, we also call A_t the *total factor productivity*.

Taking total differential and dividing both sides by Y_t,

$$\frac{\dot{Y}_t}{Y_t} = \frac{A_t F_{1t} \times K_t}{Y_t} \times \frac{\dot{K}_t}{K_t} + \frac{A_t F_{2t} \times L_t}{Y_t} \times \frac{\dot{L}_t}{L_t} + \frac{\dot{A}_t}{A_t},$$

where $F_{1t} = \partial F(K_t, L_t)/\partial K_t$ and $F_{2t} = \partial F(K_t, L_t)/\partial L_t$. Note that $A_t F_{1t}$ is the marginal product of capital and $A_t F_{2t}$ is the marginal product of labor. Denote

$$\alpha_t = \frac{A_t F_{1t} \times K_t}{Y_t}, \quad \text{and} \quad \beta_t = \frac{A_t F_{2t} \times L_t}{Y_t}.$$

If the markets for factor inputs are competitive, then α_t and β_t are the income shares of capital and labor, respectively. We then have

$$\frac{\dot{Y}_t}{Y_t} = \alpha_t \frac{\dot{K}_t}{K_t} + \beta_t \frac{\dot{L}_t}{L_t} + \frac{\dot{A}_t}{A_t}. \tag{4.12}$$

In this equation, the growth rate of the total output $\frac{\dot{Y}_t}{Y_t}$ is decomposed into three components: the growth of capital stock $\frac{\dot{K}_t}{K_t}$, the growth of labor $\frac{\dot{L}_t}{L_t}$, and technological progress $\frac{\dot{A}_t}{A_t}$. Since $\frac{\dot{A}_t}{A_t}$ is unobservable, this term has to be estimated in empirical analyses. Specifically, to estimate $\frac{\dot{A}_t}{A_t}$ in practice, we can assume that $\alpha_t = \alpha$ and $\beta_t = \beta$ are constant and run a linear regression of $\frac{\dot{Y}_t}{Y_t}$ on $\frac{\dot{K}_t}{K_t}$ and $\frac{\dot{L}_t}{L_t}$ plus a constant term. The residual term from this regression plus the constant term gives an estimate of $\frac{\dot{A}_t}{A_t}$. Technically speaking, the Solow residual is the growth in output that cannot be explained by growth in factor inputs. Hence we often call $\frac{\dot{A}_t}{A_t}$ the *Solow residual*. The contribution of the Solow residual is presumably the contribution of the total factor productivity or technological progress.

4.6 Understanding Growth

In this section, we present two theories of growth, *creative destruction* by Joseph A. Schumpeter (1883–1950) and the Lewis model named after W. Arthur Lewis (1915–1991). They are not formal mathematical models but verbal models that are described by words. Both theories are useful for explaining how macroeconomic technological progress may be achieved in the real world.

4.6.1 Creative Destruction

Creative destruction is a dynamic evolutionary process in a market economy by which creative entrepreneurs drive incumbents out of businesses so that the "technology" of the whole economy makes continuous progress. Entrepreneurs come up with new products, new technology, new managerial and marketing ideas, and other innovations. Their entry would ultimately drive uncreative incumbents out of the market, hence the term of *creative destruction*. These entrepreneurs would then become the new incumbents, trying hard to protect their market power. But a new generation of entrepreneurs would enter the market nonetheless, with even better products or ideas. The dynamic process of creative destruction goes on.

Entrepreneurs

Entrepreneurs are people who start businesses and strive for profits by taking initiatives and risks. Entrepreneurship is the act of being an entrepreneur, the dynamic process by which entrepreneurs identify business opportunities, acquire the necessary resources, and manage the resources to realize profits.

Entrepreneurship is a commendatory term. Although entrepreneurs may conduct their business solely out of personal motives, their actions often bring gains to society. For example, a successful start-up company creates new job opportunities and new products for consumers, as well as profit to its owners. And to beat the incumbents, entrepreneurs must offer higher pay to attract productive employees, produce higher-quality products, and make production more cost efficient. As the French economist Jean-Baptiste Say puts it, an entrepreneur "shifts economic resources out of an area of lower and into an area of higher productivity and greater yield." With millions of entrepreneurs working tirelessly for their own interests, the productivity of the economy as a whole improves. In other words, using the Solow model's terminology, entrepreneurs drive "technological progress."

Although we only discuss business entrepreneurship, entrepreneurship can be more general. Anyone who takes initiatives and risks to realize social gains can be called an entrepreneur. For example, a writer taking the initiative and risks to write a novel is an entrepreneur. Entrepreneurship is part of human nature, and it manifests in all areas of work. Those who have strong entrepreneurship become leaders in business, scientific research, arts, and so on.

Market Economy

The market economy is essential for creative destruction to happen. More precisely, the market must play a dominant role in picking winners, rewarding success, and bankrupting losers. If it is some government agencies that pick winners, then the true innovative entrepreneurs would generally lose out. Those who specialize in winning political favors do not typically have an edge in innovation. Nor do they have incentives to invest in research and development.

More generally, the rule of law (in contrast to "the rule of man") is essential for the market to pick winners, reward success, and bankrupt losers in a fair manner. The rule of law represents the quality of the market and the quality of market matters. The incumbents typically have more money and thus political influence. If they can buy "help" from government officials, lawmakers, police officers, and judges, then small entrepreneurs would have no chance of success in competing with large incumbents. For entrepreneurs to challenge the incumbents, the playing field must be level for everyone. This is possible only if all players, including the government, are equally and predictably bounded by the law.

The size of the market also matters. A bigger market has bigger rewards for innovation. Bigger rewards bring more entrepreneurs who challenge the status quo. Note that the market size is not the same thing as the size of an economy, measured by GDP or population. A small nation can enjoy a big market size if the nation is an integral part of the world market. Countries like Singapore and Israel are examples of such successful small open economies.

A large nation, on the other hand, can enjoy no market-size dividend if it has a segmented domestic market. The segmentation can be due to the poor infrastructure of transportation and communications. More importantly, the segmentation can be due to various forms of local protectionism. The local governments often have incentives to protect their local business and employment. Or, more sinisterly, the local officials have incentives to impose local tax and regulations for rent-seeking opportunities.

One thousand segmented local markets do not make one large market. Potential entrepreneurs in each of these local markets can only expect a small reward that a small market can afford. Many densely populated developing countries suffer from market segmentation, either due to local protectionism or poor infrastructure or both. They have a huge population, but they have small markets. India is a typical example. In the early stage of reforming and opening up, China also had a highly segmented domestic market.

Limitations

Even under the rule of law and with substantial market size, creative destruction is not a perfect process. It may not bring about "technological progress," which underpins economic growth. And it is even less certain that creative destruction will bring a better society.

First, at least some industries exhibit increasing returns to scale. Monopolies, as a result, can easily take hold in such industries. Compared to smaller potential competitors, they enjoy tremendous cost advantages simply because of their scale. More creative entrepreneurs, who may potentially produce better goods, may fail to challenge the less efficient incumbents because they have to start small. And the incumbents, facing no existential threat, have little incentive to upgrade their technology or management. The "technology" of the industry, as a result, may stagnate.

Second, the social gain from creative destruction is not guaranteed. Creativity can be used in the wrong place. For example, entrepreneurs who are shameless and creative in evading environmental laws would win over those with social responsibilities since the shameless ones enjoy cost advantages. For another example, entrepreneurs in the nutrition industry may be very creative in marketing their useless or hazardous products to credulous consumers. Those who produce truly helpful and safe products, which require expensive research and development (R&D) spending, may not compete with fraudulent producers.

Third, the gain from creative destruction is necessarily unevenly distributed. The process of creative destruction creates losers as well as winners. Although creative destruction brings overall welfare to society, the welfare may be reaped by a small percentage of the population, i.e., the successful entrepreneurs. The displaced workers in failed firms would find their skills too specific to find comparable jobs in other firms. They would have to accept a deep wage cut to find new jobs, and they would have to lower their living standards to make ends meet. Sometimes, a whole town of jobs may be lost due to the failure of a firm. The old way of life would be gone for all people in town.

Any responsible government, thus, cannot let creative destruction run its own course. The responsible government would ensure competition by breaking up monopolies. Such a government would vigorously play the cat-and-mouse games with law evaders and make sure a level playing field for all entrepreneurs. Finally, the responsible government must establish meaningful welfare programs to help losers from creative destruction. Without doing this, relentless creative destruction may destroy the institutional framework that underpins creative destruction. This dismal prospect is exactly what both Schumpeter and Marx, who first raised the idea of creative destruction, predicted.

4.6.2 The Lewis Model

W. Arthur Lewis's 1954 paper, "Economic Development with Unlimited Supplies of Labour," was instrumental in developing the field of development economics. His model characterizes how a developing country transforms its predominantly subsistence economy into a predominantly industrial one. The Lewis model is particularly relevant to the experience of China's growth. Chinese economists started to use the *Lewis turning point* to explain the emergence of labor shortages as early as 2005. This rekindled general interest, not restricted to academic circles, in Lewis's theory.

Assumptions

The Lewis model assumes that the developing country has two sectors, a small industrial sector in a few cities and the agricultural sector in the vast land around the cities. The agricultural sector supports so huge a population relative to the land that the marginal product of labor is around zero and that farmers can barely feed themselves. For this reason, we may also call the agricultural sector the *subsistence sector*. The industrial sector, in contrast, employs only a fraction of the population and sustains a high level of marginal productivity and, thus, the real wage.

The reason why the industrial sector does not immediately expand employment until the marginal productivity of labor reaches zero is that, in reality, labor is simply not available at a zero wage. To attract peasants from their accustomed way of life in the countryside, the industrialists must offer a high wage. The wage premium in the industrial sector works partly to offset the higher living cost in the city. But more importantly, the wage premium works to elevate the social image of industrial workers so that the industrial sector can continue to attract workers from the countryside. The industrial wage may also be much higher than the income of petty traders and casual laborers in the city so that industrial workers have better morale and discipline.

And industrial managers are willing to pay wages higher than the marginal labor productivity. In the modern age, economists may call it *efficiency wage*. In ancient times, the grand seigneurs were also willing to pay high wages to their servants, even though the marginal productivity of the army of servants might be close to zero. The grand seigneurs are, of course, not stupid. A loyal army of handsome or beautiful servants boosts the social prestige of the grand seigneurs.

The preceding discussions imply that, in modeling, we may regard the real wage in the industrial sector as fixed in the initial stage of development. And we

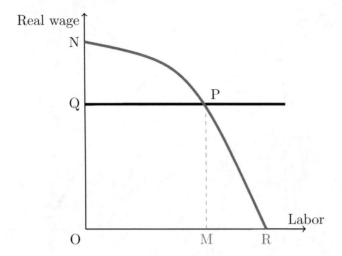

Figure 4.5 The Lewis model.

also assume that, as long as the marginal labor productivity in the subsistence sector stays around zero, the real wage in the industrial sector will remain fixed. Note that the real wage, although much higher than the marginal product of labor, should be very low, especially compared with the level in the high-income countries. The real wage would eventually rise when the labor migration from the countryside to the industrial sector starts to cause strains in agricultural production, which starts to offer higher and higher real wages. We may conjecture that, for a densely populated subsistence economy, it would take many years of industrial development to "digest" all of the underemployed labor in the subsistence sector.

Figure 4.5 gives a snapshot of a developing economy under the Lewis assumptions. NPR represents the labor demand curve. If the industrial sector increases employment of labor until the marginal product of labor reaches zero, then the industrial employment would be OR. The level of real wage, however, is exogenously given. That is, OQ. As a result, the industrial employment stands at OM. The industrial sector is profitable as a whole, with its profit (or surplus) equal to the area of QNP. The area of OQPM is the income of industrial labor.

Industrialization and Urbanization

Since the marginal product of labor in the countryside was around zero, the migration of some people to the industrial sector did not affect the agricultural output. People in the countryside might become less hungry since they have to share food with fewer people, but they would stay at the subsistence level for a prolonged time. Here, we may also invoke the Malthusian argument that people would have more children when more food is available, keeping rural households at a subsistence

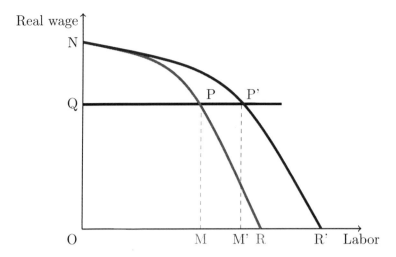

Figure 4.6 Industrialization in the Lewis model.

level of living. Rural households would then accumulate no surplus, which ensures no new investment, tying down the marginal labor productivity in the countryside.

The industrial sector, on the other hand, reinvests the profit and expands the capital stock. Since the marginal product of labor increases when more capital is available (capital–labor complementarity), the labor demand curve would shift to the right. Thus the industrial employment expands from OM to OM' (Figure 4.6).

Meanwhile, the industrial profit expands to QNP'. Thanks to the fixed (or slowly increasing) real wage, which is held down by the army of underemployed labor in the subsistence sector, the return to new capital investment can be sustained at a high level. A high level of profit attracts more investment in the capital stock and, thus, more industrial employment. The dynamic process goes on, continuously shifting the labor demand curve to the right.

This dynamic process may take the name "industrialization." As more and more people work in the industrial sector, the average labor productivity increases. Here the "technological progress" comes not from advances in science and engineering but the improvement of (labor) resource allocation.

We may also conjecture that, as more and more people migrate to the city for industrial jobs, "urbanization" takes place. If we measure urbanization by calculating the percentage of people living in the urban area, then urbanization may progress faster than industrialization. Many people may go to the city first, looking for jobs. When they cannot find one since job opportunities are inherently scarce, they may choose to settle in slums and keep looking, doing some petty trade or casual labor to get by. They, in effect, join the army of underemployed labor in the city. Their existence contributes directly to the persistently low level of the real wage.

The Lewis Turning Point

When industrialization eventually exhausts the redundant labor supply in the subsistence sector, the industrial wage will have to rise to attract more workers to the industrial sector. If the real wage does not rise, or not rapidly enough, the industrial sector will face labor shortages. During China's economic development, labor shortages occurred as early as 2004. At this point, we may say that the economy reaches the Lewis turning point.

The economic development does not stop at the Lewis turning point, though. If anything, the economic growth after reaching the Lewis turning point may be more "balanced," meaning that the share of domestic consumption will rise and the economy will become less dependent on foreign demand.

After the turning point, the investment growth would decline as the return to new investment declines (thanks to the rising labor costs). But the growth rate remains positive. The rising labor costs are not purely bad news for the capitalists, after all. Labor costs are incomes for workers. The rising labor costs imply a booming domestic consumption market for the capitalists. As the result of continued investment, the capital stock continues to accumulate, pushing up marginal labor of productivity and, thus, real wage. As pay goes up, labor's share of income would rise. Since workers' marginal propensity to consume is generally higher than that of the capitalists, the growth of total consumption expenditure may outpace the total investment expenditure. As a result, the consumption share of total expenditure would rise.

Before the Lewis turning point, the fast expansion of the industrial sector may depend on foreign demand since the growth of domestic consumption cannot match that of the domestic production, thanks to the stagnating real wage. The economy has to run a substantial trade surplus, which may lead to international trade disputes. But after the turning point, the growth of domestic consumption may outpace that of export, given that income growth is higher than the world average. As a result, the share of the net export would shrink.

Both predictions, that of rising consumption share and that of shrinking share of the net export, have proven true for China. In China, problems of labor shortage started to emerge around 2004, suggesting the advent of the Lewis turning point. The share of trade surplus topped in 2007, after which it staged a secular decline (Figure 4.7). The consumption share of GDP found the bottom in 2010, thanks to a surge in investment spending after the *Four-Trillion-Stimulus Program* enacted in 2009. After 2010, the consumption share started to climb back (Figure 4.7).

The Kuznets Curve

The celebrated Kuznets curve, named after Simon Kuznets (1901–1985), is the hypothesis that as an economy develops, the economic inequality first rises and then

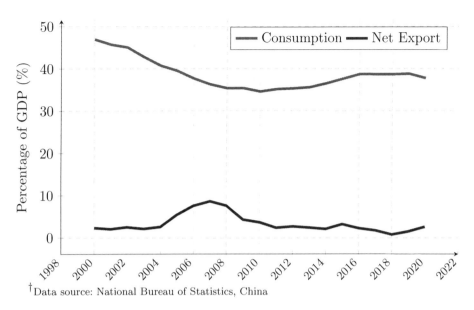

† Data source: National Bureau of Statistics, China

Figure 4.7 China's Share of Consumption and Net Export

falls (Figure 4.8). The Kuznets curve hypothesis may be formulated as a prediction of the Lewis model. When a predominantly subsistence economy starts to develop, capitalists rapidly accumulate and reinvest wealth, while the rest of the population either live in the subsistence sector or receive low wages in the industrial sector. As a result, income inequality increases. At the same time, the average income of the economy rises, thanks to, first, the surging income to capitalists and, second, the migration of workers from the subsistence sector to the industrial sector, where wages are higher.

As the economy reaches the Lewis turning point, real wages in both industrial and agricultural sectors start to rise rapidly. At the same time, return to capital stagnates or declines. Consequently, the Kuznets curve would also turn around at

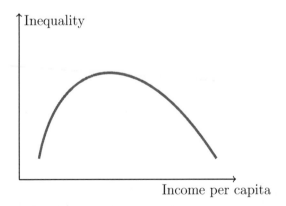

Figure 4.8 The Kuznets curve.

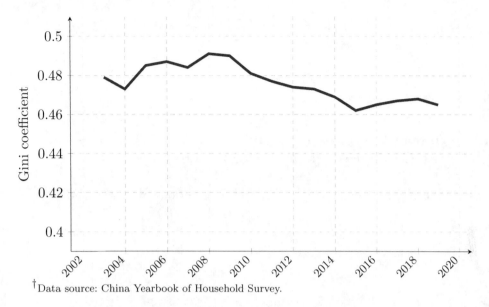

Data source: China Yearbook of Household Survey.

Figure 4.9 China's Gini coefficient of disposable income.

some level of average income, meaning that inequality would start to decline as the average income increases beyond a turning point. Figure 4.9 shows China's Gini coefficient (a well-known measure of inequality) of disposable income since 2003. It appears that China's income inequality may have reached the turning point around 2008, about the same time as talk of the Lewis turning point was widespread.

4.7   Concluding Remarks

The Solow models make it clear that sustainable growth has to come from technological progress. However, we should understand technological progress in broad terms. It is not only about the progress of science and engineering. It is also about improvement in the overall ability of a society to mobilize, organize, and manage enterprises. For developing countries, the Lewis model illuminates the point that the improvement of resource allocation may be the key to the development, at least during the initial period.

Human society is not without engines for growth. People desire better lives, and they innovate and compete. However, sustainable growth is not easy. Among all nations in the world, those that have achieved moderate growth for at least 30 years are in the minority. And the club of high-income countries remains small and exclusive. If the market is overburdened with taxes and regulations, the economy would be stagnant. If the market force rules all and everything is for sale, the economy would also be stagnant or worse. Economists have yet to agree on the set of dos and don'ts the government must obey to bring sustainable growth. But there is no controversy that the government plays a decisive role in the nation's fortune.

Exercises

(1) Suppose that the production function of the economy is Cobb–Douglas, $Y = K^\alpha L^{1-\alpha}$ and that there is no technological progress.

(a) Find the expressions for k^*, y^*, and c^* as functions of α, s, n, and δ.

(b) What is the golden-rule level for k^*?

(c) What is the golden-rule saving rate?

(2) Suppose that the production function is the constant elasticity of substitution (CES), $Y = [aK^\rho + bL^\rho]^{1/\rho}$, where a and b are both positive constants. Note that as $\rho \to 0$, the CES function becomes Cobb–Douglas.

(a) Show that the CES production function has constant returns to scale.

(b) Derive the individual production function $f(k)$.

(c) Under what conditions does $f(k)$ satisfy $f'(k) > 0$ and $f''(k) < 0$?

(3) Suppose that a differential equation characterizing the accumulation of per capita capital is $\dot{k}_t = h(k_t)$, where h is a differentiable function. If a steady-state k^* is stable, then should $h'(k^*)$ be negative or positive? Why?

(4) Let β be the fraction of working-age population (say, those who are aged between 15 and 65). Assume a 100% labor force participation rate and a 0% natural unemployment rate. Suppose that there is no technological progress, the population growth is zero, the saving rate is s, the depreciation rate is δ, and that the production function of the economy is Cobb–Douglas, $Y = K^\alpha(\beta L)^{1-\alpha}$, where L is population.

(a) Write the equation characterizing the steady state.

(b) Analyze the effect of population aging on the income per capita, Y/L.

(5) Suppose that the production function of the economy is Cobb–Douglas, $Y = K^\alpha(AL)^{1-\alpha}$, and that there is a constant rate of technological progress, g.

(a) Find the expressions for k^*, y^*, and c^* as functions of α, s, n, δ, and g.

(b) What is the golden-rule level for k^*?

(c) What is the golden-rule saving rate?

(6)   Assume that, in the Solow model with technological progress, both labor and capital are paid their marginal products.

(a) Show that MPL= $A(f(k^*) - k^* f'(k^*))$.

(b) Suppose that the economy starts with a level of per capita capital less than k^*. As k_t moves toward k^*, does the real wage grow faster, slower, or equal to the technological progress? What about the real rental price of capital?

(7)   Suppose that in the Solow model with technological progress, all capital income is saved and all labor income is consumed. Thus, $\dot{K}_t = \text{MPK}_t \cdot K_t - \delta K_t$.

(a) Derive the equation characterizing the steady state.

(b) Is the steady-state capital per capita larger than, less than, or equal to the golden-rule level?

(8)   Suppose that the individual production function is given by $f(k) = \max(Ak^{0.5} - k_0, 0)$, where $A > 0$ and $k_0 > 0$. k_0 may be interpreted as the minimum fixed cost of production.

(a) If there exists a unique steady state, then express k_0 as a function of A, n, g, δ, and s.

(b) If there exist two steady states, then derive the steady-state capital per effective labor. Which one of these two steady states is stable?

(9)   Assume that the Solow model with technological progress is at the steady state and that the production function is Cobb–Douglas, $Y = K^\alpha (AL)^{1-\alpha}$.

(a) Calculate the partial effect of a unit change in the saving rate s on k^*. (Hint: calculate $\partial k^* / \partial s$.)

(b) Calculate the elasticity of steady-state per capita output $\left(\frac{\partial y^*}{\partial s} \cdot \frac{s}{y^*} \right)$.

(**10**) Suppose that the economy has two sectors, the manufacturing sector that produces goods and the university sector that produces knowledge. The production function in manufacturing is given by $Y_t = F(K_t, (1-u)L_t A_t)$, where u is the fraction of the labor force in universities. The production function in research universities is given by $\dot{A}_t/A_t = g(u)$, where $g(u)$ describes how the growth in knowledge depends on the fraction of labor force in universities. The saving rate and the depreciation rate are s and δ, respectively.

(a) Characterize the steady state of the model.

(b) Analyze the effect of a one-time university expansion on the economy.

(c) Is there an optimal u that yields the highest income per capita?

Notes

[1] On April 26, 1980, Deng told foreign guests, "To build socialism, we must achieve higher productivity. Poverty is not socialism." （搞社会主义，一定要使生产力发达，贫穷不是社会主义。）

5

Economic Fluctuation

History doesn't repeat itself but it often rhymes. – Mark Twain

5.1 Introduction

In this chapter, we study economic fluctuation, which may be characterized by an alternating cycle of recessions and expansions. For business owners and managers weighing investment decisions, "macro traders" who want to anticipate major economic trends and policy changes, politicians facing forthcoming elections, or technocrats in some branches of the government (e.g., the central bank), economic fluctuations are almost all they care about macroeconomics.

Indeed, macroeconomics was born because of the Great Depression, the most severe recession in the twentieth century. During the Great Depression, the public found the classical approach to economic policy making no longer acceptable. The classical approach was to do nothing and wait for the economy to rebound. Classical economists would argue that the market was self-correcting and that the downturn was part of the self-correction from the previous boom. However deep the recession was, classical economists would say, the economy would get back to its potential level with full employment in the long run. But in the long run, as Keynes quipped, we would be all dead. The short-term pain of the recessions, particularly the mass unemployment, could no longer be ignored by the increasingly more democratic governments in the world.

The Great Depression prompted John Maynard Keynes to propose a theory that explained why the Depression happened and what the government could do in such circumstances. In his magnum opus, *The General Theory of Employment, Interest, and Money*, Keynes not only made a convincing diagnosis and prescription but also revolutionized the way we think about the economy as a whole. Treating the economy as a whole, Keynes introduced aggregate concepts such as aggregate demand,

111

aggregate supply, effective demand, and so on. Only after the Keynesian revolution did people find it necessary to have a separate discipline within economics – macroeconomics, different from microeconomics, which mainly deals with individual behavior.

In this chapter, we first give an empirical overview of the business cycles using Chinese and US data. Then we introduce a group of Keynesian models that rely on the sticky-price assumption. The Keynesian approach came into being as a group of neoclassical Keynesian economists, including John Hicks and Paul Samuelson, formalized Keynes's writing into mathematical models with classical flavor. Samuelson, in particular, transformed the economics profession by expressing both Keynesian macroeconomics and classical microeconomics in rigorous mathematical models. Although the Keynesian models have largely disappeared from advanced textbooks, they continue to occupy the central position in intermediate macroeconomic textbooks. The resilience is due to, first, the models' simplicity and, second, their continued relevance to the real world.

The Keynesian models, however, lost some key ideas of Keynes. The sticky-price assumption, for example, is not central to Keynes. The capital market, in contrast, is central in the determination of investment and hence employment, but it has no role in the Keynesian models. After the discussion of Keynesian models, we introduce the theory of Keynes himself and Hyman Minsky, an influential post-Keynesian economist.

5.2 Business Cycles

The business cycle is the fluctuation of output around the long-term trend of output potential. Other macroeconomic variables, such as unemployment and inflation rate, also fluctuate with the output.

Figure 5.1 shows a stylized business cycle of output and the corresponding growth rate. A cycle may start from a *peak*, where the growth rate of real output turns negative. From the peak, the economy falls in a recession. Eventually, the economy reaches the lowest point during the cycle, which we call *trough*. The trough marks the end of the recession and the beginning of an expansion. The economy continues to expand and eventually reaches another peak, finishing a business cycle and beginning a new one.

The real-world business cycles are something of great complexity. Figure 5.2 shows the time-series plots of the real GDP growth, the unemployment rate, and the inflation of the US. Several features stand out. First, real-world business cycles are highly irregular. Both the lengths of recessions and expansions vary over time.

Second, expansions are often long, and recessions (the shaded area) are often short-lived. In the past seven decades, the longest recession was the Great

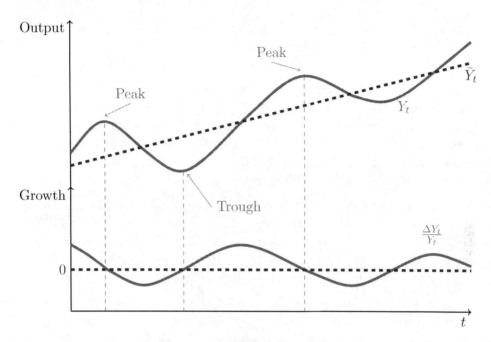

Figure 5.1 Stylized business cycles.

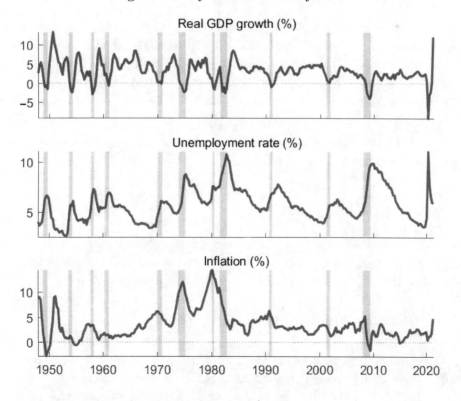

†Data source: FRED.

Figure 5.2 US business cycles.

Recession (2008Q1–2009Q2), which lasted six quarters. It was followed by the longest expansion (2009Q3–2019Q4), which lasted 42 quarters. And it was followed by the shortest recession in history, the Covid recession in 2020, which lasted two months.

Third, related to the second point, the unemployment rate rises rapidly during recessions and declines relatively slowly during expansions. During the Great Recession, for example, it took only 18 months for the unemployment rate to climb from 5.0% in April 2008 to 10.0% in October 2009. But it took 71 months for the unemployment rate to fall back to 5.0% in September 2015. As a result, the press often talks about the so-called jobless recovery.

Fourth, recessions differ in the severity of output loss or the unemployment problem. During the recent recession due to the pandemic, the US real GDP declined 9.3% from peak to trough and the unemployment rate shot up to 14.8%. And some recessions are very mild. For example, the 2001 recession lasted only eight months, with an output loss of 0.3% and a maximum unemployment rate of 6.3%.

Fifth, the unemployment rate rarely *stays* at some level. During economic expansions, it declines almost continuously until reaching a tipping point, where it reverses its course and starts to rise rapidly. The tipping point often coincides with the onset of some crisis.

Sixth, the volatility of macroeconomic variables may also vary over time. For example, inflation was volatile in the 1970s and 1980s. Then the volatility of inflation became subdued until the outbreak of the Covid-19 pandemic. In particular, the period from the mid-1980s to 2007 was known as the Great Moderation, during which the volatility of economic fluctuations was much reduced in developed countries.

Finally, the unemployment rate is conversely related to real GDP growth. Okun's law often characterizes such a relationship between output and employment. One version of Okun's law is as follows:

$$Y_t - \bar{Y} = -\gamma(u_t - u^n), \tag{5.1}$$

where $Y_t - \bar{Y}$ is the output gap, u_t is the unemployment rate, u^n is the natural unemployment rate, and γ is a positive coefficient. If (5.1) holds, then we may deduce that the unemployment rate rises when the output declines.

China's Economic Fluctuations

China's economic fluctuations are very different from those of developed countries. We often divide the postwar economic history of China into two periods, with a break in 1978, when the "Reform and Open-Up" began. We may call the first the pre-Reform era and the second the post-Reform era. We should understand, however, that the Reform was not a single event, but a process that roughly started around 1978.

The output growth in the pre-Reform era was highly volatile (See Figure 5.3). The most salient fluctuation was during 1958–1962. The output increased by 21.3% when the Chinese government launched the Great Leap Forward campaign, the aim of which was to industrialize China in a big push. However, the campaign violated almost every principle of economics. For example, it violated both the division of labor and the economy of scale when the government mobilized farmers to produce steel in small mills scattered in the countryside. The campaign soon turned into an economic disaster. The output growth ground to a halt in 1960 and declined 27.3% in 1961, when the campaign stopped. The decline in agricultural production, in particular, resulted in a devastating famine.

The "Reform and Open-Up" since 1978 has brought over 40 years of continued growth. The volatility of growth was much lower than in the pre-Reform era but much higher than in the developed countries. In the 1980s and early 1990s, the economic fluctuations were mostly driven by the reform-and-retrenchment cycle. When the reformers ruled the day, they pushed for reform initiatives that relaxed the central control on investment and prices. But this predictably led to inflation. The conservatives would then push back and used the device of central planning to cool the economy down. Once the economy was back in balance, the reformers would once again take initiatives, as the conservatives could not offer better alternatives. Thus the Reform and Open-Up continued in the fashion of "two steps forward, one step back."

Since the mid-1990s, the business cycles of China have become more and more synchronized with those in other economies, especially those of developing countries. The slowdown in the late 1990s and during 2008 and 2009, for example, coincided with the Asian Financial Crisis and the Global Financial Crisis, respectively. Note that the annual data may conceal short-term volatility. During the Global Financial Crisis, for example, China's real GDP growth slowed to 6.4% in the first quarter of 2009. Since then, however, the effects of the Four-Trillion-Stimulus program started to kick in and the economy rebounded forcefully, bringing the annual growth rate to 9.4%.

5.3   The Keynesian Cross

We first study a simple model called the *Keynesian Cross*. We use the model to understand that the economy may not produce the potential output in the short run. As a result, the economy may experience recessions and expansions.

We assume that the total expenditure of a closed economy is the sum of consumption expenditure, investment expenditure, and government expenditure:

$$TE = C + I + G,$$

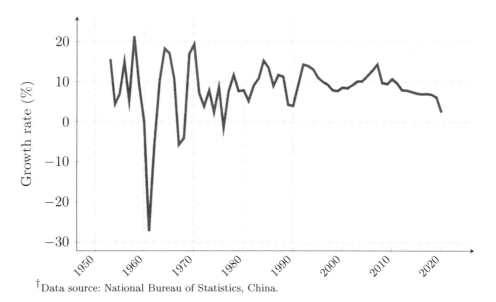

†Data source: National Bureau of Statistics, China.

Figure 5.3 Macroeconomic fluctuations in China.

where C is the consumption expenditure, I is the investment expenditure, and G is the government purchase. We further assume that the consumption expenditure is a function of disposable income:

$$C = C(Y - T),$$

where Y represents total income and T represents tax. We further assume that

$$0 < C'(\cdot) < 1 \quad \text{and} \quad C''(\cdot) < 0.$$

That is, the marginal propensity to consume (MPC) is positive, and MPC declines as the disposable income increases.

Every expenditure generates an equal amount of income on the other side of the transaction. As a result, the total expenditure has to be equal to the total income (Y):

$$Y = C(Y - T) + I + G. \tag{5.2}$$

In this model, the only endogenous variable is Y, the total income or expenditure. Other variables, including I, are assumed to be exogenous. Simple as it is, the model gives us many insights about the economy as a whole. First, total expenditure determines total income. It is not intuitive at first sight since we, in everyday life, determine expenditure according to our income. But for the economy as a whole, it is almost a tautology to say that total expenditure determines total income since they are equal by definition.

As a result, if a substantial number of people choose to reduce consumption and increase savings, then the reduced consumption expenditure would be accompanied by a reduction of total income. If a thrifty person saves more by consuming less, they

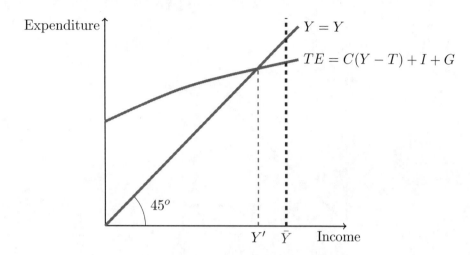

Figure 5.4 The Keynesian cross.

can maintain their income and increase their wealth. But if everyone saves more, the total income would decline, leading to reduced national wealth (via a financial crisis often associated with economic recessions). This apparent paradox is known as the *paradox of thrift*, a well-known example of the *fallacy of composition*.

Second, the equilibrium output (Y') may be below the output potential $(\bar{Y})$, as shown in Figure 5.4. Note that in the Keynesian Cross model in (5.2), the only endogenous variable is Y, the equilibrium income or expenditure. To graphically represent the solution to (5.2), we first draw the right-hand side of (5.2) as a curve, $Y = C(Y - T) + I + G$. Then we draw the left-hand side of (5.2) as a 45-degree line $(Y = Y)$. The solution of (5.2), the equilibirum total income or expenditure Y', is at the cross of the two lines.

Following Keynes, we may call Y' the *effective demand*. There is no reason, in a modern monetary economy, to believe that the aggregate demand always meets the aggregate supply at the potential output level $(\bar{Y})$. Say's law, which states that "supply creates demand," is valid only in a barter economy. In an economy with money, sellers may choose to hold money (to save) instead of spending all their income generated from transactions. If a substantial portion of the population chooses to save more money, then the total expenditure would be lower than the economy can potentially produce.

Third, to accommodate a higher income, the sum of investment and government expenditure must rise more than consumption, due to the assumption that MPC declines as the income increases. Suppose that the firms expand their production capacity in anticipation of future profit. If the increased output can be absorbed by increased aggregate demand, then total income would rise. However, since MPC declines as income increases, a larger share of the increased aggregate demand must be taken care of by investment or government expenditure.

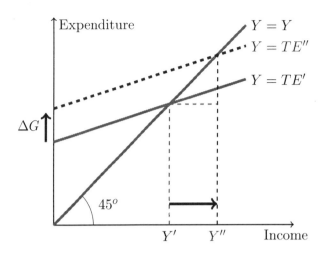

Figure 5.5 The multiplier effect.

Finally, an increase in investment or government expenditure would lead to a larger increase in total income. That is, investment or government expenditure has a *multiplier effect*. Intuitively, an increase in government expenditure generates more income, which leads to more consumption expenditure, which again generates more income, and so on.

To see this point more clearly, we may assume that the consumption function is linear, e.g., $C(Y - T) = C_0 + C_1(Y - T)$ with $C_1 < 1$, then the right-hand side of (5.2) is a straight line with a slope less than one (Figure 5.5). Now, if the government increases expenditure by ΔG, then the line TE shifts upward by ΔG, moving equilibrium income from Y' to Y''. The increase in total income is clearly larger than the initial increase in government expenditure.

Mathematically, (5.2) defines an implicit function $Y(G, T, I)$. Note that investment I is an exogenous variable in this model just like G and T. Using the implicit function theorem, we obtain

$$\frac{\partial Y}{\partial G} = \frac{1}{1 - C'(Y - T)} = \frac{1}{1 - \text{MPC}}.$$

Note that $C'(Y - T)$ is the MPC. Since MPC is less than one, $\partial Y / \partial G$ must be greater than one. It is for this reason that we call $\partial Y / \partial G = 1/(1 - \text{MPC})$ the *government expenditure multiplier*. Similarly, we have

$$\frac{\partial Y}{\partial T} = -\frac{C'(Y - T)}{1 - C'(Y - T)} = -\frac{\text{MPC}}{1 - \text{MPC}},$$

which we call the *tax multiplier*. In contrast to the government expenditure multiplier, the magnitude of the tax multiplier is not necessarily greater than one. If $\text{MPC} < 0.5$, indeed, then $|\partial Y / \partial T| < 1$.

An Example: Government Expenditure and Tax Multipliers

If we assume that the consumption function is linear, say,

$$C(Y - T) = 100 + 0.8(Y - T),$$

then MPC $= 0.8$, and

$$\frac{\partial Y}{\partial G} = \frac{1}{1 - \text{MPC}} = 5, \quad \frac{\partial Y}{\partial T} = -\frac{\text{MPC}}{1 - \text{MPC}} = -4.$$

The magnitude of the expenditure multiplier is always bigger than the tax multiplier. We can understand this point by noting that tax cuts affect disposable income, which in turn induces individuals to consume, raising aggregate demand. That is to say, the immediate effect of tax cuts on aggregate demand is moderated by MPC, which is always smaller than 1. Government spending (e.g., on public works), however, directly raises aggregate demand.

The multiplier effect is often used to justify fiscal stimulus. A multiplier greater than 1, in particular, is sometimes considered a necessary condition for government expenditures on public works. This is not necessarily the case, at least when the economy is in a deep recession and many resources (particularly the labor force) are idle. Government spending on public works would employ idle resources to build something useful, which is better than doing nothing. In other words, if opportunity costs of building public works are low, then building public works always raises aggregate welfare. A big multiplier effect is thus a plus, not a necessary condition.

We can easily extend the preceding analysis to an open economy, where part of the expenditure is on imported goods. In this case, an increase in G (even when all of it is spent on domestic goods) would bring less increase in total national income since not all income generated from transactions (i.e., G) goes to domestic households. This effect is often called *leakage* of fiscal stimulus. The leakage effect may lead to coordination failure on the world stage to combat global recessions: Every country is reluctant to implement stimulus packages that benefit other countries as well.

Note that the multiplier effect also works in the reverse direction. If the government cut spending, the reduction of national income would be more than the spending cut. If the government increases taxes, then it would lead to a reduction of national income that is proportional to the tax multiplier. If the investment or consumption expenditure declines, the immediate reduction of income would also start a chain reaction that results in a much bigger income reduction than the immediate one.

5.4 The IS-LM Model

In the Keynesian Cross model, investment is considered exogenous, and there is no role for the interest rate. As a result, there is no "crowding-out" effect predicted by classical models. More realistically, however, investment should be endogenous and may depend on, among other factors, financing cost measured by interest rate. We now present the IS-LM model that endogenizes interest rate and investment. The IS-LM model was proposed by John Hicks in 1937, and it became the leading interpretation of Keynes's theory by Keynesian economists.

In this section, we first discuss the sticky-price assumption, then study the plain vanilla IS-LM model, which is for a closed economy. The next section extends the IS-LM model to analyze open economies.

5.4.1 Sticky Price

Before introducing the IS-LM model, we first discuss the sticky-price (or nominal rigidity) assumption, which states that prices (including wages) are sticky or rigid in the short term. It is a crucial assumption for the IS-LM models in this chapter.

First, the sticky-price assumption implies that the general price level can be treated as an *exogenous* variable, simplifying analysis. Once we make the assumption, however, it would be awkward to talk about inflation, another important macroeconomic variable. Inflation will always be zero if the sticky-price assumption holds. We will relax this assumption later when we analyze inflation.

Second, under the sticky-price assumption, markets would not automatically clear. When a negative shock occurs to the aggregate demand, prices would fail to fully adjust, with a consequence that the supply side cannot operate at its full potential. Particularly, the downward wage rigidity, which has wide empirical support, would cause excess supply of labor and involuntary unemployment during recessions.

Third, under the sticky-price assumption, the classical dichotomy would fail and money would no longer be neutral. When money supply increases, for example, prices and wages would not rise proportionally. As a result, a change in money supply (monetary policy) would have some real effects.

5.4.2 The Model

IS stands for *investment* and *saving*. LM stands for *liquidity* and *money*. The IS-LM model consists of two equations corresponding to two equilibrium conditions: investment equals saving, and liquidity demand equals money supply.

IS Equation

The IS equation may be viewed as a generalization of the Keynesian Cross model in (5.2). Instead of treating the investment as exogenous, we assume that investment is a function of the *endogenous* real interest rate:

$$I = I(r).$$

And we assume that $I(r)$ is differentiable and $I'(r) < 0$. That is, a higher interest rate lowers the level of investment in the economy. The IS equation is then

$$Y = C(Y - T) + I(r) + G. \tag{5.3}$$

We may interpret the IS equation as an equilibrium in the market for goods and services. The right-hand side gives the total demand, and the left-hand side gives the total supply. Alternatively, we rewrite (5.3) as

$$I(r) = S(Y, T, G), \tag{5.4}$$

where $S(Y, T, G) = Y - C(Y - T) - G$ is the national savings. We may thus interpret the IS equation as an equilibrium in the financial market for loanable funds. We may read (5.4) as *investment equals savings*, hence the name IS.

Unlike the Keynesian Cross model, which has one equation for one endogenous variable, the IS equation contains two endogenous variables, Y and r. Hence the IS equation is not a standalone model. Any combination of Y and r satisfying (5.3) may be a possible equilibrium. All these combinations form the IS curve on the two-dimensional coordinate diagram with Y on the horizontal axis and r on the vertical axis.

IS Curve

In the IS equation, there are two endogenous variables, Y and r, and two exogenous variables, T and G. The IS equation defines an implicit function $Y(r, T, G)$. The implicit function characterizes how the total income changes with the real interest rate, given the fiscal condition expressed in T and G.

Or, equivalently, the IS equation defines an implicit function $r(Y, T, G)$, which is more suitable for graphs. We may represent the implicit function $r(Y, T, G)$ on the two-dimensional coordinate diagram in Figure 5.6, giving us the IS curve. Note that the location of the IS curve is determined by the exogenous variables. When exogenous variables change, the IS curve *shifts* on the diagram.

To see why the IS curve is downward sloping, note that a decline in r results in higher investment in (5.3). Consequently, as in the Keynesian Cross model, the total income or output Y would be higher as well.

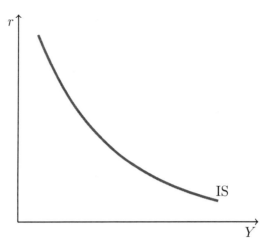

Figure 5.6 The IS curve.

Mathematically, the shape of the IS curve is determined by the slope, which is defined as

$$\frac{\partial r}{\partial Y} \equiv \lim_{\Delta Y \to 0} \frac{r(Y + \Delta Y, T, G) - r(Y, T, G)}{\Delta Y}.$$

This is a measure of how r changes with a unit change in Y, keeping T and G fixed. We can apply the implicit function theorem to obtain the following:

$$\frac{\partial r}{\partial Y} = -\frac{1 - C'(Y - T)}{-I'(r)} = \frac{1 - C'}{I'},$$

where C' and I' are shorthand for $C'(Y - T)$ and $I'(r)$, respectively. C' is nothing but the MPC and I' measures the sensitivity of investment to the real interest rate. Since $0 < C' < 1$ and $I' < 0$, we must have a negative slope, $\partial r / \partial Y < 0$.

"Move Along" or "Shift"

Fixing exogenous variables (T and G), we have a fixed IS curve on the two-dimensional diagram. When there is a change in Y, r would also change. When this happens, we say that the equilibrium point *moves along* the IS curve.

Changing any of the exogenous variables (T or G), however, *shifts* the IS curve. Suppose there are N equilibrium points on the IS curve, $(r_i, Y_i), i = 1, \ldots, N$. Increasing the government expenditure by ΔG, for example, increases every Y_i by $\Delta G/(1 - MPC)$, keeping r_i fixed. That is, the new equilibrium points are $(r_i, Y_i + \Delta G/(1 - MPC))$. That is, the IS curve shifts to the right by $\Delta G/(1 - MPC)$.

In this book, we most often analyze horizontal shifts: Fixing the endogenous variable on the vertical axis (r in the IS-LM model), we check whether an exogenous change makes the other endogenous variable on the horizontal axis (Y) bigger or smaller. If the exogenous change makes Y bigger (smaller), then we say the exogenous change shifts the curve to the right (or left).

Equivalently, we may also analyze vertical shifts: Fixing Y, we check whether the exogenous change makes r higher or lower. If it is higher (lower), then the curve shifts up (or down).

If a curve is vertical, then we can only analyze horizontal shifts. If a curve is horizontal, then we can only analyze vertical shifts.

For example, if the government increases spending by ΔG, then the IS curve would shift to the right. To see this, let's fix any real interest rate r, and analyze how the spending increase would affect Y. Fixing the interest rate means fixing the investment expenditure $I(r)$. As a result, we can apply the analysis of the Keynesian Cross, which tells us that the fiscal stimulus would increase Y by $\Delta G/(1 - MPC)$. Since this is true for every r, the increased government spending would shift the IS curve to the right (Figure 5.7).

Mathematically, note that (5.3) defines an implicit function $Y(r, T, G)$. To calculate the effect of a unit increase in G on Y, keeping r fixed, we calculate the partial derivative:

$$\frac{\partial Y(r, T, G)}{\partial G} \equiv \lim_{\Delta G \to 0} \frac{Y(r, T, G + \Delta G) - Y(r, T, G)}{\Delta G}.$$

Applying the implicit function theorem, we obtain

$$\frac{\partial Y}{\partial G} = \frac{1}{1 - C'(Y - T)} = \frac{1}{1 - \text{MPC}},$$

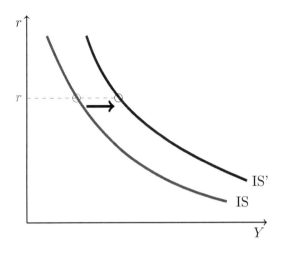

Figure 5.7 The effect of a fiscal stimulus on the IS curve.

which is exactly the government expenditure multiplier in the Keynesian Cross model. Note that the MPC in the preceding equation is a function of $(Y - T)$, the disposable income. If ΔG is small, then a ΔG-increase in government expenditure would increase Y by $\Delta G / (1 - \mathrm{MPC})$, approximately. If, furthermore, the consumption function is linear, then the approximation is exact. That is, a ΔG-increase in government expenditure would shift the IS curve to the right by exactly $\Delta G / (1 - \mathrm{MPC})$.

Similarly, we can calculate how a tax cut would shift the IS curve. We apply the implicit function theorem, and obtain the following:

$$\frac{\partial Y}{\partial T} = -\frac{C'(Y - T)}{1 - C'(Y - T)} = -\frac{\mathrm{MPC}}{1 - \mathrm{MPC}},$$

which is exactly the tax multiplier. A tax cut by the amount $\Delta T < 0$ would shift the IS curve to the right by approximately $-\mathrm{MPC} / (1 - \mathrm{MPC}) \Delta T$.

LM Equation

The LM equation characterizes money market equilibrium. We introduce an exogenous money supply M, which is assumed to be controlled by the central bank. And we introduce a function, $L(r, Y)$, to characterize the *real* demand for money (or liquidity). Denote the general price level by P, and the nominal demand for money is then $PL(r, Y)$.

We assume that a higher interest rate depresses money demand, since money (at least in the traditional sense) has zero interest rate. We also assume that a higher income boosts money demand, since higher income naturally leads to higher demand for transactions. In mathematical language, we assume that $L(r, Y)$ is decreasing in r and increasing in Y. If $L(\cdot, \cdot)$ is differentiable, then $L_1 \equiv \partial L / \partial r < 0$, $L_2 \equiv \partial L / \partial Y > 0$.

In money market equilibrium, we have $M = PL(r, Y)$, which says that money supply equals money demand. More conventionally, we write the following:

$$\frac{M}{P} = L(r, Y). \tag{5.5}$$

We may interpret the left-hand side of (5.5) as the *real* money supply. We may thus read (5.5) as *real money supply equals liquidity demand*, hence the name LM equation.

The LM equation contains two endogenous variables (Y and r) and two exogenous variables (M and P). The exogeneity of the general price level is justified by the sticky-price assumption.

Like the IS equation, the LM equation is not a standalone model. Any combination of Y and r satisfying (5.5) may be a possible equilibrium for the money market. All these combinations form the LM curve on the two-dimensional coordinate diagram with Y on the horizontal axis and r on the vertical axis.

LM Curve

Like the IS equation, the LM equation also defines an implicit function $r(Y, M, P)$, giving us the LM curve. It characterizes how the real interest rate changes with the income, given the general price level and the money supply. We now analyze the shape of the curve and how the curve shifts when M/P changes.

First, the LM equation dictates that, given any M and P, a decline in r must accompany a decline in Y (Figure 5.8). Hence the LM curve is an upward-sloping curve. To understand this intuitively, note that a decline in income would reduce the demand for money. But the money supply is fixed. Hence the interest rate must decline to maintain money market equilibrium.

More precisely, we may apply the implicit function theorem and obtain the slope of the LM curve:

$$\frac{\partial r}{\partial Y} = -\frac{L_2}{L_1} > 0. \tag{5.6}$$

There are two interesting special cases: If $L_1 = \infty$, then the LM curve would be horizontal. On the other hand, if $L_1 = 0$, then the LM curve would be vertical.

Second, if the monetary authority increases M, then the LM curve would shift to the right. To see this, suppose that we fix any r and analyze how an increase in M would affect Y. Under the sticky-price assumption, the price level P does not change. Then an increase in M increases the *real money supply*, the left-hand side of (5.5). As a result, Y on the right-hand side must rise to make the equation hold.

More precisely, note that the LM equation in (5.5) also defines an implicit function $Y(r, M, P)$. We apply the implicit function theorem and obtain

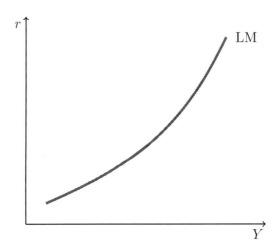

Figure 5.8 The LM curve.

$$\frac{\partial Y(r,M,P)}{\partial M} \equiv \lim_{\Delta M \to 0} \frac{Y(r,M+\Delta M,P) - Y(r,M,P)}{\Delta M} = \frac{1}{PL_2} > 0.$$

That is, if the monetary authority increases the money supply by ΔM, then the LM curve would shift to the right by $\Delta M/(PL_2)$, approximately. If the money demand function $L(r,Y)$ is linear in Y, then the approximation would be perfect.

Note that in most cases, it suffices to study horizontal shift of curves as in the preceding equation. When an upward-sloping curve (e.g., the LM curve) shifts to the right, it is equivalent to shifting upward. However, there are cases where it is necessary to study how a curve would shift vertically (e.g., if the curve is horizontal). If this is the case, we apply the implicit function theorem to the implicit function $r(Y,M,P)$ defined in (5.5) and obtain the following:

$$\frac{\partial r(Y,M,P)}{\partial M} \equiv \lim_{\Delta M \to 0} \frac{r(Y,M+\Delta M,P) - r(Y,M,P)}{\Delta M} = \frac{1}{PL_1} < 0. \qquad (5.7)$$

That is, if the monetary authority increases M, then the LM curve would shift downward. Examining (5.6) and (5.7), we may find that $L_1 = \infty$ is an interesting special case: The LM curve is *horizontal*, and monetary expansion is unable to shift the LM curve downward. We call this special case a *liquidity trap*, a situation where increases in the money supply fail to lower interest rates.

The IS-LM Model

The IS-LM model is composed of (5.3) and (5.5), both of which we rewrite here:

$$\begin{aligned} Y &= C(Y-T) + I(r) + G \\ \frac{M}{P} &= L(r,Y). \end{aligned}$$

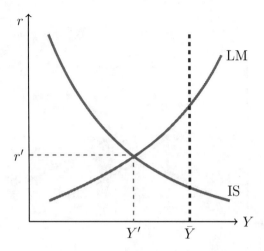

Figure 5.9 The IS-LM model.

The equilibrium of the economy is the solution to the preceding two equations, i.e., the point at which the IS curve and the LM curve cross (Figure 5.9). We may understand the point (Y', r') as the joint equilibrium in the financial market for the loanable funds and the money market. Once again, the equilibrium output Y' may or may not coincide with the output potential $\bar{Y}$.

5.4.3 The Demand-Shock Recession

Suppose that the economy is initially at the output potential ($\bar{Y}$ in Figure 5.10). If there is a negative shock to the IS curve, then the IS curve shifts to the left. As a result, the equilibrium output declines to $Y'' < \bar{Y}$. At the same time, the real interest rate falls, and, by Okun's law, the unemployment rate rises above the natural unemployment rate.

For example, a sudden decline in housing prices may depress household consumption, hence shifting the IS curve to the left. For another example, the crash of an overleveraged stock market may dent investment sentiment, also sending the IS curve to the left.

5.4.4 Policy Analysis with IS-LM

When the economy falls into a recession, the modern government is invariably under pressure to do something. The government may increase expenditures on transportation or energy infrastructure, subsidize durable-goods consumption, and so on. The government may also cut tax for businesses and households, hoping to stimulate investment and consumption. Finally, the monetary authority may inject

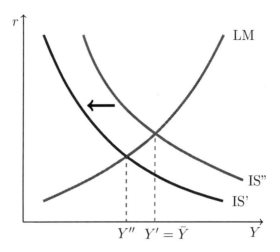

Figure 5.10 Demand-shock recession.

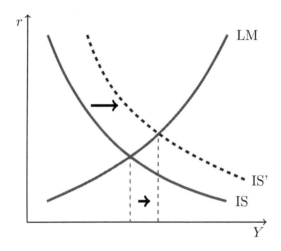

Figure 5.11 Policy analysis: fiscal stimulus.

more liquidity into the financial market, pushing down interest rates, elevating asset prices, and stimulating investment.

We may apply the IS-LM model to analyze the effect of monetary and fiscal policy on the economy. Figure 5.11 illustrates the effect of expansionary fiscal policies. If there is a fiscal stimulus, in the form of either a spending increase or a tax cut, then the IS shifts to the right, bringing higher output and employment.

At the same time, however, the real interest rate rises, and the investment expenditure declines. We call this side-effect of fiscal stimulus the *crowding-out* effect. Unlike in the classical model, however, the crowding out here is *partial*. After the fiscal stimulus, the total output will rise, but by an amount less than in the Keynesian Cross model. Recall that the Keynesian Cross model takes investment as exogenous, independent of the interest rate, hence there is no crowd-out effect.

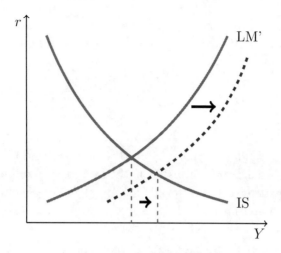

Figure 5.12 Policy analysis: monetary stimulus.

If there is a monetary stimulus, then the LM curve shifts to the right, bringing a lower interest rate and a higher output (Figure 5.12). The IS-LM model, indeed, characterizes an interest-rate channel of monetary policy transmission:

$$M \uparrow \; \Rightarrow r \downarrow \; \Rightarrow I(r) \uparrow \; \Rightarrow \; Y \uparrow.$$

Note that the direct effect of monetary stimulus (e.g., a massive liquidity injection) is to lower the nominal interest rate i. But under the sticky-price assumption, a lower nominal interest rate translates into a lower real interest rate, which businesses and households really care about. Note that there are other channels for monetary policies to affect the economy, which we will discuss later.

Mathematical Treatment

Mathematically, note that the IS-LM equations define a system of implicit functions:

$$
\begin{aligned}
Y &= Y(T, G, M, P), \\
r &= r(T, G, M, P).
\end{aligned}
$$

Note that these two implicit functions are the *solution* to the IS-LM equations, representing each endogenous variable using a function of exogenous variables. Given the values of the exogenous variables, the solution determines the equilibrium output and the real interest rate.

To analyze the effect of government policies on the output, say the effect of increasing government expenditure on the output ($\partial Y / \partial G$), we cannot use the implicit function theorem as usual, due to the fact that the implicit function $Y(T, G, M, P)$ is defined by a system of equations. There is a general version of the implicit function theorem for the system of equations, but it is difficult to remember and cumbersome to apply. Instead, we can take total differentiation of the IS-LM equations and obtain

$$
\begin{aligned}
(1 - C')dY - I'dr &= dG - C'dT \\
PL_2 dY + PL_1 dr &= dM,
\end{aligned}
$$

where $I' = I'(r)$, $L_1 = \partial L(r, Y)/\partial r$, $L_2 = \partial L(r, Y)/\partial Y$, and $C' = C'(Y - T)$ is the MPC. The total differentiation transforms the system of nonlinear equations into a linear system of equations. Now the endogenous variables become dY and dr, which we may regard as changes in Y and r, respectively. And the exogenous variables are dG, dT, and dM. Under the sticky-price assumption, we have $dP = 0$.

We may write the linear system of equations in matrix form:

$$
\begin{pmatrix} 1 - C' & -I' \\ PL_2 & PL_1 \end{pmatrix} \begin{pmatrix} dY \\ dr \end{pmatrix} = \begin{pmatrix} dG - C'dT \\ dM \end{pmatrix}.
$$

Note that changes in the endogenous variables are on the left-hand side and changes in the exogenous variables are on the right-hand side. The preceding linear system of equations is all we need for policy analysis.

To analyze the effect of government expenditure (G), we hold both T and M fixed (that is, $dT = 0$, $dM = 0$). Using Cramer's rule, we obtain

$$
\begin{aligned}
\frac{dY}{dG} &= \frac{L_1}{L_1(1 - C') + I'L_2} > 0, \\
\frac{dr}{dG} &= -\frac{L_2}{L_1(1 - C') + I'L_2} > 0.
\end{aligned}
$$

To analyze the effect of tax (T), we hold both G and M fixed (that is, $dG = 0$, $dM = 0$). Using Cramer's rule, we obtain

$$
\begin{aligned}
\frac{dY}{dT} &= -\frac{L_1 C'}{L_1(1 - C') + I'L_2} < 0, \\
\frac{dr}{dT} &= \frac{L_2 C'}{L_1(1 - C') + I'L_2} < 0.
\end{aligned}
$$

To analyze the effect of monetary policy, we hold G and T fixed (that is, $dG = 0$, $dT = 0$). Using Cramer's rule, we obtain

$$
\begin{aligned}
\frac{dY}{dM} &= \frac{I'}{P\left(L_1(1 - C') + I'L_2\right)} > 0, \\
\frac{dr}{dM} &= \frac{1 - C'}{P\left(L_1(1 - C') + I'L_2\right)} < 0.
\end{aligned}
$$

We can see that fiscal stimulus (increasing G or cutting T) would generally lead to a higher output (income) and a higher interest rate. And an expansionary monetary policy, such as quantitative easing (QE), would generally result in a lower interest rate and higher output (income). When the economy is in a recession, both policies may be helpful. However, there are two interesting special cases, where only one of them would work.

When Monetary Policy Doesn't Work

First, when $L_1 \equiv \partial L(r, Y)/\partial r = \infty$ (liquidity trap), then $dY/dM = 0$. That is, monetary policy does not affect output. But fiscal policies work:

$$\frac{dY}{dG} = \frac{1}{1 - C'}, \quad \frac{dY}{dT} = -\frac{C'}{1 - C'}.$$

In this case, the government expenditure multiplier and the tax multiplier are exactly the same as in the Keynesian Cross model. To understand this, recall that the assumption $L(r, Y)/\partial r = \infty$ implies that the LM curve is horizontal and that monetary expansion is unable to shift the LM curve downward. In this case, r becomes a constant and the IS-LM model reduces to the Keynesian Cross model.

When Fiscal Policies Don't Work

Second, when $L_1 \equiv L(r, Y)/\partial r = 0$, then $dY/dG = dY/dT = 0$. That is, fiscal policies do not affect output. But the monetary policy works in this case:

$$\frac{dY}{dM} = \frac{1}{PL_2} > 0.$$

To understand this, note that the assumption $L(r, Y)/\partial r = 0$ makes the LM equation equivalent to the classical quantity theory of money, $(M/P = kY)$, where k is constant. As a result, the LM equation alone determines the total output Y. A monetary expansion directly leads to an expansion of Y.

Graphically, the assumption $L(r, Y)/\partial r = 0$ makes the LM curve vertical. In this case, the shifting of the IS curve does not affect the output. The fiscal policies do not work, and only monetary policy matters. The Monetarists (e.g., Milton Friedman) took such a position during the stagflation in the 1970s.

Figure 5.13 illustrates the application of the IS-LM models in three scenarios: the liquidity trap, the quantity theory of money, and the normal case. From this graph, we may say that the so-called Monetarist revolution did not refute Keynesian economics, but applied Keynesian economics to a particular situation.

5.4.5 Interest Rate Policy

Central banks in the real world have a dominant influence on short-term interest rates without targeting any level of money supply. A typical practice is to define a

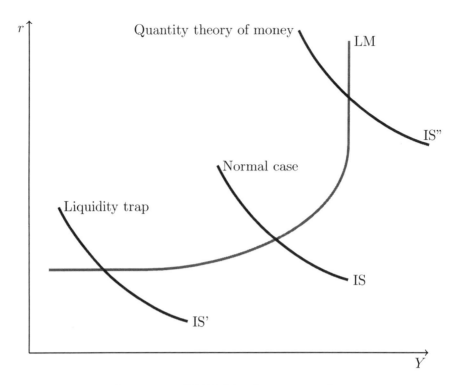

Figure 5.13 IS-LM in three scenarios.

narrow corridor for the overnight interest rate at which banks lend to each other. For example, the US Federal Reserve sets a small range for the federal funds rate (FFR). As of October 31, 2020, the target range for FFR is 0.00–0.25%. For another example, the European Central Bank sets a rate on its deposit facility, which acts as the floor of the interest rate corridor, and a rate on its marginal lending facility, which acts as the ceiling. In addition, ECB also sets a rate on its main refinancing operations (MRO), in which banks can borrow liquidity from the Eurosystem against collateral on a weekly basis. As of October 31, 2020, the rate on the ECB deposit facility is −0.5%, the rate on the marginal lending facility is 0.25%, and the rate on MRO is 0%.

For the simplicity of analysis, we may assume that the central bank sets the interest rate. Money supply changes when the interest rate changes. To implement an interest rate cut, for example, the central bank may inject an adequate amount of liquidity, increasing the base money. The interest rate cut may also stimulate bank lending, thus expanding the broad money. In other words, the policy rate may be regarded as exogenous, while the money supply may be regarded as endogenous.

To model interest rate policy, we may modify the IS-LM as follows:

$$\begin{cases} Y &= C(Y - T) + I(r) + G \\ r &= \bar{r} \\ \frac{M}{P} &= L(r, Y), \end{cases}$$

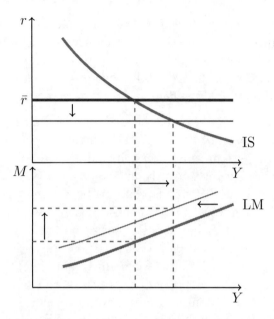

Figure 5.14 An interest rate cut.

where $\bar{r}$ is the exogenous policy rate. In this model, the money supply M is endogenous. Given the policy rate $\bar{r}$, the IS equation solely determines the total output or income. The money supply then automatically adjusts to meet the demand for money, which is determined by the policy rate and the equilibrium income. To see how a cut in the policy rate may expand the economy, see the upper panel of Figure 5.14. And the rate cut must be accompanied by an increase in money supply, as shown in the lower panel of Figure 5.14.

5.5 Open-Economy IS-LM Models

We now extend the IS-LM model to analyze open economies. We first discuss different types of exchange rate regimes, which make a difference in model analysis. Then we consider models for *small open economies*, whose excess saving or saving deficit does not affect the world interest rate. And we also consider a model for a *large open economy*. In the following, we assume free international capital flows, which implies a common real interest rate in the world. The common real interest rate is exogenous to small open-economy models but endogenous to the large open-economy model.

5.5.1 Exchange Rate Regime

An exchange rate regime is how a monetary authority manages its currency related to other currencies and the foreign exchange market. There are two major types: floating (or flexible) exchange rate and fixed (or pegged) exchange rate.

In a floating exchange rate regime, the exchange rate is allowed to fluctuate freely in the foreign exchange market. The monetary authority may or may not intervene with the foreign exchange market. If the monetary authority does not intervene with the foreign exchange market, we call it a *clean float*. Otherwise, we may call it *managed float* or *dirty float*.

In a fixed exchange rate regime, the currency of a small economy is pegging to a reserve currency (e.g., USD, Euro) at a particular exchange rate. And there are different forms of pegging in history, including the gold standard, monetary union (e.g., Euro area), currency boards, and so on. In a typical fixed exchange rate regime, the monetary authority stands ready to buy or sell the foreign currency at a predetermined exchange rate. If the domestic currency tends to appreciate, the monetary authority has to "sell" domestic currency and buy the foreign currency in the foreign exchange market. For the monetary authority, "selling" domestic currency is injecting money into the economy, expanding the money supply. If the domestic currency faces depreciation pressure, the monetary authority has to do the opposite, "buy" domestic currency and sell the foreign currency. To buy domestic currency is to withdraw liquidity from the market and decrease the money supply.

The advantage of a floating exchange rate is that the country can make monetary policies independently from other central banks in the world. As we can see in the preceding discussion, if the exchange rate is pegged to a reserve currency, the money supply has to change with the occurrences of appreciation/depreciation pressure. The monetary authority is thus unable to pursue objectives other than the defense of the fixed exchange rate. The disadvantage of the floating exchange rate is that the economy has to live with an exchange rate that is often excessively volatile.

The advantage of having a fixed exchange rate (often with a major trading partner) is mainly the stability of the exchange rate, which facilitates international trade and investment. For countries with a poor record of responsible monetary policy, fixing the exchange rate with a major foreign currency is a way of "importing" responsible monetary policy from abroad. Defending the exchange rate can often rally more political support than conducting responsible monetary policy.

The disadvantage of the fixed exchange rate is, first, the loss of the independence of monetary policy. Second, to defend the fixed exchange rate against speculative attacks, the country has to accumulate a substantial amount of *foreign exchange reserve*. The foreign exchange reserve must be liquid and safe, which necessarily implies a low return to reserve assets. If a country has a higher return on domestic

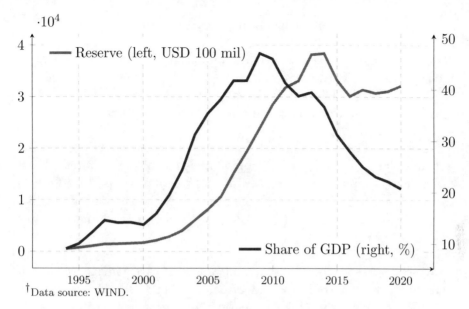

Figure 5.15 China's foreign reserve.

investment, then maintaining a massive low-return foreign exchange reserve is costly to the welfare of the country.

From 1995 to 2005, China pegged RMB to the US dollar. To maintain the peg, and especially to keep RMB stable even after the "7.21 Reform" of 2005, China accumulated a massive foreign reserve. In absolute terms, China's foreign reserve reached an all-time high of USD 3.84 trillion in 2014, which amounts to 36.5% of GDP that year (Figure 5.15). Since the foreign reserve is mainly invested in safe assets with high liquidity, e.g., the US treasury bonds, the return to foreign reserve is very low. It is a curious fact that a fast-growing country like China, in which capital is presumably scarce and return to investment is high, lends a tremendous amount of money at generous terms to a developed country like the US. The welfare loss to China is obvious. And this is the price to pay for maintaining a stable exchange rate with respect to the US dollar.

China's Exchange Rate Regime

The currency of China is called Renminbi (RMB), meaning "people's money." Interestingly, there are two (largely) segmented markets for RMB, the onshore RMB (CNY) market and the offshore RMB (CNH) market. CNH is a clean float and CNY is a managed float.

The managed float of CNY works as follows.[1] On each trading day, the People's Bank of China (PBC) announces central parity rates (CPR) for important currencies around 9:15 A.M. The most important CPR is the one for USDCNY, the exchange rate of CNY with respect to USD. CPR's for other currencies (e.g., JPY) are consistent with market rates (e.g., USDJPY).

CPR serves as the benchmark, and the market exchange rates can fluctuate within a trading band of 2% around CPR. Heavy trading of CNY exchange rates takes place in the interbank foreign exchange market, which opens at 9:30 A.M. and closes at 11:30 P.M.

In contrast, the offshore market (mostly in Hong Kong and Singapore) for CNH trades around the clock. And there is no trading band on CNH exchange rates. The trading volume of CNH, however, is minuscule compared to that of CNY in the onshore market.

CPR has become the main instrument for PBC to manage CNY exchange rates. Currently, PBC uses "the previous closing rate plus changes in the currency basket" to determine CPR.[2] The previous closing rate in the onshore market reflects the demand for and supply of foreign currencies. And the consideration of changes in the currency basket allows CNY to be relatively stable with respect to a basket of currencies.

5.5.2 Modeling a Small Open Economy with a Floating Exchange Rate

We now introduce a small open-economy model with a floating exchange rate. The model, together with the small open-economy model with a fixed exchange rate, is often called the Mundell–Fleming model.

We may imagine that there are only two economies in the world, one small and the other large. The large economy is much bigger than the small, to the extent that the large economy determines the world real interest rate, while the small economy has no influence at all on the interest rate. The small economy is a price taker.

The Model

The model is a close relative to IS-LM, consisting of two equations:

$$Y = C(Y - T) + I(r^*) + G + X(e) \tag{5.8}$$

$$\frac{M}{P} = L(r^*, Y), \tag{5.9}$$

where r^* is the world interest rate, and $X(e)$ is the net export, which is a decreasing function of the nominal exchange rate e. Under the sticky-price assumption, changes in the nominal exchange rate are equivalent to changes in the real exchange rate.

We may rewrite the IS equation in (5.8) as

$$S(Y, T, G) - I(r^*) = X(e),$$

where $S(Y, T, G) \equiv Y - C(Y - T) - G$ is the national saving. Now we may understand the IS equation as an equilibrium condition in the foreign exchange market. The supply side of the foreign currency is $X(e)$, which is earned from net export. The demand side is the excess saving $S(Y, T, G) - I(r^*)$, which has to flow out of the country.

Note that the LM equation is the same as in the plain-vanilla IS-LM model, except that the interest rate is now exogenous. That is, the monetary policy of the small open economy cannot change the interest rate.

The two endogenous variables in the model are Y and e. The IS equation defines an implicit function $Y(e)$. Since a lower e corresponds to a higher Y (using the Keynesian Cross analysis), the IS curve is downward sloping. There is only one endogenous variable Y in the LM equation, which uniquely determines Y. Hence the LM curve is vertical. Figure 5.16 illustrates the joint equilibrium in the foreign exchange market and the money market.

The Effect of Fiscal and Monetary Policies

Suppose that the economy is in a recession, producing less than the output potential. If the government conducts fiscal stimulus (e.g., increasing government expenditure), then the IS curve shifts to the right. But the LM curve is vertical. The rightward shift of the IS curve only produces an appreciation of the domestic currency, which fully "crowds out" the effect of the fiscal stimulus.

If the monetary authority conducts monetary stimulus, then the LM curve shifts to the right. This leads to the depreciation of the domestic currency and higher output and employment. Indeed, the small open-economy model with a floating exchange rate characterizes an *exchange rate channel* of monetary policy transmission:

$$M \uparrow \ \Rightarrow \ e \downarrow \ \Rightarrow \ X(e) \uparrow \ \Rightarrow \ Y \uparrow.$$

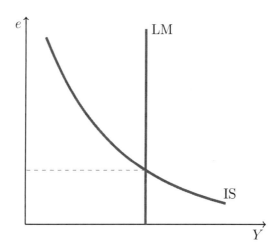

Figure 5.16 IS-LM curves of the small open economy with floating exchange rate.

That is, although the monetary authority of the small open economy cannot cut the interest rate, it can still depreciate its currency to stimulate the economy.

We may also analyze another interesting scenario: The world interest rate r^* rises. This may happen when a large economy tightens its monetary policy. For the small open economy, the IS curve shifts to the left, and the LM curve shifts to the right, producing a depreciation of the domestic currency and, somewhat counterintuitively, a higher output. The increased output is brought about by the currency depreciation, which stimulates exports. This experiment illustrates the merit of the flexible exchange rate, which acts as a buffer between global monetary conditions and the domestic economy. If the exchange rate is not flexible, then the *global tightening* (in the form of rising r^*) would transmit to the domestic economy.

5.5.3 Modeling a Small Open Economy with a Fixed Exchange Rate

Now we consider a small open economy with a fixed exchange rate. To maintain the fixed exchange rate, the monetary authority of the small economy stands ready to sell the foreign currency using foreign reserve when there is depreciation pressure, or buy the foreign currency when there is appreciation pressure, at the fixed exchange rate. Selling foreign currency means withdrawing domestic currency from the economy, and buying foreign currency means issuing domestic currency into the economy. Since both operations would change the money supply, the money supply in the small open economy with a fixed exchange rate is necessarily *endogenous*.

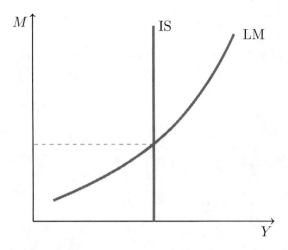

Figure 5.17 IS-LM curves of the small open economy with fixed exchange rate.

The Model

The IS-LM model of the small open economy with a fixed exchange rate is given by
the following:

$$Y = C(Y - T) + I(r^*) + G + X(e^*) \qquad (5.10)$$

$$\frac{M}{P} = L(r^*, Y), \qquad (5.11)$$

where r^* is the world interest rate and e^* is the fixed exchange rate. The endogenous
variables are output (Y) and money supply (M), and the exogenous variables include
r^*, e^*, T, G, and P.

It is clear that the IS equation in (5.10) determines the level of output or income,
Y, regardless of the money supply (M). As a result, if we draw the IS curve on the
two-dimensional coordinate system with Y on the horizontal axis and M on the
vertical axis, then the IS curve would be vertical (Figure 5.17). In the LM equation
(5.11), higher M would correspond to higher Y. As a result, the LM curve is upward
sloping (Figure 5.17).

The Effect of a Foreign-Demand Shock

Suppose that a major trade partner goes into recession and that the net export
declines. For example, the US economy plunged into recession in 2008. It was a
foreign-demand shock for many countries, including China.

If a small economy is initially at full employment, producing the potential
output, then the foreign-demand shock would shift the IS curve to the left, causing a
foreign-demand-shock recession. Note that economies with fixed exchange rates are
more vulnerable to foreign-demand shocks. In an economy with a flexible exchange

Table 5.1 China's slowdown in 2008–2009.

Quarter	Real GDP growth (YoY growth, %)	Export to the US (YoY growth, %)
2008Q1	11.5	5.4
2008Q2	10.9	12.0
2008Q3	9.5	15.3
2008Q4	7.1	0.7
2009Q1	6.4	−14.8
2009Q2	8.2	−18.5
2009Q3	10.6	−16.7
2009Q4	11.9	0.6

[†]Data source: WIND.

rate, currency depreciation may prevent the economy from going into recession, as shown in the analysis of the small open-economy model with a floating exchange rate.

Case Study: China's Slowdown in 2008–2009

China's GDP in 2007 was about 26% of the US GDP. At the same time, although the RMB exchange rate was no longer pegged to USD, it was still very inflexible – so inflexible that it was called a *crawling peg*. Consequently, we may apply the small open-economy model with a fixed exchange rate to China's economy back then.

From 2005 to the first half of 2008, China maintained double-digit real GDP growth rates, thanks to the domestic investment boom and the US consumption boom. As the Global Financial Crisis erupted in the US, the US demand for Chinese goods took a nosedive. In the first quarter of 2009, the Chinese export to the US declined 14.8% compared with the same quarter in 2008. In the first quarter of 2009, the slowdown of the Chinese economy reached the bottom at 6.4% (see Table 5.1). Starting from the second quarter of 2009, however, the Chinese economy started to rebound vigorously, thanks to the massive Four-Trillion-Stimulus program. The export to the US did not start to rebound until the fourth quarter of 2009.

The Effect of a Fiscal Stimulus

Suppose that the economy is in a recession, producing less than the output potential. If the government conducts fiscal stimulus, say increasing the government expenditure, then the IS curve shifts to the right, raising both output and money supply. To understand why money supply would expand, recall that in the small open economy with a floating exchange rate, fiscal stimulus would tend to strengthen the domestic currency. To keep the domestic currency from appreciation, the monetary authority has to issue domestic currency and buy the foreign currency, hence the monetary expansion.

Note that the small open-economy model with a fixed exchange rate does not predict any "crowding-out" effect: The increase in output is the same as the rightward shift of the IS curve. This is because both the interest rate and the exchange rate in the IS equation are fixed. The interest rate is the world interest rate, which the small economy cannot influence. The exchange rate is held constant by the monetary authority, which in effect cooperates with the fiscal authority by conducting a monetary expansion.

The Effect of Global Monetary Tightening

We may also analyze another interesting virtual experiment: Suppose that the world real interest rate rises. This may happen when the US starts to raise interest rates. Since the US dollar is the dominant funding currency in the international monetary system, the US monetary tightening is equivalent to a global monetary tightening.

In the small open-economy model with a fixed exchange rate, the global monetary tightening would shift the IS curve to the left and the LM curve to the right, resulting in lower output and money supply. That is, we have a combination of economic recession and tightened monetary policy.

To understand why the money supply has to be tightened, note that the rise in the world interest rate puts depreciation pressure on the domestic currency (using the analysis of the small open-economy model with a floating exchange rate). Defending the fixed exchange rate, the monetary authority has to buy the domestic currency, which is to withdraw money from the economy.

The prediction from this virtual experiment rhymes with many episodes in the history of international finance. Whenever the US interest rate rises substantially, many small countries with rigid exchange rates would experience economic slowdown, monetary tightening, and even currency and banking crises. The Asian Financial Crisis in the late 1990s was a vivid example.

Case Study: The 1997–1998 Asian Financial Crisis

The Asian Financial Crisis started in 1997 and gripped much of East Asia and Southeast Asia (see Table 5.3). Among the most affected are Thailand, Indonesia, and South Korea. Malaysia and the Hong Kong Special Administrative Region of China were also badly hit.

The seed for the crisis was sown in the early 1990s when financial liberalization accelerated in Asia. Financial liberalization generally includes the removal of credit

Table 5.2 The federal funds rate, dollar index, and the Asian exchange rates.

	Fed. funds Rate (%)	Dollar Index	Exchange rates (per dollar)		
			Baht	Won	Rupiah
1993	3.02	89.9	25.3	805.8	2,110
1994	4.20	88.4	25.2	806.9	2,200
1995	5.84	83.4	24.9	772.7	2,308
1996	5.30	87.2	25.4	805.0	2,383
1997	5.46	93.9	31.1	953.2	4,650
1998	5.35	98.5	41.3	1,400.4	8,025
1999	4.97	97.0	37.9	1,189.8	7,085
2000	6.24	101.8	40.2	1,130.9	9,595

[†]Data source: WIND.

control, interest rate liberalization, privatization of banking, removal of capital account restrictions, and so on. Policy makers at the time generally believed in the free-market doctrine that financial liberalization was good for economic development. However, with inadequate financial regulation and macroprudential management, financial liberalization made the financial system fragile and prone to crisis.

The liberalization of capital account transactions (e.g., foreign lending, portfolio investment), in particular, played an important role in the Asian Financial Crisis. After the liberalization, international money poured into the region to search for higher yields. And local banks and firms ventured out to borrow the US dollar and Japanese yen, two popular funding currencies, at much lower interest rates than they can get domestically.

The Asian economies were booming even before financial liberalization. The massive capital inflow after the liberalization led to overheated economies and asset bubbles. Beneath the apparent prosperity, however, there was a combination of currency mismatch (liability in foreign currency, revenue in local currency) and term mismatch (short-term debt, long-term investment) in many Asian countries. A disaster was waiting to happen when banks and firms were in heavy foreign short-term debt and their investment was in the nontradable sector, real estate in particular.

Several factors contributed to the eruption of the crisis. An important one is the global monetary tightening. The average US federal funds rate in 1993 was 3.0%, which was very low by historical standard. From 1994, however, the US Federal Reserve started to raise interest rates. It rose to 4.2% and 5.8% in 1994 and 1995, respectively. And it stayed around 5.4% from 1996 to 1998. At the same time, the US dollar started to appreciate against other currencies. The dollar index climbed from around 83.4 in 1995 to around 93.9 in 1997 and 98.5 in 1998 (Table 5.2).

As the global monetary condition tightened, Asian currencies were under pressure. For example, the Thai Baht exchange rate was kept around 25 Baht/USD before July 1997. Although the government pledged to defend Baht, it lacked foreign reserves to make the pledge credible. Massive speculative attacks forced the Thai government to float the Baht on July 2, 1997, a date that marked the beginning of the Asian Financial Crisis. The devaluation of the Thai Baht started chain reactions that led to a regionwide crisis.

After the floating, Baht devalued quickly and the Thai government had to ask for assistance from the International Monetary Fund (IMF), which was supposed to act as the lender of last resort for member countries. Although the IMF did provide a rescue package, it demanded fiscal and monetary tightening on the Thai government and restructuring and reform on the financial sector. The fiscal and monetary tightening made the recession worse. And the chaotic financial restructuring sparked panic runs on many financial institutions in 1998. Later, IMF applied the same approach to other Asian countries and arguably deepened the crisis.[3]

Based on its model, the IMF projected a mild recession for Thailand in 1997 and a 3.5% GDP growth in 1998. However, the Thai economy went into a much deeper recession in 1998, with real GDP declining 7.6% in the local currency and 24.3% in dollar terms.

In Indonesia, the economy contracted 5.4% in dollar terms in 1997 thanks to the devaluation of the Indonesian Rupiah. The next year was much worse. The economy declined 13.1% in local currency and 32.9% in dollar terms. The mass unemployment, coupled with cutbacks in food and fuel subsidies for the poor (thanks to the fiscal tightening), prepared for violent social disruptions. During the May 1998 riots of Indonesia, mobs and organized gangs attacked the Chinese Indonesian communities, including vandalizing shops and sexually assaulting women. This further damaged confidence in the Indonesian economy.

In South Korea, the economy contracted 5.3% in dollar terms in 1997 thanks to the devaluation of the Korean Won. And the next year was more catastrophic. Although the real GDP contracted a mere 5.5% in the local currency, the dollar-denominated GDP declined by 57%.

Although there was speculation that China might follow other Asian countries and devalue its currency, China's Premier Zhu Rongji made it clear that China would not do it. By 1997, China had kept CNY pegged to the USD at 8.3 for over two years. The capital flow into China was mainly in the form of direct investments such as factories. Hence there was little capital flight when the crisis broke out. Furthermore, China had strict controls on capital flow, and it had enough foreign exchange reserves. When China pledged to keep the peg, therefore, it was credible.

There are important lessons to be learned from the Asian Financial Crisis. First, cross-border capital flow, especially in the form of short-term debt, is destabilizing for open economies. Capital control is helpful for developing countries to maintain macroeconomic stability.

Table 5.3 The impact of the Asian Financial Crisis.

| | Real GDP growth (local currency) | | | GDP growth (in USD) | | |
	Thailand	S. Korea	Indonesia	Thailand	S. Korea	Indonesia
1994	8.0	9.2	7.5	13.8	13.3	17.9
1995	8.1	9.6	8.2	15.4	14.0	22.1
1996	5.7	7.6	7.8	8.1	12.8	7.5
1997	−2.8	5.9	4.7	−18.0	−5.3	−6.8
1998	−7.6	−5.5	−13.1	−24.3	−57.0	−32.9
1999	4.6	11.3	0.8	11.4	43.6	29.7
2000	4.5	8.9	4.9	−0.2	19.1	15.7

[†]Data source: WIND.

Second, the crisis made it clear there was no lender of last resort for individual countries. Even for countries with relatively flexible exchange rates, if without capital control, they could not allow their currency to freefall since the devaluation might have bankrupted firms and banks in short-term foreign debt. To maintain a certain degree of exchange rate stability, countries have to insure themselves by accumulating foreign exchange reserves. And this is exactly what happened after the Asian Financial Crisis.

Many Asian countries, including China, built "war chests" of foreign reserves. Since foreign reserves were mostly in the US treasury bonds, building foreign reserves meant lending (or exporting savings) to the US. Consequently, former Federal Reserve chair Ben Bernanke complained in 2005 that the Asian reserve building contributed to a "saving glut" that kept the US long-term interest rate low despite the fact the Fed was raising the short-term interest rate.[4] The ultralow long-term interest rate arguably fueled the US housing bubble, the burst of which led to the 2008 Global Financial Crisis.

5.5.4   A Model of a Large Open Economy

The large open economy differs from the small one in that the capital outflow of the large open economy would have an impact on the world interest rate. We use $F(r)$ to denote the net capital outflow, which is assumed to be a function of the real interest rate r. Since more capital outflow from the large economy depresses the world interest rate, we assume that $F(r)$ is a decreasing function, i.e., $F'(r) < 0$. And we use $X(e)$ to denote the net export, which is assumed to be a decreasing function of the nominal exchange rate e.

We consider the following model:

$$Y - C(Y - T) - G \;=\; I(r) + F(r), \tag{5.12}$$

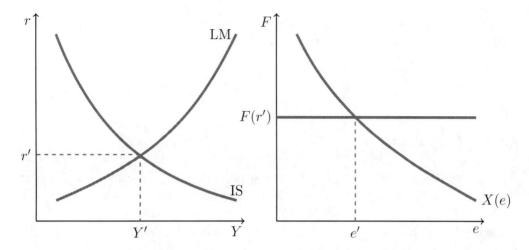

Figure 5.18 The large open economy model.

$$\frac{M}{P} = L(r, Y), \tag{5.13}$$

$$F(r) = X(e). \tag{5.14}$$

The equation in (5.12) is the IS equation, describing the equilibrium in the market for loanable funds (or equivalently, the market for goods and services). The equation in (5.13) is the familiar LM equation, characterizing the equilibrium in the money market. The equation in (5.14) characterizes the equilibrium in the foreign exchange market, where the net export is the supply side and the net capital outflow is the demand side.

In this model of three equilibrium conditions, there are three endogenous variables: Y, r, and e. All other variables, including the sticky price P, are exogenously given. The model looks complicated, but it is easy to solve. Note that the exchange rate e does not appear in the first two equations. So Y and r can be determined as in the usual IS-LM model. With r determined, we can determine e by solving the equation in (5.14). Graphically, Figure 5.18 shows how the model can be solved. The analysis based on the model is straightforward.

Indeed, the directional prediction of policy impact on Y and r is the same as predicted by the usual IS-LM model. Quantitatively, however, there are some differences. For example, the effect of fiscal stimulus would be smaller than in the closed-economy IS-LM model, thanks to the *leakage* through trade. Recall that a fiscal stimulus would drive up the interest rate, which boosts the domestic currency. The appreciation of the domestic currency, in turn, discourages exports and stimulates imports. Thus the effect of fiscal stimulus leaks to foreign countries.

A monetary stimulus, however, may have a bigger impact on output and employment than in the closed-economy IS-LM model. The monetary stimulus not only drives down the interest rate, which stimulates domestic investment, but also devalues the domestic currency, stimulating the net export. That is to say, the large open-economy model characterizes a dual-channel monetary transmission:

$$M \uparrow \; \Rightarrow \left\{ \begin{array}{l} r \downarrow \; \Rightarrow I(r) \uparrow \\ e \downarrow \; \Rightarrow X(e) \uparrow \end{array} \right\} \; \Rightarrow Y \uparrow.$$

5.5.5   A Summary

A closed economy can be regarded, conceptually, as an extremely large economy. Indeed, the economy of the earth must be closed since there is no interstellar trade so far. From the closed-economy model, we learn that a fiscal stimulus would raise the output and the real interest rate. And a monetary stimulus would also raise the output but lower the real interest rate.

On the other extreme is the small open-economy model, where the interest rate is exogenously given. If the exchange rate is fixed, a fiscal stimulus may raise output and employment. Monetary stimulus, however, is ruled out since monetary policy is no longer independent under the fixed-exchange-rate regime. If the small open economy has a floating exchange rate, it would enjoy an independent monetary policy. A monetary stimulus would lead to the depreciation of the domestic currency, which stimulates output by stimulating foreign demand. Fiscal stimulus, in contrast, is completely ineffective since the appreciation of the exchange rate would lower net export, offsetting the effect of increased government expenditure or a tax cut.

The large open-economy model analyzes an intermediate case between the closed economy and the small open economy with a floating exchange rate. The policy effect on the large economy is something between the effect on the closed economy and that on the small open economy. For example, the effect of a fiscal stimulus on the output would be positive since the effect of the same policy on the closed economy is positive and that on the small open economy with a floating exchange rate is zero. The effect on the large open economy would not be as large as on a closed economy, though, thanks to the leakage through trade.

5.6   The Keynesian AD-AS Models

Under the sticky-price assumption, we treat the general price level as exogenous in the IS-LM models. To analyze inflation, however, we must allow price to change, and thus treat price as endogenous in models. In this section, we endogenize price and introduce Keynesian AD-AS models that deal with both output and inflation.

Conceptually, we may regard the models in this section as *medium-run* models, in contrast to the short-run models that assume sticky prices and the classical long-run models that assume flexible prices. In the medium run, prices are subject to change but not as flexible as making monetary policy ineffective.

5.6.1 Aggregate Demand (AD)

From IS-LM to AD

Treating P as endogenous, we may reinterpret the IS-LM model as a special Keynesian AD-AS model:

$$Y = C(Y - T) + I(r) + G \tag{5.15}$$

$$\frac{M}{P} = L(r, Y) \tag{5.16}$$

$$P = \bar{P}. \tag{5.17}$$

The preceding model has three endogenous variables, Y, r, and P, and three equations. We may group the first two equations, (5.15) and (5.16), together, characterizing the aggregate demand (AD). Note that, given any price level P, the first two equations determine, as in the IS-LM analysis, an *effective demand*. The schedule of effective demand with respect to a whole range of P gives us the AD curve.

On the other hand, (5.17) characterizes the aggregate supply (AS) under the sticky-price assumption. The sticky-price assumption reduces a general AD-AS model to the IS-LM model, which is a simple AD-only model.

Mathematically, given a set of exogenous variables (G, T, M), we can solve the IS and LM equations for an equilibrium price level P (eliminating r, one of the endogenous variables). In other words, the IS-LM equations define an implicit function $P(Y, G, T, M)$, which we call the AD curve. Note that Y is an endogenous variable in $P(Y, G, T, M)$, and that G, T, and M are exogenous variables that may shift the AD curve.

To study the shape of the AD curve, we fix T, G, and M, and take total differentiation of both IS and LM equations:

$$dY = C'(Y - T)dY + I'(r)dr,$$
$$0 = L(r, Y)dP + P\left(L_1(r, Y)dr + L_2(r, Y)dY\right).$$

We have thus transformed the IS-LM model into a *linear* model with endogenous variables being dY, dr, and dP. Eliminating dr from this system of equations, we obtain

$$\frac{dY}{dP} = -\frac{I'L}{P\left(L_1\left(1 - C'\right) + I'L_2\right)} = -\frac{I'M}{P^2\left(L_1\left(1 - C'\right) + I'L_2\right)}.$$

Since $I' < 0$, $L_1 < 0$, $0 < 1 - C' < 1$, we have $dY/dP < 0$, indicating a downward-sloping AD curve.

Figure 5.19 illustrates the graphical derivation of the AD curve. A decline in the price level P increases the real balance of the money supply. This shifts the LM

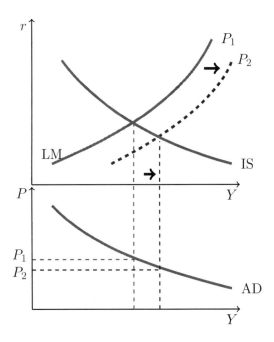

Figure 5.19 Derivation of the AD curve, $P_1 > P_2$.

curve to the right, yielding a higher effective demand Y. Hence the decline in P corresponds to a higher Y. In other words, the AD curve is downward sloping.

To understand the mechanism behind the downward-sloping AD curve, note that the increase in the real money supply (brought by a decline in P) tends to lower the real interest rate, which further stimulates the investment demand, a major component of the aggregate demand.

And recall that the downward-sloping AD curve cannot be taken for granted in macroeconomics. As discussed in Chapter 3, the fact that almost every good and service has a downward-sloping demand curve does not prove a downward-sloping AD curve. To take this curve for granted, we may commit the *fallacy of composition*. The IS-LM model, as we have seen, illustrates the Keynesian argument for the downward-sloping AD curve.

The Effects of Fiscal and Monetary Policies

Fiscal and monetary policies can shift the AD curve. To see how the AD curve shifts horizontally, we can fix P and examine the effects of the changes in exogenous variables (G, T, M) on Y. But this is exactly the policy analyses based on the IS-LM model. We know the following from the analysis in Section 5.4.4:

$$\frac{dY}{dG} > 0, \quad \frac{dY}{dT} < 0, \quad \text{and} \quad \frac{dY}{dM} > 0.$$

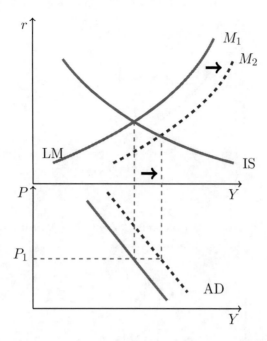

Figure 5.20 The effect of a monetary expansion on the AD curve, $M_1 < M_2$.

This says that increased government expenditure, a tax cut, and monetary expansion can all shift the AD curve to the right, meaning that, at every price level P, the aggregate demand Y increases. Figure 5.20 illustrates the effect of a monetary expansion on the AD curve.

Using the AD curve, we can analyze the effect of policies on inflation, in the short run and in the long run. First, in the short run, the sticky-price assumption implies that the aggregate supply curve is horizontal ($P = \bar{P}$). The shift of the AD curve thus would fail to produce any inflation (Figure 5.21).

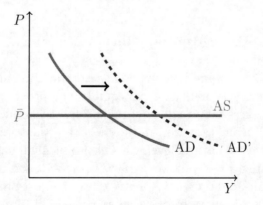

Figure 5.21 Short-run effect of a stimulus.

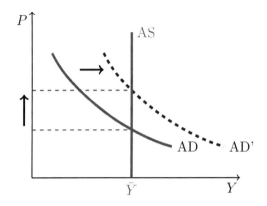

Figure 5.22 Long-run effect of a stimulus.

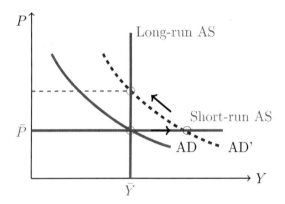

Figure 5.23 From short-run to long-run equilibrium.

In the long run, however, the sticky-price assumption does not hold, and the economy would produce the output potential $\bar{Y}$ regardless of the price level. In this case, the aggregate supply curve would be vertical ($Y = \bar{Y}$). The shift of the AD curve to the right thus would only produce inflation and fail to raise output (Figure 5.22).

From Short-Run to Long-Run Equilibrium

We may combine short-run and long-run analyses to analyze an unnecessary stimulus. Suppose the economy is in its long-run equilibrium, producing the output potential $\bar{Y}$. But policy makers may want to stimulate the economy anyway, perhaps for a better prospect of staying in power. In the short run, the stimulus measures would raise the output above the natural level without producing much inflation, thanks to the sticky price. As time goes by, however, factor prices (labor, material, energy, etc.) would rise in the overheated economy, forcing firms to adjust production plans. Eventually, the economy would move from the short-run equilibrium back to the long-run equilibrium at $\bar{Y}$, but with a higher price level. See Figure 5.23 for an illustration.

The preceding narrative is a typical classical argument against government stimulus. However, if we start from an output level *below* the output potential, we can have an argument that is much friendlier to stimulus measures. An output level below the output potential is almost always associated with a high unemployment rate and low inflation (or even deflation). At this point, a fiscal or monetary stimulus would raise the output, reduce the unemployment rate, and start a virtuous cycle toward full recovery. This can be achieved without stirring much inflation since many resources are idle when the output is below the potential.

So knowing the state of the economy is important for making a policy judgment. Indeed, a sensible policy maker can be compared to a physician treating a sick man. He should make all efforts to know about the physiological condition of the sick. He should also try his best to know what has shocked the sick away from the healthy equilibrium. A fever caused by a flu should be treated differently from one caused by injury. For an economic policy maker, he should make all efforts not only to know how the economy is performing but also what kind of shock is affecting the economy. For example, inflation that is caused by demand shocks (e.g., asset bubble, investment boom) should be treated very differently from inflation that is caused by supply shocks (a severe drought, the formation of an international oil cartel, etc.).

Supply Shocks

If a shock reduces the supply of factor inputs or productivity, we call it a *negative* or *adverse* supply shock. A *positive* or *favorable* supply shock, in contrast, increases the supply of factor inputs or productivity. The Industrial Revolution, for example, is a favorable supply shock since it increases the productivity of the economy.

Policy makers do not have to respond to favorable supply shocks, since they generally increase social welfare without bringing inflation risks. The adverse supply shock, however, calls for policy makers' attention since it not only brings inflation but also reduces output and employment.

A famous example of adverse supply shock (or price shock) happened in 1973, when the Organization of Petroleum Exporting Countries (OPEC) restricted oil supply. Consequently, the oil price soared, raising the cost of production all over the world. The rise in production costs pushed up the general price level. We often call inflation that is brought by increases in factor prices (labor, raw material, energy, etc.) cost-push inflation.

Given the aggregate demand curve, the exogenous increase in the general price level would shift the AS curve upward, resulting in a lower equilibrium output (Figure 5.24). The combination of inflation and economic stagnation is famously termed *stagflation*.

Is it sensible to use monetary tightening to bring down the inflation caused by the supply shock? The monetary tightening would shift the AD curve to the left,

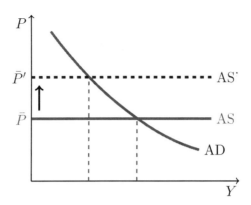

Figure 5.24 Stagflation.

aggravating the recession and unemployment problem. This policy is not favorable, compared to doing nothing and waiting for inflation to come down.

Another policy option, which we may call the *accommodative* approach, is to conduct monetary or fiscal stimulation to raise aggregate demand and reduce unemployment. The accommodative approach would shift the AD curve to the right where it restores the output to the natural level. However, the stimulus may stoke fears of even higher inflation.

The stagflation is, thus, a challenging situation for policy makers. Historically, the stagflation in the 1970s undermined support for Keynesian economics and policy making.

Case Study: The Oil Shocks in 1973 and 1979

In October 1973, the OPEC proclaimed an oil embargo on Western countries that supported Israel during the Yom Kippur War. The embargo caused an oil crisis that raised oil and fuel prices dramatically in the Western world. The price of oil in the US, for example, had risen nearly 400% within half a year. This was historically called the first oil crisis.

The second oil crisis happened when the Iranian Revolution succeeded in 1979, replacing a pro-Western authoritarian monarchy with an anti-Western theocracy. The revolution created a widespread panic, sending oil prices doubling within the next year. As if to confirm the panic, the Iran–Iraq War broke out in September 1980. As a result, Iran's oil production almost came to a stop, and Iraq's oil output also dropped substantially.

Both oil crises led to stagflation in the Western world. In the US, for example, inflation rose to double digits after each of the oil crises. Meanwhile, real GDP growth declined to negative territory (Figure 5.25).

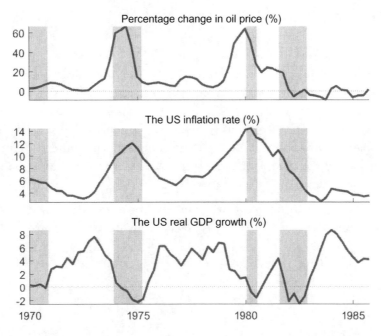

†Data source: fred.stlouisfed.org.

Figure 5.25 The US stagflation in the 1970s and 1980s.

5.6.2 Aggregate Supply

The horizontal AS curve (under the sticky-price assumption) and the classical vertical AS curve are two special cases of a general theory of aggregate supply, which we now discuss.

The Case for an Upward-Sloping AS Curve

Recall that the AS curve is the relationship between the general price level P and the total real output that the firms are willing to supply. We may characterize the AS curve by the following function:

$$P = P(Y, Z),$$

where Z is a vector of exogenous variables that may shift the AS curve, and $\partial P/\partial Y > 0$, that is, the AS curve is upward sloping. That the AS curve is upward sloping can be intuitively understood using the "imperfect information" argument. Suppose that each firm in the economy produces a single good and there are many different goods in the market. If we assume that each firm has imperfect information on the overall price level, then, without perfect information, they may mistake an overall price rise as a rise in the relative price of the good that they produce. If the overall price level rises, many firms make more efforts to produce more, hence the upward-sloping AS curve.

We may further specify the AS equation in a linear form:

$$P = EP + \phi\left(Y - \bar{Y}\right), \tag{5.18}$$

where Y is output, $\bar{Y}$ is the output potential, P is the price level, EP is the expected price level, and ϕ is a parameter that measures the sensitivity of price to the deviation of output from the natural level. If the price level rises above the expectation, the output will exceed the output potential; if the price level declines, then the economy underperforms its potential. In this linear AS model, both $\bar{Y}$ and EP are exogenous variables. In particular, EP is the intercept of the AS curve, and changes in EP shift the AS curve along the vertical direction.

The linear AS equation in (5.18) can also be derived using the sticky-price argument. Assume that there are two types of firms in the economy:

(a) Flexible-price firms, which set prices according to

$$P_f = P + \gamma\left(Y - \bar{Y}\right), \quad \gamma > 0.$$

(b) Sticky-price firms, which set the price by

$$P_s = EP.$$

Let $0 < s < 1$ be the fraction of sticky-price firms. The overall price level would be

$$P = sP_s + (1 - s)P_f = sEP + (1 - s)\left(P + \gamma\left(Y - \bar{Y}\right)\right).$$

Rearranging the terms, we obtain

$$P = EP + \frac{(1 - s)\gamma}{s}\left(Y - \bar{Y}\right).$$

Obviously this is the same equation as in (5.18) with $\phi = (1 - s)\gamma/s > 0$. If we draw the price level P on the Y-axis, which is conventional in economics, the AS curve has a positive slope of ϕ.

The slope of the AS curve is an important parameter for an economy. If the slope approaches infinity, then the AS curve would become vertical, i.e., the classical AS curve. The imperfect-information argument for the upward-sloping AS curve tells us that the AS curve would be steeper for those economies with a volatile aggregate price level, where people would learn to differentiate relative price changes from overall inflation. The sticky-price argument tells us that the AS curve would be steeper for those economies with a higher average level of inflation, where prices are relatively more flexible. Combining these two arguments, we may safely say that the AS curve would be steeper in economies with high and volatile inflation. It is thus no wonder that the classical approach to economics made a comeback in the 1970s, an era marked by exactly high and volatile inflation in developed countries.

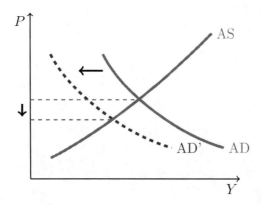

Figure 5.26 The effect of a negative AD shock.

Demand-Shock Recession Revisited

Suppose that the economy is initially at the full-employment level. If there is a negative shock to the aggregate demand (e.g., reduced investment sentiment), then the AD curve shifts to the left (Figure 5.26), resulting in an economy that produces less than the output potential. Meanwhile, the price level declines, resulting in deflation.

Deflation may further reduce aggregate demand. First, deflation makes the existing debt more difficult to service. It is equivalent to transfering wealth from debtors to creditors. Debtors are typically younger, having higher marginal propensity to consume, and are generally more entrepreneurial than creditors. Therefore, deflation may depress both consumption and investment.

Even an expectation of deflation may immediately dent aggregate demand. We may consider the following IS-LM model:

$$Y = C(Y - T) + I(i - E\pi) + G, \qquad (5.19)$$

$$\frac{M}{P} = L(i, Y), \qquad (5.20)$$

where i is the nominal interest rate, and $E\pi$ is the expectation of inflation. In this model, the investment expenditure is a function of the ex ante real interest rate. And the endogenous variables are Y and i. Note that the expectation of deflation corresponds to a negative $E\pi$. When $E\pi$ turns from positive to negative, the IS curve will shift to the left, resulting in less output or income.

Responding to Demand Shocks

Relatively speaking, policy makers are more ready to respond to demand shocks than to supply shocks. As seen earlier, the government may conduct expansionary monetary or fiscal policies to stimulate aggregate demand when the economy slides into a recession.

And when there is a positive shock to the aggregate demand (e.g., a surge in investment sentiment) and inflation becomes a problem, then the government may raise interest rates (monetary tightening) or tax rates (fiscal tightening). The tightening would shift the AD curve to the left and cool down the economy.

Case Study: The Great Depression

Before the Great Depression, there was a spectacular bull market on Wall Street in the 1920s. People believed that the bull market was going to last forever, including the famous American economist Irving Fisher. And brokerage firms offered high-leverage financing for their customers to take advantage of the roaring market.

In late October 1929, the US stock market finally crashed. The initial crash led to forced selling by those who bought stocks with borrowed money and who had received "margin calls." A vicious cycle thus began. The stock crash turned the previous extreme optimism into extreme despair. New investment expenditure of the US economy almost came to a stop. The quick deterioration of the real economy further fed back to the stock market.

We may regard the Great Depression as an extreme version of the demand-shock recession. By mid-1932, the Dow Jones Industrial Average (DJIA) had lost almost 90% of its market value. The investment expenditure declined by a similar rate. The real output declined by about 30%. And the unemployment rate rose to 25% in 1933. Meanwhile, the economy went into deflation in 1930 and intensified in 1931. The deflation also contributed to the continued weakness.

The Great Depression did not hit China until 1932. The reasons why China escaped the initial shock waves were twofold. First, the Chinese economy in the 1920s and 1930s was agrarian, and it was not dependent on exporting to foreign markets. Second, the silver-based Chinese currency depreciated against major currencies that were on the gold standard. For example, a Chinese yuan was about $0.71 US in 1927. In 1930 and 1931, the exchange rate dropped to $0.21 US per yuan.[5] The sharp depreciation protected the agricultural sector and stimulated import-substituting industries. Furthermore, the overseas Chinese bought silver and sent their wealth home. The consequent monetary expansion led to a short-lived boom in China when other parts of the world suffered from deflation.

However, the silver stopped flowing into China in 1932 and started to flow out, although initially on a moderate scale. In 1934, the silver outflow became a serious problem when the US passed the Silver Purchase Act, which required the US government hold a quarter of the currency reserves in silver. In 1934 alone, silver worth 257 million yuan flowed out of China, and this did not include the silver smuggled out of the country. At the same time, the silver price doubled within a year. To the Chinese economy, this meant a dramatic appreciation of its currency and a radical monetary tightening due to the outflow of silver.

As a result, deflation finally hit China hard. From 1931 to 1934, farm prices fell 58%. Farmers were especially hard hit, since their taxes were fixed cash obligations. And the weather did not help. Drought and floods wreaked widespread devastation in 1934–1935. The rice harvest in 1934 was 34% below that of 1931.[6] Note that even in 1931, Chinese peasants were close to subsistence level. The Great Depression meant mass unemployment in the West, but famine and depopulation in China. It was under such circumstances that the Nationalist government gave up the silver-based currency in 1935.

The Phillips Curve

If the AS curve is upward sloping and fixed, shifts of the AD curve will produce changes in output and employment, along with inflation. Suppose that the economy is at the full-employment level and there is a negative shock (e.g., a financial crisis) to the aggregate demand. The shock would shift the AD to the left, resulting in less output, higher unemployment, and lower inflation, producing an inverse relationship between unemployment and inflation. The inverse relationship also remains when the economy starts to expand as long as the boost to the economy comes mainly from the demand side. The government may conduct fiscal or monetary stimulus, shifting the AD curve to the right. As a result, output increases, unemployment declines, and inflation rises.

The celebrated Phillips curve is a hypothesis that there exists an inverse relationship between unemployment and inflation (Figure 5.27). As shown in the preceding analysis, the Phillips curve essentially suggests that short-term shocks to the economy mainly come from the demand side. When A.W.H. Phillips (1914–1975) first published his result in 1958, inflation was not a big concern. So policy makers thought that, based on the Phillips curve, they might reduce unemployment by stoking up inflation.

One of the modern versions of the Phillips curve takes the following form:

$$\pi = E\pi - \alpha(u - u^n) + v, \tag{5.21}$$

where π is the inflation rate, $E\pi$ is the expected inflation, u is the unemployment rate, u^n is the *natural rate of unemployment*, and v is a random shock to inflation.

Roughly speaking, inflation expectation is the average view of future inflation. Note that the expectation can be self-fulfilling: When everyone expects prices to go up, prices will go up as consumers hasten to purchase and sellers hesitate to sell.

We may call $(u - u^n)$ the *cyclical unemployment*, which is the deviation of the unemployment rate from the natural level. And α is a positive parameter that measures the sensitivity of inflation to cyclical unemployment. A drop in cyclical

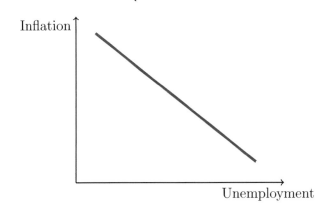

Figure 5.27 The Phillips curve.

unemployment leads to the so-called *demand-pull inflation*. Note that when the unemployment rate drops, more workers have jobs, and they have more income to spend, hence there is higher demand in the economy.

We assume that natural rate of unemployment u^n is stable over time and independent of the cyclical unemployment. We call this assumption the *natural-rate hypothesis*. An alternative hypothesis is *hysteresis*, which states that the natural rate of unemployment may be time varying and that the level of the unemployment rate depends not only on the current state of the economy but also on the historical path. For example, a sustained period of unemployment may make the skill set of the unemployed obsolete, hence permanently raising the unemployment rate.

Finally, we may call the random shock v the *supply shock* and the inflation caused by v the *cost-push inflation*.

The Phillips-curve equation in (5.21) can be derived as follows. Let $p_t = \log(P_t)$. We modify the short-run AS equation in (5.18) as follows:

$$p_t = E_{t-1}p_t + \phi(Y_t - \bar{Y}) + v_t,$$

where we add a supply shock v_t and $E_{t-1}p_t$ represents the expectation of p_t given information available at time $t-1$. Subtracting p_{t-1} from both sides of the equation, we obtain

$$\pi_t = E_{t-1}\pi_t + \phi(Y_t - \bar{Y}) + v_t. \tag{5.22}$$

Note that $\pi_t = p_t - p_{t-1}$ and that $E_{t-1}p_{t-1} = p_{t-1}$. Plugging in Okun's law, $(Y_t - \bar{Y}) = -\gamma(u_t - u^n)$, we obtain the Phillips-curve equation:

$$\pi_t = E_{t-1}\pi_t - \alpha(u_t - u^n) + v_t,$$

where $\alpha = \phi\gamma$. The Phillips curve indicates a trade-off between inflation and unemployment: It may take the cost of inflation to reduce unemployment.

Thanks to (5.22), we may also say that the trade-off is between inflation and the output gap. And we may call $1/\phi$ the *sacrifice ratio*, which measures the

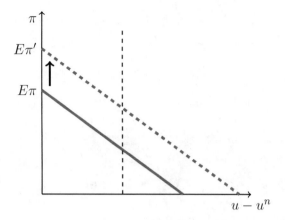

Figure 5.28 The Phillips curve with inflation expectation.

percentage of a year's real GDP growth that must be forgone to reduce inflation by one percentage point.

Examining the equation in (5.21), we see that the Phillips curve may be unstable due to the presence of v and $E\pi$, both of which can shift the Phillips vertically. When supply shocks (e.g., oil shock) were noteworthy in the 1970s, for example, the inverse relationship between unemployment and inflation all but disappeared.

Expectation also plays an important role in making the Phillips curve unstable. Under the *rational expectation* hypothesis, which states that people form expectations using all relevant information and that the expectation is correct on average, the expected inflation would increase as soon as policy makers consider a stimulus package. Consequently, the Phillips curve shifts upward immediately, foiling the attempt to trade more inflation for less unemployment (Figure 5.28). In the end, inflation may be stoked up with no reduction in unemployment.

In other words, there may be no trade-off between inflation and output (employment) when people can correctly evaluate policies and adjust their expectations of inflation. However, the nonexistence of a trade-off between inflation and output (employment) is not necessarily bad news. The good news is that, if the rational expectation hypothesis holds, it may be painless to combat inflation. In other words, a credible policy maker may bring down inflation without causing any increase in unemployment.

The rational expectation hypothesis is valuable for theoretical analysis. For empirical analysis, however, the inflation expectation requires more concrete forms. We may measure the inflation expectation by conducting a survey, asking a carefully chosen sample of people their opinions on inflation. We may also employ econometric models to predict inflation and use the predicted value as expected inflation. The simplest econometric model for predicting inflation assumes that the one-period-ahead inflation equals the current inflation:

$$E_{t-1}\pi_t = \pi_{t-1}.$$

This assumption is called the *adaptive expectation of inflation*. If this assumption holds, then inflation tends to stay at the current level, implying persistence (or inertia) in the movement of inflation.

5.6.3   A Simple Dynamic AD-AS Model

A static model specifies a set of *simultaneous* relations among all variables. Given an external shock, the endogenous variables shift to another equilibrium immediately and stay there. To study the time-dependent transition from one equilibrium to another, we need dynamic models.

A dynamic model specifies a set of time-dependent relations, which necessarily involves lags of endogenous variables (predetermined variables). For example, if we assume adaptive expectation, the Phillips curve has the form $\pi_t = \pi_{t-1} - \alpha(u_t - u^n) + v_t$, which becomes a dynamic model. Note that the Phillips curve equation is a difference equation, in contrast to the differential equations we repeatedly use in Chapter 4. The differential equations describe smooth changes over time, while difference equations allow nonsmooth changes.

We first consider a static linear AD-AS model:

$$\begin{aligned} Y_t &= 100 + 0.4P_t + u_t, \\ Y_t &= 400 - 0.6P_t + v_t, \end{aligned}$$

where u_t and v_t denote shocks to the supply and the demand, respectively. Note that the model has two endogenous variables (Y_t and P_t), two exogenous variables (u_t and v_t), and two equations. We can *solve* the model and obtain

$$\begin{aligned} P_t &= 300 + (v_t - u_t), \\ Y_t &= 220 + \frac{1}{5}(3u_t + 2v_t). \end{aligned}$$

By "solve," we mean representing endogenous variables using exogenous variables as in the preceding example. Note that although the variables have time subscript, this is still a static model. In this model, a unit negative shock to u_t would result in a unit instantaneous price increase and a 0.6 decline in Y_t. The shock does not affect the future price or output.

If the AS curve does not shift, i.e., $u_t = 0$, then we have

$$\begin{aligned} P_t &= 300 + v_t, \\ Y_t &= 220 + 0.4v_t. \end{aligned}$$

This says that if shocks come only from the demand side, then price and output move together, which is consistent with a downward-sloping Phillips curve since the output is inversely related to the unemployment rate.

Now we assume that the aggregate supply reacts to the lagged price level. Then the model becomes

$$
\begin{aligned}
Y_t &= 100 + 0.4P_{t-1} + u_t, \\
Y_t &= 400 - 0.6P_t + v_t.
\end{aligned}
$$

The slight change makes the model dynamic, in which a past shock would affect the current and future economy. In this model, Y_t and P_t are endogenous variables, u_t and v_t are exogenous shocks, and P_{t-1} is a predetermined variable. In solving a dynamic model, we may treat predetermined variables as exogenous variables.

We may define a *steady state* of the dynamic model as the state in which the price is constant and there are no shocks ($u_t = v_t = 0$). It is easy to see that in the steady state, we have $P_t = 300$ and $Y_t = 220$.

In the dynamic model, an exogenous shock leads to a series of changes to endogenous variables. For example, suppose that the economy is initially at the steady state ($P_0 = 300$ and $Y_0 = 220$) and that there is a one-period negative shock to the AS at $t=1$ (say, $u_1 = -1$). Other than this, the supply and demand shocks remain zero, $u_t = 0$ for $t > 1$ and $v_t = 0$ for all t.

The supply shock immediately reduces output and raises the price at $t = 1$. And the effect of the supply shock on the economy will not stop at $t = 1$. In the next period, Y_2 and P_2 depends on P_1, which further depends on u_1. Figure 5.29 shows a simulation study of the dynamic effect of the preceding supply shock on price and output in the simple AD-AS model. Note that if the demand shock is absent, the model produces an inverse relationship between price and output. We can do the simulation in Figure 5.29 using an Excel spreadsheet. Interested readers may want to play with the Excel file "simple_adas.xlsx" available at http://jhqian.org/macrobook.

5.6.4 A New Keynesian Dynamic AD-AS Model

We now present a more useful dynamic AD-AS model, which contains three equations: (i) an IS equation; (ii) a "Phillips curve" equation; and (iii) a monetary policy rule. We first specify the three-equation model. Then we solve the model, that is, we represent each endogenous variable with exogenous and predetermined variables. Finally, we apply the model to macroeconomic analysis.

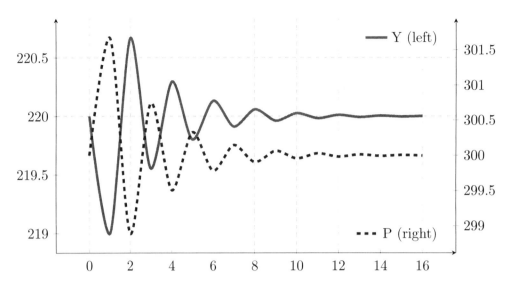

Figure 5.29 Dynamic effect of a supply shock.

The Model and the Solution

We first specify an IS equation as follows:

$$y_t = \bar{y} - \alpha(r_t - r^*) + u_t,$$

where $y_t = \log Y_t$, $\bar{y} = \log \bar{Y}$, r_t is the real interest rate, u_t is the demand shock, α is a constant measuring how demand responds to changes in r_t, and r^* is a constant called the *natural rate of interest*. Based on the IS equation, we may understand r^* as the real interest rate that makes output equal to output potential in the absence of demand shocks.

We further specify r_t as the ex ante real interest rate:

$$r_t = i_t - E_t\pi_{t+1},$$

where i_t is the nominal interest rate and $E_t\pi_{t+1}$ is the expected next-period inflation at period t. Note that E_t denotes *conditional expectation* using information available at time t.

Then we use the Phillips-curve-like equation in (5.22) to model the dynamics of inflation:

$$\pi_t = E_{t-1}\pi_t + \phi(y_t - \bar{y}) + v_t,$$

where $(y_t - \bar{y})$ is the *output gap*, v_t is the *supply shock*, and ϕ is a constant measuring how inflation responds to the output gap.

Finally, to complete the model, we assume that the monetary authority determines the nominal interest rate by the following rule:

$$i_t = \pi_t + r^* + \theta_\pi(\pi_t - \pi^*) + \theta_y(y_t - \bar{y}),$$

where π^* is the inflation target; θ_π and θ_y are constants measuring how the monetary authority would respond to inflation and output gap, respectively; and r^* is the natural rate of interest. Based on this monetary policy rule, we may understand r^* as the real interest rate in a perfect state of the economy where the output equals the output potential and inflation equals the inflation target.

The preceding monetary policy rule implies that the monetary authority has two objectives: (1) Keep a moderate inflation rate; and (2) promote output and employment. The famous Taylor rule for the US Fed is given by

$$\text{FFR} = \text{inflation} + 2 + 0.5(\text{inflation} - 2) + 0.5(\text{GDP gap}),$$

where FFR represents the federal funds rate, which is the main target variable for the US Federal Reserve. The Taylor rule assumes that the natural rate of interest for the US economy is 2%. When inflation reaches the target 2% and the GDP gap is zero, then FFR should be 4%.

To make the conditional expectation $E_{t-1}\pi_t$ more concrete, we assume adaptive expectation of inflation (i.e., $E_{t-1}\pi_t = \pi_{t-1}$). Putting all the preceding equations together, we have

$$y_t = \bar{y} - \alpha(i_t - \pi_t - r^*) + u_t, \tag{5.23}$$

$$\pi_t = \pi_{t-1} + \phi(y_t - \bar{y}) + v_t, \tag{5.24}$$

$$i_t = \pi_t + r^* + \theta_\pi(\pi_t - \pi^*) + \theta_y(y_t - \bar{y}). \tag{5.25}$$

In this model, the endogenous variables are y_t, π_t, and i_t. The exogenous variables are $\bar{y}$, π^*, r^*, u_t, and v_t. And there is a predetermined variable: π_{t-1}.

It is useful first to define a steady state. Here we define the steady state as the state where inflation is constant and there are no shocks, $u_t = v_t = 0$ for all t. It is easy to see that in such a steady state, $y_t = \bar{y}$, $\pi_t = \pi^*$, $i_t = \pi^* + r^*$, and $r_t = r^*$. Thus, real variables (y_t, r_t) do not depend on monetary policy, and monetary policy only influences the nominal variables (π_t, i_t). Hence the steady state satisfies the classical dichotomy and monetary neutrality.

There are three equations and three unknowns (endogenous variables). We may solve the system of equations and obtain

$$\pi_t = a_1(\pi_{t-1} + v_t) + a_2\pi^* + a_3 u_t,$$

$$y_t = \bar{y} + a_4(\pi^* - \pi_{t-1} - v_t) + a_5 u_t,$$

where $a_1 = \frac{1+\alpha\theta_y}{1+\alpha\theta_y+\phi\alpha\theta_\pi}$, $a_2 = \frac{\phi\alpha\theta_\pi}{1+\alpha\theta_y+\phi\alpha\theta_\pi}$, $a_3 = \frac{\phi}{1+\alpha\theta_y+\phi\alpha\theta_\pi}$, $a_4 = \frac{\alpha\theta_\pi}{1+\alpha\theta_y+\phi\alpha\theta_\pi}$, and $a_5 = \frac{1}{1+\alpha\theta_y+\phi\alpha\theta_\pi}$. Similarly, we may represent i_t as linear functions of exogenous and predetermined variables, simply by plugging the preceding solutions to π_t and y_t to the monetary policy rule in (5.25).

To apply the model, we must assign values to α, ϕ, θ_π, and θ_y. A natural approach would be to statistically estimate these parameters using data. But

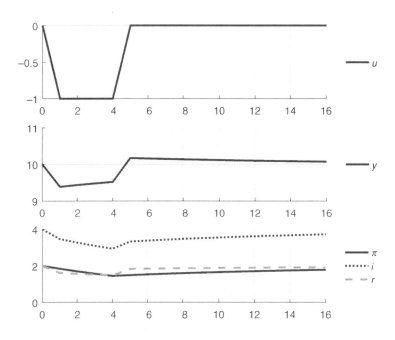

Figure 5.30 Dynamic analysis of a demand-shock recession.

statistical estimation is most often infeasible. Instead, economists often rely on *calibration*, an approach that directly assigns values to the parameters in the model, drawing on empirical and experimental studies. Here, we simply set $\alpha = 1$, $\phi = 0.25$, $\theta_\pi = 0.5$, and $\theta_y = 0.5$. Furthermore, we assume $\bar{y} = 10$, $\pi^* = 2$, and $r^* = 2$. Next, we perform a couple of experiments on the model.

Demand-Shock Recession

Suppose that the economy is initially at the steady state and that there are four consecutive negative shocks to the IS equation, $u_1 = u_2 = u_3 = u_4 = -1$, each period representing a quarter. From the fifth quarter, the demand shock u_t is back to zero, and $u_t = 0$ for $t > 4$. Figure 5.30 shows the dynamics following the shock.

The demand shock produces a recession that lasts only one quarter. However, the output gap remains negative for four quarters. From the second quarter, the economy starts to recover, thanks to the expansionary monetary policy (i.e., the real interest rate declines). In the fifth quarter, when the demand shock ends, the output is already above the output potential. At the same time, the monetary policy shifts to tightening, raising the real interest rate. The continued monetary tightening prevents the economy from further overheating. The output declines and converges to the output potential in the long run.

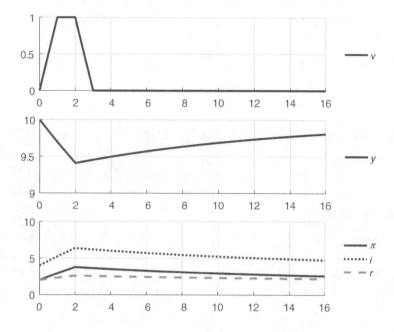

Figure 5.31 Dynamic analysis of a supply-shock recession.

As the output declines in the recession, inflation also declines. The decline of both output and inflation leads to aggressive cuts in the nominal interest rate, from 4% to below 3% in the fourth quarter. The aggressive monetary policy prevents inflation from steep declines. From the fifth quarter, inflation starts to pick up. But it stays below the target inflation and slowly converges to the target.

Supply-Shock Recession

Suppose that the economy is initially at the steady state and that there are two consecutive shocks to the Phillips-curve equation, $v_1 = v_2 = 1$. These shocks directly push up inflation. Hence we may interpret them as supply shocks or price shocks. From the third quarter, the supply shock v_t is back to zero, $v_t = 0$ for $t > 2$. Figure 5.31 shows the dynamics following the shock.

The supply shocks produce a recession that lasts two quarters. The economy starts to recover from the third quarter when the supply shock ends. The recovery, however, is slow. In the 16th quarter, the output is still below the potential.

The reason behind the slow recovery is that inflation rises substantially when the supply shocks occur. Inflation rises from 2% to nearly 4% in the second quarter. In contrast, output only declines by 0.6%. According to the monetary policy rule, the central bank should give higher priority to the inflation problem. Therefore, the central bank raises the nominal interest rate aggressively from 4% to 6.4% in the second quarter. The real interest rate rises during the recession. The hawkish monetary policy helps reduce inflation but slows down the recovery in output.

Interested readers may use the Excel file "dynamic_adas.xlsx," available at `http://jhqian.org/macrobook`, for other experiments on the New Keynesian dynamic AD-AS model.

5.7 Keynes Theory of Employment and Investment

The IS-LM and AD-AS models are interpretations of Keynes's theory by the mainstream Keynesian or New Keynesian economists. These models are popular because they, using simple mathematics, have clear formulations with clear implications.

The mathematical models, however, lose some key insights of Keynes. In this section, we give an outline of Keynes's key ideas in his masterpiece, *The General Theory of Employment, Interest, and Money*.[7] The central questions are: (a) What determines the level of employment? (b) What determines the investment?

5.7.1   Theory of Employment

Keynes proposes an AD-AS model of employment that looks like the Keynesian Cross model. He postulates an *aggregate demand function* to characterize the demand side of the economy as a whole:

$$D = f(N),$$

where D is the proceeds (or revenue) that firms expect to receive from the employment of N workers. Note that the demand curve for a firm characterizes the changing quantity of a commodity that will be purchased at varying prices. For the economy as a whole, however, we cannot measure the total output in any simple unit, such as a ton. Instead, Keynes uses the number of workers employed to measure the total output. On the other hand, D corresponds to *price*, and it may be called the aggregate demand price. Keynes assumes that the aggregate demand function is increasing in N. That is, demand increases with employment.

On the supply side, Keynes postulates an *aggregate supply function*:

$$Z = \phi(N),$$

where Z is the *aggregate supply price* of the output from employing N workers. The term "aggregate supply price" needs a definition and some explanation. Keynes defines it as follows:

> ... the aggregate supply price of the output of a given amount of employment is the expectation of proceeds which will just make it worth the while of the entrepreneurs to give that employment.

In a market economy, entrepreneurs make employment (thus, production) plans to maximize their profits. For a firm employing N_i workers, the manager may expect a minimum amount of proceeds, D_i. If he expects a revenue lower than D_i, he will reduce employment. Since both N_i and D_i can take simple summation, it is conceptually clear that, in aggregate, there is a minimum amount of proceeds that the whole entrepreneur class requires to employ a varying amount of total employment. The aggregate supply price is exactly the minimum amount of proceeds to induce a certain amount of employment.

The aggregate supply price should be higher than the expected factor costs, including wage costs in particular. We may assume that $Z = W \cdot N + R$, where W is the average wage, $W \cdot N$ is the total wage bill, and R represents the sum of economic profits and other factor costs. R may or may not increase as entrepreneurs consider more employment of labor. But it is unlikely that R decreases as entrepreneurs consider increasing labor inputs. To induce more employment, thus, the aggregate supply price must increase. As a result, the aggregate supply function is also increasing in N (Figure 5.32).

Furthermore, we may establish two facts about the AD and AS curves: (i) The AS curve has a steeper slope than the AD curve; and (ii) the AS curve is below the AD curve when the employment level N is very low. As a result, the AD and AS curves will have an intersection, which determines the equilibrium employment level N' and the effective demand D'. If the aggregate supply price is lower than the aggregate demand price for a given value of N, then firms will increase employment and production, driving up factor costs and hence the aggregate supply price, up to the level of employment for which Z has become equal to D. If the aggregate supply price is higher than the aggregate demand price for a given value of N, then firms will find it unprofitable to offer so much employment. They will cut costs by slashing jobs and scaling down production to the level of employment for which Z has become equal to D. In other words, the entrepreneurs maximize their expectation of profits at the intersection of the AD and AS curves.

To see why the AS curve has a steeper slope than the AD curve, we note that wages are income to workers, and workers' consumption expenditure is a major part of the aggregate demand for entrepreneurs. Recall that the marginal propensity to consume is less than one, hence workers consume only part of their increased income. If we hold the average wage W constant, the increase of employment ΔN will bring an increase of $W \cdot \Delta N$ in the aggregate supply price. The increase in the aggregate demand price, however, will be only $MPC \cdot (W \cdot \Delta N) < W \cdot \Delta N$. That is to say, as more employment increases wage bills, the aggregate supply price rises faster than the aggregate demand price.

To see why the AS curve is below the AD curve when the employment level N is very low (say, far below the full-employment level), note first that the labor costs (and hence the aggregate supply price) should be very low if jobs are scarce. Second, note that people usually try hard to maintain a certain level of consumption,

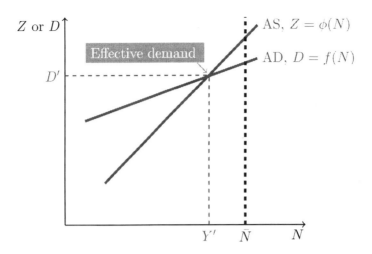

Figure 5.32 Aggregate demand and aggregate supply.

even when their incomes decline during recessions. When current income cannot cover current consumption, they may draw on their past savings. In the worst case, people have to maintain a minimal level of consumption just for survival. If there are no savings to draw from, they have to borrow from others, which is to draw on other's savings. Although the labor income goes down together with the labor costs during economic downturns, the aggregate consumption is more resilient thanks to the possibility of drawing on savings and borrowing. As a result, the aggregate demand price will be higher than the aggregate supply price when N is far below the full-employment level.

The intersection of the AD and AS curves determines, on the one hand, an equilibrium level of employment N' and, on the other hand, the *effective demand* D', which refers to the expected proceeds that just equal the necessary proceeds that make the employment of N' profitable to entrepreneurs.

There is no reason to believe that the intersection always falls on the full-employment level $\bar{N}$. Suppose that the economy is initially at the full-employment equilibrium, that is, $N' = \bar{N}$. If there is a negative shock to investment sentiment or propensity to consume, then the AD curve will shift downward. If the AS curve fails to shift downward by the same amount, then the new equilibrium employment will be less than $\bar{N}$. Note that sticky price, sticky wage in particular, may prevent the AS curve to adjust adequately for full-employment.

Keynes calls his theory of employment a *general* theory, in contrast to the classical theory, which he regards as a special case. The classical theory, as in Say's law, postulates that *supply creates its own demand*. As a result, the AD and AS curves must overlap, and competition between entrepreneurs must expand employment up to full employment. But Say's law holds only when money serves only as a medium of transactions. To assume that Say's law holds is equivalent to assuming that there are no obstacles to full employment. The repeated occurrence of prolonged mass unemployment, however, contradicts the classical doctrines.

5.7.2   Theory of Investment

The Importance of Investment

In Keynes's eyes, investment is important because the investment demand fills the gap between the effective demand and the consumption demand at the equilibrium employment level. As a result, the fluctuation of investment demand drives business cycles.

To see this, we may omit the effect of foreign trade and government expenditure and decompose the effective demand Y into two components:

$$Y = C(Y) + I,$$

where $C(Y)$ denotes an aggregate consumption function, which Keynes calls *propensity to consume*, and I denotes the demand derived from new investment. Note that we should understand Y within the consumption function as the aggregate income. We simplify analysis by assuming that the effective demand equals the aggregate income, which differs from the effective demand in Keynes's General Theory by a user cost of capital.

The propensity to consume and the new investment, together, determine the effective demand and the volume of employment. If there is insufficient new investment, the effective demand has to decline and, with it, the volume of employment. Indeed, a decline in the new investment, as analyzed in the Keynesian Cross model, may have a multiplier (negative) effect on total income and employment.

Since the marginal propensity to consume is less than one and it generally declines as income increases, the investment demand is especially important for wealthy societies, which have wider gaps between the aggregate income and the consumption expenditure. For a wealthy society, which typically enjoys a high productive power, investment means not only the possibility of future growth but also the necessity of maintaining the current living standards. But bad times hit. When a recession or depression occurs, the new investment demand may take a nosedive, forcing many to lose jobs, despite the fact that they are willing to work. Keynes calls this phenomenon the *paradox of poverty in the midst of plenty*.

Marginal Efficiency of Capital

It is of utter importance to study how investment fluctuates in the economy. Keynes in the General Theory offers a much richer account than the simple investment function in the IS-LM models.

Keynes introduces the concept of the *marginal efficiency of capital* to characterize the profitability of new investments. He defines the marginal efficiency of capital as

> the rate of discount which would make the present value of the series of annuities given by the returns expected from the capital-asset during its life just equal to its supply price.

Here, the series of annuities refers to the future cash flow of an investment or capital asset. We may also call it the *prospective yield* of the investment. The *supply price* of a capital asset refers to the price that would just induce the production of an additional unit of such assets. A more familiar name for the supply price is *replacement cost*.

In mathematical terms, we first denote the series of *expected* annuities by $Q_1, Q_2, \ldots, Q_n$. The marginal efficiency of capital is the discount rate r_m that solves the following equation:

$$\text{Supply price} = \frac{Q_1}{(1 + r_m)} + \frac{Q_2}{(1 + r_m)^2} + \cdots + \frac{Q_n}{(1 + r_m)^n}.$$

The key word in this definition is *expected*. The current and past returns to a capital asset are irrelevant. Entrepreneurs, when deliberating new investment, have to form expectations of future yields.

For any given type of capital, new investment would depress the marginal efficiency of capital, mainly because the expected annuities per unit of capital would decline when the capital becomes more abundant. Equivalently, for each type of capital, there is a schedule of new investment corresponding to different marginal efficiencies of capital. We may aggregate all these schedules across different types of capital and obtain an economywide schedule of new investment corresponding to different marginal efficiencies of capital. Keynes calls this the investment demand schedule or the schedule of the marginal efficiency of capital.

Entrepreneurs as a whole will add new investment until there is no longer any class of capital asset with a marginal efficiency of capital higher than the current interest rate. To help understand this, Keynes introduces the *demand price* of a capital asset as the present value of the expected annuities discounted by the interest rate r:

$$\text{Demand price} = \frac{Q_1}{(1 + r)} + \frac{Q_2}{(1 + r)^2} + \cdots + \frac{Q_n}{(1 + r)^n}.$$

If the supply price of a capital asset is lower than the demand price or, equivalently, if $r_m > r$, then entrepreneurs will supply such capital assets, that is, add new investment.

The Inducement to Invest

The marginal efficiency of capital is defined in terms of the expectation of future yield and the current supply price of capital assets.

The supply price of capital assets may be mainly determined by the current technology and prevailing factor prices, such as wages and prices of energy and resources. A technological revolution, for example, may bring a lower supply price, which stimulates investment. In most historical periods, however, technology should be stable in the short term. Wages are notoriously sticky or stable in the short term. Therefore, in the absence of major supply shocks that may result in large fluctuations in energy and resource prices, the supply price of capital assets should be relatively stable.

The expectation of future yield, however, is often subject to major revisions, resulting in large fluctuations in the marginal efficiency of capital. The long-term expectation, in particular, is on extremely precarious ground. Often it is not that it is difficult to forecast future yields, but that there is a lack of confidence in the forecasts. In modern terms, there are not only risks that can be dealt with using probability distributions but also uncertainties that make any long-term expectation cautious and subject to sudden revisions.

Keyes regards the fluctuation in the marginal efficiency of capital as the cause of business cycles. The optimistic evaluation of the marginal efficiency of capital leads to overinvestment in the later phase of economic expansion. For a time, the feverish investment brings higher profits to corporations and confirms the optimism of the investors. Such a self-reinforcing activity, however, is also self-defeating. Sooner or later, the game has to stop since the feverish accumulation of capital would depress the marginal efficiency of capital. When this happens, optimism gives way to pessimism. As a result, the marginal efficiency of capital may collapse suddenly. The ensuing collapse in new investment leads to the collapse of the effective demand and thus an economic recession.

The recession continues as long as the marginal efficiency of capital is lower than the interest rate. The dismal state of the economy may change for the better when (i) the monetary authority slashes the interest rate to below the marginal efficiency of capital; (ii) the expectation of future yield improves as business confidence restores; and/or (iii) the supply price of capital declines by an amount enough for the marginal efficiency of capital to exceed the rate of interest.

The Role of the Stock Market

The stock market exerts a decisive influence on the rate of new investment. If the stock market valuation is low, then there is little incentive for entrepreneurs to make new investments since they can purchase capital assets in the stock market. If the valuation is high, then the entrepreneurs are more than willing to build new assets and try to float them, exploiting the high valuation.

The stock market provides for entrepreneurs and investors with a *conventional valuation* of almost every type of capital asset. The conventional valuation is imperfect but indispensable, because the expectation of future yields, especially the long-term expectation, rests on precarious grounds. The convention, however, has its weak points. That is, the convention itself is built on precarious grounds. Keynes lists five factors that contribute to the precariousness of stock market expectation of future yields.

First, as more and more shares are owned by retail investors or people who have no special knowledge of businesses, the stock market's overall ability to value assets has declined.

Second, short-term fluctuations in profits tend to have excessive influence on the market. Keynes gives two examples: (i) The share prices of American ice companies are seasonally higher in summer and (ii) the recurrence of holidays may raise the market valuation of the British railway substantially.

Third, the conventional valuation of the stock market results from the mass psychology of a large number of ignorant individuals. The mass psychology, or opinion, may suddenly change due to factors unrelated to the prospective yield. In some abnormal times, the market may be subject to waves of optimistic and pessimistic sentiment. Although individual participants may be rational, the stock market as a whole may behave like a mad man. And the irrational behavior is, sadly, legitimate since there is really no solid ground for forecasting future yields.

Fouth, even professional investors and speculators are concerned not with making superior forecasts of future yields, but with foreseeing changes in the conventional valuation a little ahead of the others. In the ideal world, the professionals will correct the vagaries of the ignorant investors to their own benefits. For example, if the ignorant bid up the share price for no fundamental reasons, the professionals will sell the share to the ignorant (possibly buy a similar stock with similar fundamentals) for a profit. Those who succeed in such games would be contributing to society, in that a more proper valuation of assets leads to more reasonable and stable investment.

In the real world, however, the *value investors*, who employ all available information to calculate the stream of future yields by the best methods available, may not dominate the market. Instead, the speculators whose only job is to guess crowd psychology may dominate the market valuation. There are several factors that may work against the predominance of the value investors.

For one, human nature desires quick results. It is exciting to make quick money, and less immediate gains are discounted at a high rate. Furthermore, to ignore short-term fluctuations, the value investors must have greater resources for safety and should avoid leverage. As Keyes says, "markets can remain irrational longer than you can remain solvent." Finally, when a committee is in charge of evaluating investment performance, the value investor will face the most criticism. The committee may not only pay excessive attention to short-term results but also penalize the *contrarian* character that is valuable to successful value investing. "Worldly wisdom teaches us that," Keynes says, "it is better for reputation to fail conventionally than to succeed unconventionally."

Fifth, once a collapse has occurred, the market recovery requires a revival of not only speculative confidence but also the confidence of banks to provide credit. The process of recovery can be lengthy.

In conclusion, the conventional valuation offered by the stock market has deep flaws. The violent fluctuations in the mass psychology of investors and speculators drive the fluctuations in the conventional valuation of prospective yields, which further drives the fluctuations in new investment, which further drives the business cycles. Keynes does not believe that investment should be solely determined by the stock market. He says,

> When the capital development of a country becomes a by-product of the activities of a casino, the job is likely to be ill-done.

On "Animal Spirit"

The instability of our economy comes not only from speculation but also shocks to the "delicate balance" between spontaneous optimism, which leads to actions, and cold mathematical expectation, which leads to inaction.

Keynes observes that a large proportion of our positive activities come as a result of the *animal spirit*, a spontaneous urge to do something. Undoubtedly, enterprises that are born out of hopes benefit society as a whole. If humans are all cold calculators of future benefits and costs, inaction would be the rule of human society, which then would not achieve the levels of prosperity enjoyed today.

The animal spirit, however, requires a supportive political and social atmosphere. Since the prosperity of our economy depends on the delicate balance of animal spirit and cold calculations, a shock to the political or social atmosphere may tip the balance and change the whole picture.

5.8   Minsky's Financial Cycle

The IS-LM and AD-AS models help us understand why, in recessions, an economy may employ less labor than the labor supply, producing less than the potential level of output. We have also studied how policies such as government expenditure, tax cuts, and monetary easing may get the economy back to the full-employment level.

However, we should not get the impression that the full-employment equilibrium is the norm and that fluctuations are exceptions. We should understand the concept of equilibrium as a dynamic process: Both the full-employment economy and the underemployment economy are in equilibrium. And, importantly, the full-employment equilibrium is as transitory as the underemployment equilibria.

When the economy gets back to the full-employment level, for example, the increased optimism will induce more investment. More investment will lead to higher corporate profit and labor income, reinforcing optimism. Meanwhile, asset prices keep rising and credit conditions keep loosening, as borrowers are more willing to borrow and lenders are more willing to lend. Full of inner dynamism, our economy cannot stay quietly anywhere. As soon as it recovers from a recession and reaches the full-employment state, it will move on to overheat.

The inner dynamism manifests itself most evidently in finance. While Keynes focuses on the role of the stock market, Hyman Minksky develops a theory that centers on the banking industry and the credit market. In his *Stabilizing an Unstable Economy*, Minsky characterizes a three-stage financial cycle. During the stage of *hedge finance*, the economy is dominated by *hedge units*, firms whose cash flows (from capital assets or other financial contracts) are sufficient to cover all cash-payment commitments (interests and principals) now and in the future. At this stage, the economy just starts to recover from a recession. The hedge units may be survivors from the previous financial crisis or new firms grown up from a conservative financial environment, which is also the legacy of the previous crash.

As the economy continues to recover, however, more firms become *speculative units* or even *Ponzi units*. For speculative units, the cash flow may be lower than cash-payment commitment (due to existing debt) in some short-term periods. Speculative units expect to borrow more to cover the gap. And typically, they expect to roll over their debts when they mature. Compared to hedge units, the viability of speculative units depends not only on business conditions (i.e., cost and revenue) but also on conditions of the financial system.

For Ponzi units, the cash-payment commitment is not only higher than the cash flow but also higher than its income. Ponzi units expect to borrow more or sell assets to meet their future cash-payment commitments. As we can see, Ponzi units are even more vulnerable to worsening conditions in the financial system than speculative units. They need bankers who do not care about their worsening balance sheets. And they need the prices of their assets to go higher and the liquidity of these assets to be adequate.

At the later stage of an economic boom, more and more hedge units become speculative, and more and more speculative units become Ponzi. It happens not just because entrepreneurs and their bankers become more optimistic. It may also happen when revenues from new investments into some crowded industries are lower than expected, or when costs of business (interest rate, wage, etc.) rise substantially, forcing hedge units into speculative units, speculative units into Ponzi units.

When a substantial number of corporations engage in speculative or Ponzi finance, the financial markets and the economy become fragile. And the tendency for a robust economy dominated by hedge units to become a fragile one dominated by speculative or Ponzi units is engrained in our financial economy since engaging in speculative or Ponzi finance is highly profitable in a robust economy dominated by hedge units. The profitability of speculative and Ponzi finance will attract more converts, who will generate more credit and raise the demand for assets. The ensuing rise in asset prices will attract more converts to speculative or Ponzi units. The cycle repeats until the financial system is extremely fragile. At the final stage, only a small shock may be enough to tip the financial market to a crisis.

During the crisis, former speculative or Ponzi units may be liquidated, or they may go through debt restructuring, which is an effort to transform speculative or Ponzi units into hedge units. At least for a while, survivors of the business community and bankers will shy away from speculative and Ponzi finance. Thus, a robust economy dominated by hedge units reemerges. The financial cycle, which propels the business cycle, goes on.

Note that the financial cycle does not simply repeat in the same style. Every cycle is different because financial markets are structurally changing over time. In the aftermath of each crisis, a responsible government has to identify what has gone wrong and tries to strengthen regulations to prevent that from happening again. However, when panic gives way to optimism on the part of market participants and when alertness gives way to complacency on the part of regulators, financial innovations will come back to life and make new forms of speculative and Ponzi finance possible.

Every cycle is, of course, also similar, especially in that there is always a bust following a boom. To modify Mark Twain's famous quote, the history of economic fluctuations doesn't repeat itself, but it often rhymes.

5.9   Concluding Remarks

In this chapter, we study a series of models that address short-run economic fluctuations. All these models share a common feature: The market is assumed to be imperfect in some way. The IS-LM models rely on the sticky-price assumption, which says that prices and wages are not flexible enough for markets to clear automatically. The AS model and the Phillips curve rely on the argument of sticky price or imperfect information. Keynes bases his theory of business cycles on an imperfect capital market. And, in the same spirit, Minsky describes a boom-and-bust financial cycle that drives expansions and recessions in the economy.

The economic history of the world speaks to the fact that the market economy is unstable. It was unstable before the government became big enough to influence the economy. It is still unstable after the government has become big and special institutions and policy instruments have been developed to smooth business cycles.

Stabilizing an unstable economy is a very difficult job. But it is also a job that all responsible governments have to do. We leave this to the next chapter.

Exercises

(1) Suppose that the aggregate output (Y) is a linear function of the employed people (N), $Y = \gamma N$, with $\gamma > 0$. Calculate the multiplier effect of government expenditure on the level of employment (i.e., $\partial N / \partial G$) in the Keynesian Cross model.

(2) Consider the Keynesian Cross model. Suppose that the government imposes a flat-rate income tax, $T = \tau Y$, $0 < \tau < 1$. Calculate the government expenditure multiplier, and compare with the case of a lump-sum tax (T is fixed).

(3) Consider the Keynesian Cross model with international trade. Suppose that the equilibrium condition is given by

$$Y = C + I + G + EX - IM,$$

where both the consumption (C) and the import (IM) are linear functions of the disposable income:

$$
\begin{aligned}
C &= 1000 + 0.75(Y - T) \\
IM &= 100 + 0.5(Y - T).
\end{aligned}
$$

We regard I, G, T, and the export (EX) as exogenous. Calculate the government expenditure multiplier and compare it with the closed-economy case.

(4) Suppose that the IS equation is given by

$$
\begin{aligned}
Y &= C(Y - T, r) + I(r) + G \\
C(Y - T, r) &= a + b \cdot (Y - T) - c \cdot r \\
I(r) &= d - e \cdot r,
\end{aligned}
$$

where $a > 0$, $0 < b < 1$, $c > 0$, $d > 0$, and $e > 0$ are all constants.

(a) Given an increase in G, say ΔG, how and how much does the IS curve shift?

(b) If there is an improvement in investor sentiment, say, $I(r)$ becomes

$$I(r) = 2d - e \cdot r,$$

then how and how much does the IS curve shift?

(5) Suppose that LM equation is given by

$$\frac{M}{P} = L(r, Y) = f \cdot Y - g \cdot r,$$

where f and g are both positive constants.

(a) Given an expansion of the money supply, say ΔM, how and how much does the LM curve shift?

(b) If there is a one-time price shock from P to $1.1P$, then how and (approximately) how much does the LM curve shift?

(6) Suppose that the IS and LM equations are as follows:

$$
\begin{aligned}
\text{IS:} \qquad Y &= C(Y - T, r) + I(r) + G, \\
C(Y - T, r) &= a + b \cdot (Y - T) - c \cdot r, \\
I(r) &= d - e \cdot r, \\
\text{LM:} \qquad \frac{h \cdot M}{P} &= L(r, Y), \\
L(r, Y) &= M_0 + f \cdot Y - g \cdot r,
\end{aligned}
$$

where a, b, c, d, e, f, g, h, and M_0 are all positive constants and $b < 1$.

(a) Given an increase in G, say ΔG, calculate the government multiplier effect. Compare your result with (i) the Keynesian Cross case, $c = e = 0$; and (ii) the case where $c = 0$.

(b) If $f = h = 0$, does a monetary stimulus raise output? Does a fiscal stimulus work?

(c) If $g = 0$, does a monetary stimulus raise output? What about a fiscal stimulus?

(7) Consider the usual IS-LM model:

$$
\begin{aligned}
Y &= C(Y - T) + I(r) + G, \\
\frac{M}{P} &= L(r, Y).
\end{aligned}
$$

(a) If the government increases spending by ΔG and the central bank attempts to keep the interest rate unchanged, then how should the central bank do? (Do a quantitative analysis.)

(b) If the central bank manages to do this, what would be the government spending multiplier in this case?

(8) Consider a small open economy, and assume that the net export depends on not only the exchange rate but also the total income,

$$X = X(e, Y).$$

Note that X is decreasing in Y. More income leads to more consumption of imported goods. Analyze the effect of a fiscal stimulus on the economy when the foreign exchange rate regime is

(a) Floating.

(b) Fixed.

(9) Consider the small open-economy model with a floating exchange rate, and assume that the price level is specified as follows:

$$P(e, w) = wP_d + (1 - w)P_f/e,$$

where P_d is the price level for domestically produced goods, P_f is the price level for the imported goods, and $w \in (0, 1)$ is the share of the domestic-product consumption.

(a) Draw the IS-LM curves for this model.

(b) Analyze the effect of a negative foreign-demand shock on the economy, that is, the net export declines for every e.

(c) Suppose that there is a one-time shock (for example, the outbreak of African swine fever raises the pork price) to the domestic price, say P_d rises by ΔP_d and stays at $P_d + \Delta P_d$. Analyze the effect on the economy.

(10) Suppose that in the large open economy, the net export depends on total income as well as the exchange rate:

$$X = X(e, Y),$$

where $\partial X/\partial Y < 0$. Analyze the effect of a decline in investment sentiment on the exchange rate.

(11) A senior advisor once told the US president, Donald Trump, that trade deficit did not represent "losing." He said that the trade deficit was a sign of American strength and that the better the US economy, the larger was the trade deficit. How do you understand this claim? Can you use a model to justify the claim?

(12) Suppose that the IS and LM equations are as follows:

$$
\begin{aligned}
\text{IS:} \quad Y &= C(Y - T) + I(r) + G, \\
C(Y - T) &= a + b \cdot (Y - T), \\
I(r) &= d - e \cdot r, \\
\text{LM:} \quad \frac{M}{P} &= L(r, Y), \\
L(r, Y) &= M_0 + f \cdot Y - g \cdot r,
\end{aligned}
$$

where a, b, d, e, f, g, h, and M_0 are all positive constants and $b < 1$.

(a) Derive the AD equation from the IS and LM equations.

(b) How does the AD curve shift when there is a negative shock to the investment sentiment. Specifically, the investment function becomes $I(r) = d - d_0 - e \cdot r$, where $d_0 > 0$.

(13) Draw the AD curves for the following models:

(a) The small open-economy model with a floating exchange rate.

(b) The small open-economy model with a fixed exchange rate.

(14) In addition to the imperfect-information argument and the sticky-price argument, can you think of other arguments for the case of an upward-sloping AS curve?

(15) If the AS curve is upward sloping, then how should the unemployment rate correlate with the inflation if

(a) The shocks come mainly from the demand side (e.g., investment sentiment, foreign demand).

(b) The shocks come mainly from the supply side (e.g., technology).

(16) Consider the simple dynamic AD-AS model in Section 5.6.3. Describe the dynamic response of the model to a one-period demand shock. How would you modify the model to produce an inverse relationship between output and price?

(17) Consider the New Keynesian dynamic AD-AS model in Section 5.6.4. Suppose that the economy is at a steady state and that the central bank decides to target inflation only ($\theta_y = 0$). At the same time, there is a demand shock. Compare the economic performance in the new monetary regime with the case where $\theta_y = 0.5$.

Notes

[1] For a detailed analysis of China's exchange rate regime, we refer to Su and Qian (2021), Structural Changes in the RMB Exchange Rate Mechanism, *China & World Economy*, 29 (2), 1–23.

[2] People's Bank of China, 2016, China Monetary Policy Report, Quarter One, Available from: www.pbc.gov.cn/en/3688229/3688353/3688356/3706393/index.html.

[3] For a forceful critique of IMF policies during the Asian financial crisis, read Joseph Stiglitz's *Globalization and Its Discontents*, New York: W. W. Norton.

[4] Ben Bernanke, The Global Saving Glut and the U.S. Current Account Deficit, March 10, 2005, www.federalreserve.gov/boarddocs/speeches/2005/200503102/.

[5] Dietmar Rothermund, 1996, *The Global Impact of the Great Depression 1929–1939*, New York: Routledge.

[6] *The Cambridge History of China*, Volume 13, Republican China 1912–1949, Part 2, edited by John K. Fairbank and Albert Feuerwerker, Cambridge: Cambridge University Press.

[7] For a gentle introduction to *The General Theory*, I refer to Dudley Dillard's *The Economics of John Maynard Keynes: The Theory of Monetary Economy*, New Jersey: Prentice Hall.

6

Stabilization Policies

It is an enduring principle of governance to keep prepared for the unforeseen.
– Wei Zheng (580–643)[1]

6.1 Introduction

Almost all modern governments attempt to stabilize the economy. Especially when the unemployment problem intensifies during a recession, the government is under pressure to do something. And modern governments have enormous power to influence the economy. The government is often the biggest spender in the economy. And, through the central bank, the government can influence interest rates and exchange rates. With great power comes great responsibility. The question is how to wield that power to achieve the common good. For the objective of economic stabilization, we hope that the government's actions are *countercyclical*, meaning that they stimulate the economy when it is in downturns and cool down the economy when it overheats. And we hope that the government avoids *procyclical* policies, which would add fuel to a booming economy and tighten a depressed one.

In IS-LM and AD-AS models, we have considered fiscal and monetary policies that may be useful for smoothing the business cycles. However, to simplify analyses, we simplify fiscal and monetary policies so much so that they reduce to three variables: government expenditure (G), tax (T), and money supply (M). In the real world, fiscal and monetary policies are far more complicated than the three variables can characterize.

In this chapter, we briefly describe how, in the real world, the government may stabilize the economy. We first examine the role of the so-called automatic stabilizers. Then we go deeper into discretionary fiscal policies. Then we study monetary policy in more detail. Finally we study how a government may safeguard the financial system by acting as the lender of last resort and conducting macroprudential policies.

6.2 Automatic Fiscal Stabilizer

Modern governments are big. They take a substantial share of national income by taxation, and they are the biggest spender in the economy. The fiscal policies of the modern government can have a big impact on economic stability. Before the study of discretionary fiscal policies, we first discuss the role of *automatic fiscal stabilizers*.

Automatic stabilizers are relatively fixed features of the fiscal establishment that may dampen economic fluctuations without taking discretionary actions. We may divide automatic stabilizers into two groups, tax stabilizers and spending stabilizers.

6.2.1 Tax Stabilizers

Many categories of taxes, including the personal income tax, corporate income tax, and sales tax, are automatic stabilizers because their revenue automatically declines when the economy contracts.

In particular, if the personal income tax is *progressive*, then it would be an even stronger automatic stabilizer. To see this, note that when a recession leads to widespread declines in personal income, people may be subject to a lower marginal tax rate under the progressive tax system. Thus the tax revenue will decline more rapidly than under a flat-rate tax system.

Marginal Tax Rate of China's Personal Income Tax (PIT)

China implements a seven-step progressive PIT system. The taxable income is total income minus various deductions, including an allowance of 5,000 Yuan per month.

	Annual taxable income (Yuan)	Marginal tax rate (%)
1	≤36,000	3
2	(36,000–144,000]	10
3	(144,000–300,000]	20
4	(300,000–420,000]	25
5	(420,000–660,000]	30
6	(660,000–960,000]	35
7	>960,000	45

Similarly, enterprise income tax (EIT) is also a better automatic stabilizer than value-added tax (VAT) or business tax (on gross receipts). EIT is on profits, which decline rapidly when a recession hits the economy. VAT and business tax, however, are on business activities. Even if firms do not generate profits, they have to pay VAT or business taxes as long as they are in operation. The tax revenue from VAT or business tax also declines in recessions, but not as fast as the revenue from EIT.

6.2.2 Spending Stabilizers

The spending stabilizers are mainly transfer payments to the unemployed and the poor. When the economy enters a recession, more people will claim unemployment benefits as they lose jobs. As a result, the fiscal spending on unemployment "insurance" automatically increases. The same is true for transfer payments to the poor.

General social security payments, such as retiree benefits, are also automatic stabilizers in a sense. Since they are stable over time, the share of social security payments in the GDP automatically rises in recessions and declines in expansions. Thus they are also a stabilizing force for the economy.

6.2.3 The Importance of Automatic Stabilizers

Automatic stabilizers are very important to economic stability. Once in place, they work automatically, without any delay, and throughout the cycles. Discretionary policies, in contrast, are often delayed responses: It takes time for policy makers to recognize that there is something wrong going on; it takes time for politicians and technocrats to draw up plans; it takes time for a policy to exert effects on the economy. It is not uncommon that when a discretionary policy finally has effects, the problem (e.g., recession) that the policy is intended to solve has been over.

Therefore, policy makers should consider policy effects on economic stability when they deliberate on the reforms of tax code, transfer payments, and social security programs. The more automatic stabilizers, the better. The fewer "automatic destabilizers," the better. For example, although a balanced budget seems moral, the balanced-budget constraint is an automatic destabilizer since it forces the government to cut spending in recessions, when tax revenues decline, and to increase spending in expansions.

6.3 Discretionary Fiscal Policy

A discretionary policy is based on the judgment of policy makers under a particular situation, as opposed to a policy set by a predetermined rule. Discretionary fiscal policies are taxation and expenditure by the government for the purpose of dampening economic fluctuations.

6.3.1   Direct Government Expenditure

The discretionary fiscal policy may be direct government expenditures, tax cuts, or incentives. The direct expenditure may be the provision of more public goods. For example, the government may decide to upgrade public education, public security, and so on. It may also be investments in new roads, new generations of communications networks, electricity grids, and so on.

Note that these policies also promote long-term growth. But the timing of policies is important since they have a strong impact on the short-term demand of the economy. It would be best if public spending is *countercyclical* as well as progrowth.

6.3.2   Tax Cuts or Incentives

The tax cuts or incentives may be for households or businesses. Tax cuts for households put more money in consumers' pockets and induce them to consume more. If a tax cut is permanent, the effect on consumption would be stronger than in the case of a temporary cut. But even if the tax cut is temporary, it may still stimulate consumption due to the myopia of consumers or the *liquidity effect*. To understand the latter, note that if consumers are liquidity constrained, or unable to borrow, the tax cut will relax their borrowing constraint and thus stimulate consumption temporarily.

Tax cuts for businesses help to increase profit margins and may stimulate investment. To directly stimulate investment, the government may also provide temporary tax credits for businesses engaged in investment. For tax credits to have timely effects, they have to be temporary. Otherwise, businesses may adopt the usual wait-and-see attitude during recessions, delay investment until there is less uncertainty, and enjoy the tax credit later.

6.3.3   Deficit and Debt

Expansionary fiscal policies, discretionary or not, often lead to a budget deficit, which is the shortfall in tax revenue to pay for the expenditure. There are two ways to finance the deficit: issuing debts and printing money. The latter is illegal in many countries, including China. However, the central bank's seigniorage profit is part of government revenue, although a small part in normal times. And it is legal, and common, for central banks to purchase government bonds in open-market operations.

Thus it is bond issuance that mainly finances the budget deficit, which necessarily increases government debt. Here, the budget deficit is a *flow* variable, and government debt is a *stock* variable.

For individual households, the budget deficit is something to avoid. Any responsible head of household would try to "make ends meet." But for a nation, a self-imposed balanced-budget constraint is unnecessary and counterproductive. To see that, we first note that government budget deficit is net income to the private sector. Furthermore, an increase in government debt is an increase in assets held by the private sector. And government debts are safe assets, at least when exchange rate risk may be ignored. During financial crises, financial institutions often seek to sell risky assets and purchase safe assets such as government bonds. If there are not enough government bonds, it will take longer for financial institutions to "normalize" their balance sheets.

Second, we note that the balanced-budget constraint makes the fiscal policy necessarily procyclical. Under the balanced-budget constraint, when the economy enters a recession, the government would have to reduce spending since the tax revenue declines during recessions. When the economy overheats, the government would have to increase spending since the tax revenue rises during booms.

There is no natural virtue about a balanced budget for a government. Fiscal policies should be judged by the effects on the economy, not by whether the budget is balanced.[2] However, this argument takes for granted a responsible government. If the people have a strong distrust of the government, then the balanced-budget constraint is a powerful tool to rein in erratic government behavior such as fighting unnecessary foreign wars, building vanity projects, and so on.

6.3.4 Ricardian Equivalence

If we omit the role of money printing, we may say that the government can either raise taxes to finance the budget deficit or borrow from the market. Since the government has to pay off the debt, the choice is "tax now or tax later." The well-known doctrine "Ricardian equivalence" says that, under some stringent conditions, this choice does not matter, and tax cuts would fail to stimulate demand. If consumers and firms are forward looking, then they would anticipate future tax hikes when the government cuts taxes now. They save the money rather than being fooled into consumption or investment.

Even David Ricardo himself does not believe that the Ricardian equivalence holds in reality. He points out that individuals do not behave as rationally as required by the theory. Instead, individuals often take myopic views of the tax burden.

There is another problem with the Ricardian equivalence doctrine. The government can issue long-term bonds to finance the deficit. Compared to the government, people have short lives. When middle-age individuals receive more income from a tax cut financed by a 30-year bond, they may consider it a definite gain. The debt will be paid off by the next generation.

One reply is that people care about their descendants and do not want to leave an excessive tax burden to future generations. Modern economists, indeed, prove that the Ricardian equivalence continues to hold with the availability of long-term financing, under some additional assumptions.[3] In particular, they assume that people can borrow or lend any amount at the same interest rate as the government enjoys.

In the real world, however, consumers have credit constraints, and they have to pay interest rates much higher than the government. Tax cuts are equivalent to an "inclusive" loan with an interest rate as low as the government bond. Despite the possibility of tax hikes in the future, the current tax cuts are, therefore, a definite gain to the current-generation consumers. Thus the current tax cut may result in larger aggregate demand.

Furthermore, there is no reason that the government has to pay off all its debt at some point. The government may roll over the debt infinitely. Indeed, if the economy is growing, the debt burden can increase as well. Therefore, we should not avoid the budget deficit as a sin and try to minimize government debt as much as possible. What is important is to avoid wasteful spending and put the budget deficit to good use.

6.3.5   The Limitations

First, we have mentioned earlier that the discretionary policy may be a delayed response to a crisis. After policy makers recognize the problem, draw up plans, go through political processes, and implement the plan, the crisis may already be over. Note that it also takes time for a policy to transmit to the economy.

Second, the interest costs of debt may become a burden if the government debt rises too fast. Suppose that the debt/GDP ratio rises to 300% and that the interest rate is 2%. Then the interest costs would be 6% of GDP every year.

Here, we need to consider the effect of internal debt and external debt separately. If the government borrows from its citizens, then it adds to its internal debt. For interest payments of the internal debt, the government raises taxes and transfers them to the owners of government bonds, who are also citizens. Thus, the interest payments to the internal debt do not increase the overall burden on the economy, just like transfer payments. But unlike the usual transfer payment, the interest payments may be regressive, i.e., transferring wealth from the poor to the rich.

If the government borrows from foreigners, then it adds to its external debt. A substantial level of external debt may be more problematic for the economy than an equivalent level of internal debt. Since the interest payment on the external debt transfers wealth from citizens to foreigners, it is equivalent to a new tax on the economy in the future. Unlike the usual tax, which may be used to provide domestic public goods, the new tax will be for nothing. Therefore, if the level of external

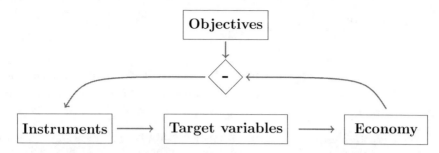

Figure 6.1 Monetary instruments, target variables, and objectives.

debt rises too fast, the interest payments may become an unbearable burden on the economy.

Finally, external debt usually has a currency mismatch, especially for small economies. The interest and principal payments may be in a unit of foreign currency. But the tax revenue is in domestic currency. The currency mismatch, if on a large scale, may make the country vulnerable to the *self-fulfilling currency crisis*. Suppose that there is depreciation expectation, due to some other weaknesses in the country (e.g., political instability). Investors may move portfolios out of the country, and speculators may short the currency to such an extent that the government finds it unable to service its external debt. Consequently, there may be a sovereign default and a currency devaluation larger than justified by the economic weakness.

6.4   Monetary Policy

Monetary policy refers to policies deliberated and implemented by the monetary authority, i.e., the central bank, to achieve some *objectives* set by the government or lawmakers. The objectives of monetary policy include price stability, full employment, economic growth, financial market stability, and possibly exchange-rate stability. To achieve these objectives, the central bank tries to manipulate some *intermediate target variables* such as the interest rate on overnight borrowing, growth of money supply, and so on. To manipulate target variables, the central bank employs a variety of *policy instruments* such as open market operations (OMO), required reserves, central bank loans, liquidity facilities, and so on. Figure 6.1 illustrates the relationship among objectives, target variables, instruments, and the economy.

Note that monetary policy, like fiscal policy, attempts to dampen economic fluctuations. In the language of control system, Figure 6.1 shows a *feedback loop*. And we hope that monetary policy achieves a *negative* feedback loop. The central bank constantly assesses the economic conditions, comparing reality to its objectives. When the economy shows signs of recession, the central bank attempts to stop the trend by deploying monetary stimulus. When the economy starts to overheat, the central bank also tries to stop the trend, by tightening liquidity.

6.4.1   Objectives

The most important objective of monetary policy is to maintain price stability. Many central banks indeed have explicitly adopted *inflation targeting*, a standard framework for monetary policy.

Different central banks may interpret price stability differently. The European Central Bank (ECB) defines price stability as inflation below 2%. The Bank of England (the central bank of the UK), under the inflation-targeting framework, sets 2% as the target, allowing for a maximum deviation of one percentage point. Even the US Fed, which has a dual mandate (promoting full employment as well as price stability), has an aim for 2% inflation. Generally, developing countries allow higher inflation targets. For example, the Reserve Bank of India targets 4% and allows for a maximum deviation of two percentage points.

There are two reasons why policy makers around the world set a positive inflation target rather than a zero inflation target. First, moderate inflation facilitates downward adjustment of real wages in the face of adverse shocks, thus alleviating unemployment problems. As James Tobin famously says, *inflation greases the wheels of the labor market.*[4]

Second, positive inflation provides some cushion against deflation. When the economy slows down or enters a recession, inflation typically declines. If inflation is initially positive, then there is a period of disinflation, during which inflation is still positive. It is hoped that the recession will be over before inflation declines to zero. Otherwise, when inflation becomes deflation, the economy may fall victim to the *debt deflation spiral.* During the debt deflation spiral, deflation increases the debt burden and thus depresses consumption and investment. This reduced aggregate demand puts more downward pressure on prices, completing a vicious cycle.

The second most important objective of monetary policy is to promote full employment. Since output and employment have a stable relationship (Okun's law), the full-employment objective is equivalent to one that targets a zero output gap. And since the output potential is generally growing, the objective of a zero output gap may be further translated into a growth target. The Chinese government, for example, has an annual target for real GDP growth. And in its "five-year plans," it also sets a five-year target for average growth rate in the next five years.

For countries with a fixed exchange rate or, to a lesser extent, managed float, the central banks have to maintain exchange rate stability. As we have discussed earlier, this objective may dominate domestic concerns such as inflation and unemployment. If that is true, then we say that the country does not have an *independent* monetary policy. To achieve exchange rate stability while retaining some degree of monetary-policy independence, the central bank must keep an eye on the balance-of-payment conditions. It may implement restrictions on cross-border capital flows when necessary.

Finally, monetary authorities are also responsible for maintaining stability in the financial system. A stable financial system is essential for the working of modern economies. Since the financial system is inherently unstable, maintaining financial stability is a daunting task for central banks. We may understand the central bank's role in financial stability in two senses: crisis management and the prevention of future crises. After a crisis has broken out, the central bank has to intervene and perform as the lender of last resort. To prevent the next crisis, the central bank has to perform macroprudential regulation and oversight. We will examine these roles in more details later.

6.4.2 Intermediate Target Variables

Intermediate target variables are those that are vitally important to the economy and that are manipulable by the monetary authority. Traditional central banks used to control money supply or the growth of it, as is assumed in the quantity theory of money or IS-LM. Since the 1980s, central banks in the developed world have generally converged to the practice of targeting for short-term money market interest rates (see Table 6.1). The US Federal Reserve, for example, targets the federal funds rate (FFR), which is the interest rate banks charge when they lend excess reserves to other banks on an overnight uncollateralized basis.

In normal times, a central bank usually has one target variable. However, when the central bank finds the single target variable inadequate, it may target additional variables such as long-term interest rates. For example, in response to the 2008 financial crisis, the Fed first slashed the federal funds rate to almost zero. Finding this inadequate for dealing with the deepening crisis, the Fed started to conduct quantitative easing (QE), which was essentially targeting the quantity of reserves. Soon after the second round of QE concluded, the Fed announced Operation Twist to lower the long-term interest rate, which also became a target variable for the Fed.

Monetary policy that relies on interest rates as target variables is often called the "price-based" monetary policy since interest rates are essentially the price of (future) money. In contrast, monetary policy that targets money supply is called the "quantity-based" money policy. In normal times, the price-based monetary policy is generally more effective than the quantity-based policy since changes in interest rates directly change financial costs in the economy. However, during deep recessions, the target interest rates may hit the zero lower bound. And, for various reasons, the monetary authority may be reluctant to cut interest rates below zero. Under such circumstances, the monetary authority may switch to quantity-based policies such as QE.

China is in transition from quantity-based to price-based monetary policy making. The People's Bank of China (PBC) used to target money (M2) growth. The development of capital markets and shadow banking, however, makes M2 less connected with the financing activities in the economy. From around 2012, PBC toned

Table 6.1 Objectives, target variables, and instruments of major central banks.

	Objectives	Target variables	Key instruments
China	Price stability, economic growth	Interbank seven-day repo rate, loan prime rate	Open market operations
Eurozone	Price stability	Overnight market interest rate	Main refinancing operations, marginal lending facility, deposit facility
Japan	Price stability	Uncollateralized overnight call rate	Open market operations
UK	Price stability	Short-term money market interest rate	Bank rate
US	Full employment, price stability	Federal funds rate	Interest on reserves

down the importance of the M2 target. PBC started to use an alternative measure called aggregate financing to the real economy (AFRE), which is the total volume of financing provided by the financial system to the economy during a certain period.

Meanwhile, PBC has been pushing for the "liberalization" of interest rates, which is to let the market determine interest rates. The "liberalization" of interest rates paved the way for price-based policy making.[5] An important milestone was reached when PBC reformed the formation mechanism of the loan prime rate (LPR) in August 2019. After the reform, LPR became the benchmark loan interest rate for commercial banks and one of the target variables of PBC. Compared to the previous benchmark loan rate, which was set by the central bank, LPR is market based, and its variation reflects changing demand and supply of funds. At the same time, PBC uses the medium-term lending facility (MLF) rate to exert influence on LPR. So we have the following *bank-lending channel* of monetary policy transmission:

$$\text{MLF Rate} \Rightarrow \text{LPR} \Rightarrow \text{Loan interest rates} \Rightarrow \text{Economic activities.}$$

Another target variable of PBC is the interbank seven-day repo rate (DR007). PBC uses the rate of its repo or reverse repo operations (a type of open-market operations) to influence the interbank seven-day repo rate.

6.4.3   Monetary Policy Instruments

To manipulate target variables, central banks have a variety of policy tools that we call monetary policy instruments. The usual instruments include open-market operations (OMO), reserve requirements, interest rates on central bank deposits, standing lending facilities, forward guidance, and so on.

Open-Market Operations

Through OMO, a central bank adjusts the supply of reserves, which further influences the money supply. OMO may take the form of purchasing or selling securities, often government bonds. When the central bank sells securities, it effectively withdraws liquidity from the financial system. When the central bank purchases securities, it effectively injects liquidity into the financial system.

OMO may also take the form of repo (repurchase operation) or reverse repo. In a repo operation, the central bank lends temporarily with collaterals, in effect injecting liquidity into the market. In a reverse repo, the central bank borrows temporarily (say, seven days) from the market with collaterals, in effect withdrawing liquidity from the market. The reverse repo may be regarded as a deposit facility. Both repo and reverse repo are conducted using auctions.

China's PBC conducts repo operations regularly. The interest rate on these repo operations has become an important policy signal to market participants. Note that there is a difference in terminology. China's repo operation is equivalent to the reverse repo operation in the US, and China's reverse repo is equivalent to the US's repo.

Central bank intervention of the foreign exchange market is also a type of OMO. When the central bank supports a weak domestic currency, it has to sell foreign currency and buy domestic currency, withdrawing liquidity from the market. When the central bank wants to devalue a strong domestic currency, it has to buy foreign currency and sell domestic currency, injecting liquidity into the market.

Reserve Requirement

The reserve requirement is the minimum amount of reserve commercial banks must hold at the central bank. The reserve requirement is often expressed in the *reserve requirement ratio*, which is the ratio of the required reserve to the total deposits. The reserve requirement may serve a macroprudential purpose, preventing banks from lending excessively. But it may also serve as a monetary policy instrument that influences the *money multiplier*, which further influences the money supply.

To understand the role of the reserve requirement in influencing the money supply, note that the *base money* (or *monetary base, high-powered money,* etc.) consists of two components: currency in circulation (or physically in commercial banks' vaults), and the reserve:

$$B = C + R,$$

where B represents base money, C denotes currency in circulation, and R represents reserve, which is banks' deposits at the central bank.

Note that the money supply also consists of two components: currency in circulation and deposits (demand or saving deposits). For example, M1 in China includes currency in circulation and demand deposits. Let M denote the money supply; we thus have the following:

$$M = C + D,$$

where D represents deposits. M may be any measure of the money supply. Broader measures such as M2 include less liquid deposits such as savings deposits.

If we further define the currency ratio and the reserve ratio,

$$c = \frac{C}{D}, \quad r = \frac{R}{D},$$

respectively, then we have the following:

$$M = \frac{1+c}{c+r} B.$$

For broader money-supply measures such as M2, c is small. Hence the money supply is largely determined by base money (B) and the reserve ratio (r). Given a level of base money, lower r results in larger money supply. We may call $m = (1+c)/(c+r)$ the *money multiplier*. Note that the reserve requirement ratio (RRR) is the smallest possible reserve ratio for banks. When banks are active in lending, the reserve ratio may hit RRR. Under such circumstances, the central bank may influence the money multiplier by adjusting RRR.

In most of the developed countries, reserve requirements do not serves as a monetary instrument. In fact, there are no reserve requirements in Canada, the UK, New Zealand, Australia, and Sweden. The US also abolished reserve requirements in March 2020. Of course, this does not mean that banks can create money without limit. Banks have to satisfy *capital adequacy* requirements, which are more important than reserve requirements even in countries with reserve requirements.

However, China's reserve requirement remains high. As of November 2020, China's RRR is 12.5% for large banks. And China used to adjust the ratio fairly frequently. In 2008 alone, PBC adjusted the ratio 10 times, first raising RRR eight times to control economic overheating and inflation, and then cut it twice to combat the worsening Global Financial Crisis.

Interest on Reserves (IOR)

Banks may deposit at the central bank more than required. The extra amount is often called *excess reserves*. Central banks use the interest rate on reserves to influence both the level of excess reserve and the money market interest rate. If the central bank raises the interest rate on the reserve, then banks would hold more excess reserve, thus reducing lending activity. At the same time, IOR may serve as the *reservation rate* in the interbank money market, the lowest rate that banks are willing to accept for lending out their funds. Adjusting IOR may thus influence the money market interest rate.

The US Federal Reserve recently clarifies that IOR is the "primary tool of monetary policy implementation," which helps steer the FFR into the target range.[6]

PBC pays interest on both required reserves and excess reserves. Normally, the interest rate on the required reserves is much higher than on the excess reserves. As of November 3, 2020, for example, the interest rate on the require reserves is 1.62%, while that on the excess reserves is 0.35%. IOR is not a primary instrument for PBC. Since the 2008 Global Financial Crisis, PBC rarely adjusts IOR.

Standing Lending Facilities (SLF)

SLF is a mechanism by which the central bank makes short-term loans to financial institutions *on request*. SLF has different names in different central banks. The US Fed calls it the *discount window*, the ECB the *marginal lending facility*, the Bank of England the *operational standing facility*, and the Bank of Japan the *complementary lending facility*. It is a common feature of central banking.

Like the reverse repo, SLF loans require collaterals. Unlike the reverse repo operation, it is financial institutions, in need of liquidity, that initiate SLF operations. The interest rate on SLF is an important monetary policy rate. If the central bank lowers the interest rate on SLF, then it encourages borrowing from the central bank, thus expanding the base money.

China's PBC started the SLF in 2013. A typical SLF loan in China, however, has a relatively longer maturity than SLF loans in other major central banks. The typical SLF maturity in China is one to three months, while SLF loans in other countries are typically overnight. A bank in need of overnight liquidity support has to go to the interbank market.

Medium-Term Lending Facility (MLF)

PBC introduced MLF in September 2014 as a medium-term liquidity tool. Through MLF, PBC lends to banks against adequate collaterals, so as to supply base money. The term of the MLF loans is typically one year. PBC's MLF is similar to the "longer-term refinancing operations" of ECB.

In recent years, PBC has been using the MLF rate as the medium-term policy rate, which guides the loan prime rate (LPR). And LPR has become the benchmark rate for bank loans in China. By adjusting the MLF rate, the central bank may influence the cost of financing in the economy through LPR.

Forward Guidance

Forward guidance refers to the effort by the central bank to provide information about the likely future course of monetary policy. Forward guidance is a relatively new instrument. The Bank of Japan started to use forward guidance in 1999, and the Fed experimented with it in the early 2000s. Since the 2008 Global Financial Crisis, other central banks also embraced forward guidance as an indispensable instrument.

For example, the ECB began forward guidance in July 2013 when the ECB said that it expected interest rates to remain low for an extended period. Such forward guidance, by reducing policy uncertainty, may reduce the term premium of interest rates, leading to higher economic activity. Such effects may be achieved even without large-scale open-market operations.

Forward guidance may or may not commit the central bank's future course of action. If a forward guidance explicitly commits a future course of policies, we may call it *Odyssean* forward guidance.[7] If a forward guidance merely *forecasts* the economy and the central bank's actions, we may call it *Delphic* forward guidance.[8] Odyssean forward guidance is stronger than Delphic forward guidance since the former reduces policy uncertainty more than the latter. However, the public understands that the central bank may deviate from the Odyssean forward guidance in the future if the economy takes an unexpected turn. Thus the effect of Odyssean forward guidance may depend on the reputation and credibility of the central banker.

Window Guidance

Window guidance is another form of the central bank's communications with the market. In contrast to forward guidance, which is open to the public, window guidance is often closed-door and only with a few selected banks. Between 1961 and 1991, Bank of Japan used window guidance to directly affect bank lending. For the same purpose, PBC of China has been using window guidance since it stopped setting credit plans in the late 1990s.

The banks that receive window guidance may or may not comply. They have to weigh the costs of compliance with the benefits, which include the availability of liquidity support from the central bank or other policy conveniences.

The effectiveness of window guidance depends not only on the central bank's leverage over the banks but also the importance of bank lending in the financial system. If the share of total bank lending in the total financing declines, a phenomenon known as *disintermediation*, then window guidance will become less effective. To understand the term "disintermediation," note that bank lending is called *indirect finance*, meaning that the savers finance the lender through the intermediation of banks. In contrast, bond and equity issuance is called *direct finance*, meaning that buyers of the bonds and stocks directly finance the issuer.

Finally, note that there are other monetary policy instruments employed by central banks. Nowadays, almost all central bankers believe in the value of transparency and predictability. As a result, the websites of central banks around the world provide rich information on the objectives, target variables, and policy instruments. Interested students are encouraged to explore these websites.

6.4.4   Interest Rate Corridor

The interest rate corridor (or channel) is now a common operating framework for central banks to control the volatility of the short-term money market interest rate, or simply the *short rate*.

The ceiling of the corridor is defined by the interest rate at which central banks lend to depository financial institutions that we call *banks*. In practice, the ceiling is often provided by the interest rate on SLF (or the discount window). In theory, no borrower would be willing to accept an interest rate higher than the rate at which they can borrow from the central bank.

The floor of the corridor is defined by the interest rate at which central banks borrow from the market. In practice, it is often the interest rate on excess reserves or deposit facility. In theory, no lender would be willing to accept an interest rate lower than what the central bank pays on its borrowing. Both ceiling and floor rates are determined by central banks.

The demand curve for the reserves is flat (perfectly elastic) at the ceiling rate, because no one would be willing to borrow in the money market at a higher rate than the central bank loan charges (Figure 6.2). The demand curve is also flat at the floor, because banks would be willing to borrow an infinite amount of reserves if the market rate were slightly below the floor rate. (They may lend [deposit] them to the central bank for an instant profit.) Between the ceiling and the floor, the demand curve is downward sloping. As the short rate declines, the opportunity cost of holding excess reserves declines, making banks willing to hold more reserves.

Between the ceiling and the floor, the supply curve is also upward sloping, because a higher rate induces banks with excess reserves to lend more to the market. At the ceiling rate, the supply curve becomes perfectly elastic because the central bank may supply an infinite amount of reserves at this rate, at least in theory. At the floor rate, banks are indifferent between supplying reserves to the market and keeping money idle at the central bank (receiving the floor rate). If the short rate is slightly below the floor rate, there would be no supply at all. Hence the supply curve at the floor rate is also flat (Figure 6.2).

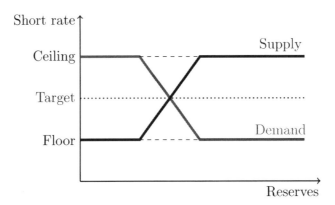

Figure 6.2 Interest rate corridor.

Conventional Monetary Policy

In conventional central banking, the central bank uses open-market operations to shift the supply curve so that the equilibrium market rate stays close to the target rate.

More practically, a central bank will estimate the quantity of reserves that will be demanded given the target rate and the quantity of reserves that will be supplied by other banks. If the quantity demanded at the target rate exceeds the supply, then the central bank injects the difference into the market by asset purchases or repo operations. If the supply at the target rate exceeds the demand, then the central bank withdraws the difference from the market by asset sales or reverse repo operation.

As experience accumulates over time, the central bank can learn to estimate the gap between supply and demand at the target rate fairly accurately. Of course, even if the central bank fails to get an accurate estimation, the existence of the corridor ensures that the market rate does not go out of the bounds.

Unconventional Monetary Policy

Since the 2008 Global Financial Crisis, most of the developed countries have been conducting unconventional monetary policies. A key characteristic of the unconventional monetary policy is the ample supply of reserves. We may call such a monetary policy framework the *ample-reserves regime.*

Under the ample-reserves regime, the central bank makes sure that the supply curve crosses the demand curve at the floor rate, which coincides with the target rate (Figure 6.3). Note that the floor rate can be negative. For example, the floor rate in the Eurozone is the interest rate on the deposit facility (DF). As of November 2020, the DF rate is -0.5%.

In the age of ample reserves, the corridor system reduces to the floor system.

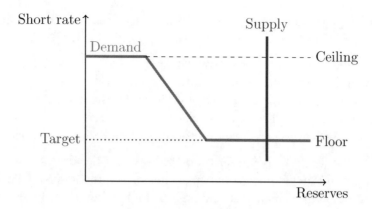

Figure 6.3 Interest rate corridor with ample reserves.

And the floor rate becomes the most important policy instrument. In comparison, OMO becomes less important because its job reduces to one that only ensures ample reserves. In the US, the IOR has become the key policy instrument.

6.4.5   Monetary Policy Rule

A monetary policy rule characterizes how a central bank responds, by manipulating the target variable, to changes in economic conditions. Note that central banks do not generally follow any policy rule. But their responsiveness to changing economic conditions leads to an *empirical* relation between the target variable and economic objectives such as inflation and unemployment. If such a relationship is relatively stable over time, the rule may give some guidance for central bankers.

The most well-known monetary policy rule is the Taylor rule, which was proposed by John B. Taylor in 1993. According to the Taylor rule, the target interest rate (e.g., the federal funds rate in the US) responds to the inflation gap and the output gap in the following fashion:

$$i_t = \pi_t + r^* + \theta_\pi(\pi_t - \pi^*) + \theta_y(y_t - \bar{y}), \tag{6.1}$$

where i_t is the target rate, π_t is the inflation rate, r^* is the *natural rate of interest* that we discuss shortly, π^* is the inflation target, y_t is the logarithm of the total output, $\bar{y}$ is the logarithm of the potential output, and θ_π and θ_y are constants measuring how the monetary authority would respond to the inflation gap $(\pi_t - \pi^*)$ and the output gap $(y_t - \bar{y})$, respectively.

The natural rate of interest, r^*, or neutral rate of interest, was invented by the Swedish economist Knut Wicksell, who defines the natural rate of interest as a real short-term rate that makes output equal to potential (natural) output with constant inflation. If the Taylor rule in (6.1) is perfectly effective, in the sense that it keeps the economy at the state of zero output gap and zero inflation gap, then r^* will be the prevailing real interest rate in such a perfect economy. The natural rate of interest is unobservable. Taylor assumed that $r^* = 2\%$ for the US economy.

Both θ_π and θ_y should be positive. By specifying $\theta_\pi > 0$, the Taylor rule says that the central bank should raise the target interest rate faster than inflation. For example, if $\theta_\pi = 0.5$ and inflation rises by 1%, then the central bank should raise the target rate by 1.5%. The idea that the nominal interest rate should rise faster than inflation (to effectively control inflation) is often called the *Taylor principle*.

If both θ_π and θ_y are positive, then the Taylor rule also achieves a trade-off between two conflicting objectives. An expansionary monetary policy leads to a higher output (or employment) at the cost of higher inflation. If we fix $\theta_\pi = 0.5$, then the parameter θ_y controls how much weight to put on output or employment. The smaller θ_y, the lower weight on output or employment. If $\theta_y = 0$, then the Taylor rule reduces to a strict version of inflation targeting that pays little attention to the output (employment) gap.

6.4.6   Monetary Policy Transmission

In the previous chapter, we discussed two traditional channels of monetary policy transmission. The first is the interest rate channel implicit in the closed-economy IS-LM model: Monetary expansion leads to a decline of the interest rate, which stimulates the investment. The second is the exchange rate channel implicit in the small open-economy with a floating exchange rate: Monetary expansion devalues the domestic currency, which stimulates the net export.

In reality, even the interest rate channel is not as simple as the IS-LM model describes. Through either open-market operations or policy rate adjustments, the monetary authority directly influences short-term interest rates in the money market. And changes in short-term interest rates transmit to the real economy via multiple channels.

First, the short rate influences banks' deposit and lending rates. The money market is an alternative source of funding for banks. A lower money market rate induces banks to offer lower deposit rates for savers and lower lending rates for borrowers. Lower deposit rates encourage consumption, and lower lending rates encourage investment financed by bank lending. Conversely, higher deposit rates lead to more savings and less consumption and discourage investment financed by bank loans.

Second, the short rate influences the risk appetite of financial institutions. Institutions such as insurance companies and pension funds usually have relatively rigid built-in expectations about the return to capital. For example, pension funds usually target an annual return of 7–8%. Other institutions, under shareholders' pressure on short-term performance, may also fall victim to such rigid expectations. A low short rate thus often compels financial institutions to "hunt for yield" by taking more risks. Consequently, banks may make risky loans to small businesses that are willing to pay higher interest rates. And institutional investors may scramble to buy risky corporate bonds, making bond financing cheap for risky investments. Conversely, a higher short rate discourages risk taking.

Third, the short rate influences asset prices. A lower short rate leads to higher prices of not only risky bonds but also almost every other asset. To understand this, note first that a lower short rate corresponds to a lower discount rate for future cash flows, which translates into a higher asset price, the present value of the future cash flows. Furthermore, a low short rate also corresponds to an abundant supply of liquidity, which encourages speculations in the financial markets. Higher liquidity itself elevates asset prices since it makes investors feel safe holding the assets.

Rising stock and housing prices would have "wealth effects" on consumers. Consumers who feel richer may increase spending. The housing price is particularly important. A rising housing price may encourage the purchase of houses, which would lead further to spending on durable household goods. Rising asset prices also relax borrowing constraints on businesses. Assets, whether financial or real (land, houses, etc.), are collaterals for borrowing. Higher asset prices imply higher borrowing power.

Conversely, a higher short rate leads to lower asset prices, which make consumers feel poorer and, thus, reduce consumption. In particular, a declining housing price discourages housing purchases and depresses the consumption of household durables. Lower asset prices also lead to worsening credit conditions for businesses due to the lower value of collaterals.

Last but not least important, the actions and forward guidance of the monetary authority directly change the expectation of consumers and businesses. First, a change in the market expectation of future interest rates immediately affects the current long-term interest rates. For example, if the central bank pledges to keep the short rate at a low level for a long time, then the long-term interest rate will decline immediately. Second, the monetary authority may guide the market expectation toward an equilibrium of stability. The presence of expectation often gives rise to the problem of *multiple equilibria*, some of which may be undesirable. For example, if people expect inflation to rise substantially, then substantial inflation will realize as a result of hastened purchases and hoarding. This phenomenon is also known as *self-fulfilling prophecy*. If, however, the monetary authority pledges to maintain price stability and if the pledge is credible, then the market expectation will be anchored for the good low-inflation equilibrium.

The preceding discussion on the transmission of monetary policy is by no means exhaustive. Monetary policies may have more subtle ways to influence the economy. Furthermore, different channels of transmission may reinforce each other dynamically. For example, lower deposit and lending rates stimulate spending on consumption and investment, contributing to higher inflation expectation. The elevated inflation expectation, in turn, contributes to a lower real interest rate, stimulating consumption and investment.

6.5 Financial Stability

As Hyman Minsky argues, financial instability often underlies the instability of a modern economy. To stabilize the economy, the government must keep an eye on the health of the financial industry. When a financial crisis erupts, the government often has to intervene and acts as the savior. And to prevent the next crisis, the government has to strengthen regulation and oversight. The former role is known as the *lender of last resort*, and the latter is essentially what *macroprudential policy* is all about. Both responsibilities, in most countries and at least partly, falls on the monetary authority.

6.5.1 Lender of Last Resort

Financial crises usually involve "runs" on financial institutions. For example, panic savers may want to withdraw deposits from banks. If all savers do this, even healthy banks will go bankrupt. Such *bank runs* can also happen to other modern financial institutions such as investment banks, insurance companies, and so on, which rely on short-term financing. If the market suspects the viability of an institution, then no one will be willing to lend to the institution. Even if the institution is otherwise healthy, it will fail due to the lack of liquidity. Under such circumstances, only the central bank is able to intervene and perform the role of the lender of last resort.

Indeed, after Lehman Brothers failed during the 2008 Global Financial Crisis, other investment banks and insurance companies also became suspect. Even Goldman Sachs and Morgan Stanley, the last two US investment banks, suffered from "run." In response, the Fed introduced several short-term credit and liquidity facilities to help stabilize markets. And Goldman Sachs and Morgan Stanley were heavy users of these facilities.

The possibility of central bank assistance, however, may encourage financial institutions to take excessive risks, paving the way for future crises. This problem is known as *moral hazard*. Managers may go out of their way to expand the balance sheet, hoping that their institutions will become "too big to fail."

Aware of the moral hazard problem, the central bank may make it clear that it won't save those institutions that have taken excessive risks. However, when a crisis does happen, refusing to be the lender of last resort may become a choice too costly to the financial market and the economy. This problem is an example of *time inconsistency*. The central bank is in a similar position as a stern father who threatens to spank his kid severely for certain misbehavior. But when the kid does misbehave, the father may have to scale down the punishment, possibly under the pressure of the mother and the grandparents.

6.5.2 Macroprudential Policy

Macroprudential policies refer to rules and actions that promote the stability of the financial system as a whole. In contrast, we may call supervisory or regulatory policies for individual financial institutions "microprudential policies."

We may define the stability of the financial system as the absence of systemic vulnerabilities, which may include asset bubbles, excessive risk taking by banks, excessive debt (households, corporations, local governments), and so on. It is challenging, if not impossible, to ensure the persistent stability of the financial system. Too often, an emerging bubble is indistinguishable from healthy reaction to economic expansion. The ever-evolving shadow banking makes it even more difficult to identify problems. Even when problems are identifiable, intervention at an early stage may be politically infeasible. Groups who benefit from asset and credit bubbles may criticize the macroprudential authority for being excessively active, threatening economic freedoms. Often it is too late when the macroprudential authority identifies a systemic vulnerability and decides to act on it. And the action to stop a bubble often causes the bubble to burst. China's stock market panic in 2015 provides a vivid example.[9]

Rules on Leverage

The macroprudential policy may take the form of rules on the maximum leverage financial institutions can take. For example, the macroprudential authority (domestic or international) typically imposes a capital adequacy requirement on commercial banks. That is to say, banks must set aside enough capital buffers for negative shocks. A required reserve ratio serves a similar purpose as the capital adequacy requirement, limiting the leverage of banks' lending business.

There are also rules on leverage that apply to individuals or households. The macroprudential authority typically imposes a minimum margin requirement for margin trading of stocks. Brokers must apply the minimum rules to customers, but they are free to apply more stringent requirements.

The macroprudential authority may also set a minimum down-payment ratio for home buyers. For example, China requires first-time homebuyers to make down payments of at least 30 percent, and, in some cities, the second-time home-buyers must make down payments of at least 70 percent. The down-payment requirement effectively reduces the average leverage of homebuyers.

For consumer loans in general, the authority may also set a cap of the debt-payment-to-income ratio. In the US, the Consumer Financial Protection Bureau (CFPB) sets a cap of 43% for the debt-payment-to-income ratio, which is the total monthly debt payments divided by the gross monthly income. In China, banks have an implicit cap of 50% for the debt-payment-to-income ratio.

Financial Market Entry

The macroprudential policy may also take the form of restrictions on market entry. For example, in most countries, a new bank has to obtain a license to operate. Licensing requires the attainment of some minimum standards on financial and operational soundness. The license can be expensive, meaning that the process of obtaining one is difficult, especially for nationwide operations. An expensive license acts as an ultimate threat to the new bank. If it behaves irresponsibly, then the authority may revoke the license.

The market entry restriction on financial institutions, and financial regulation in general, is justified by the fact that the financial industry exhibits externality due to its interconnected nature. Banks lend to each other. Insurance companies write insurances (on bonds and companies) that other financial firms trade and hold. And investment banks are counterparties to almost all other financial firms. One bank's default risk, thus, is another's counterparty risk. One bank's default may lead to the collapse of the entire financial system, as shown in Lehman Brother's downfall in 2008. Therefore, the social cost of one bank's default far exceeds the costs to the shareholders of the bank, hence the externality. Left to their own devices, shareholders of financial firms will take more risk than a benevolent social planner would allow.

Limiting Speculations

The macroprudential policy may also take the form of restrictions on speculation. The stock market and housing market are particularly prone to speculative bubbles, thanks to the visibility and accessibility of the two markets to retail investors. Speculative bubbles are usually the product of word-of-mouth feedback loops. An initial rise in asset price attracts new retail investors into the market. Their entry pushes the asset price even higher, attracting even more investors into the game. This a positive feedback loop that the policy makers want to break.

Stock Market

In the stock market, retail investors have neither the ability or patience to analyze businesses. They contribute nothing to the market but liquidity. The marginal benefits of increased liquidity to "price discovery" may quickly decline to zero as the army of retail speculators rush into the market. As more money chases the limited supply of stocks, the stock prices soar far above the level that the fundamentals can sustain. The feedback loop requires, however, a continuous flow of new money into the market. When almost everyone has entered and has been talking passionately about stock picks, days of the bull market would be numbered. When the market crashes, the wealth of a large population will be damaged, leading to a sudden contraction of aggregate consumption. If there are not many retail investors, then the impact of a stock crash on consumption will not be as big.

It is thus desirable from the perspective of a benevolent social planner that the access to stock speculation should be restricted to a limited circle, just like the access to casinos should be limited. The "every man a speculator" culture is not good for the economy, whether "bears" or "bulls" dominate the stock market. Gambling in the stock market does not require any special knowledge or expertise. So almost everyone from any occupation can participate, with a strong emotional satisfaction that derives from the gambling instinct in human nature. The emotional satisfaction is the strongest during the bull market, where the pleasure of making money quickly and the satisfaction of the gambling instinct reinforce each other. The term "stock mania" accurately describes such a state of mass mental disease. When a stock mania captures a substantial portion of the population, human capital as a whole is subject to a hit. It is a waste of human capital for every man to become a speculator because it is against the principle of division of labor.

To limit stock speculation, the government may tax stock transactions. For example, China levies a small stamp tax on stock transactions. More potently, the government may tax capital gains, especially short-term capital gains. In the US, short-term capital gains are taxed at the investor's ordinary income tax rate, with the definition of "short-term" being a year or less. Long-term capital gains are taxed at a lower rate. Note that such taxes on transactions or capital gains are extremely unpopular. The financial industry is clearly in opposition to any such taxes. So are retail investors, though they as a whole lose money in the stock market almost all the time.

For more dangerous types of trading, such as margin trading, futures, options, and so on, the government may impose minimum eligibility requirements. For example, to qualify for opening a margin account in China, investors should have tradable securities or cash worth at least 500,000 CNY. The eligibility requirements often include a minimum understanding of the risks involved in trading. But this is just part of the paperwork. Brokerages are more than happy to open whatever accounts for investors as long as they satisfy the minimum financial requirements.

Housing Market

The feedback loop in the housing market can be even stronger than in the stock market. The rise of housing prices not only attracts but also scares new buyers into the market. Unlike stocks, houses are real assets that everyone has to live in, either owning or renting one. And the quality of housing directly determines the quality of living. Especially in countries where homeownership is treasured and envied, purchasing a home is almost a necessary investment. Young couples who are waiting for marriage, for example, cannot wait to buy a home when they find that housing prices are rising.

Furthermore, investment in homes has built-in leverage. Even a down payment of 30% implies a leverage ratio of more than three. When housing prices rise, thus, the wealth of homeowners rises dramatically. This serves an irresistible word-of-mouth advertisement for home purchases. Even in countries where land supply is elastic (e.g., the US), housing prices can rise fast as speculative demand surges, as illustrated in the housing bubble of the US in 2004–2006. In countries where land supply for homebuilding is relatively inelastic, say, due to regulation of land use, speculative demand can easily send housing prices sky high.

When housing prices are rising, the economy can easily overheat. First, to satisfy speculative demand, housing developers cannot wait to build more homes. Residential construction competes for resources from other sectors, leading to a larger share of residential construction in GDP. Second, home purchases lead to demand for home renovation and household durable goods. Finally, the wealth effect of rising housing prices leads to consumption booms in general.

When housing prices start to decline, however, all these sources of demand will disappear. Furthermore, the leverage in home purchasing will start to bite the households that take too much debt and the whole economy. Since the house is usually the biggest asset for a household, the decline of housing value can easily make the "net worth" of household negative. In countries where personal bankruptcy is not allowed, people have to cut consumption, so as to "save out of" the negative net worth. In countries where personal bankruptcy is convenient, people may choose to foreclose their home en masse. This would cause trouble for banks and other financial institutions that hold mortgages, mortgage-backed securities (MBS), or other derivatives on home mortgages. The 2008 subprime mortgage crisis of the US was a vivid example.

To limit speculation in the real estate market, governments around the world have introduced various measures. There are numerous kinds of transaction taxes, such as stamp tax, capital gain tax, and so on. There is also the property tax that affects the "carry cost" of property holding. Note that the major objective of the property tax is not macroprudential but financing the government, especially the local government. And there are outright restrictions on home purchases and mortgage loans. China offers many examples of such policies.

6.6   Concluding Remarks

The most important job of stabilization policies is to keep the system robust so that it can withstand shocks, which will always come. Due to various imperfections discussed in Chapter 5, the real-world market is far from self-correcting. In particular, the financial market, if left alone, may become so fragile that a small shock is enough to crash the whole system. History tells us that the ultimate "correction" in the form of financial and economic crises is too costly for the society. Thus, it is the responsibility of the government to install fiscal automatic stabilizers and conduct macroprudential policies.

As mentioned earlier, macroprudential policy is difficult. Rapid asset price inflation is not necessarily an emerging bubble, which is often indistinguishable from a healthy reaction to economic expansion. The ever-evolving shadow banking makes it even more difficult to identify problems. It thus requires professional expertise on the part of regulators to identify and solve problems at the early stage. But professional expertise is expensive, and capable regulators, who are typically low-paid public servants, may easily be recruited by the financial industry. Furthermore, regulators often have to overcome political resistance to take early actions on an emerging bubble since those who benefit from bubbles will always oppose them. It remains a great challenge for governments around the world to build an effective macroprudential authority.

Notes

[1] Wei Zheng (魏徵, 580–643) is a famous advisor to Emperor Taizong of Tang. "备豫不虞，为国常道"，唐·吴兢《贞观政要·纳谏》载魏征语。

[2] This view was first proposed by Abba Lerner (1943), Functional Finance and the Federal Debt. *Social Research*, 10 38–51.

[3] For example: Robert J. Barro (1974), Are Government Bonds Net Wealth? *Journal of Political Economy*, 82 (6): 1095–1117.

[4] James Tobin (1972), Inflation and Unemployment, *American Economic Review*, 62, 1–18.

[5] Yi Gang (the governor of the People's Bank of China), 2021, China's Interest Rate System and Market-Based Reform of Interest Rate, *Financial Research* (in Chinese), 495 (9), 1–11.

[6] Jane Ihrig and Scott Wolla (2020). Let's Close the Gap: Revising Teaching Materials to Reflect How the Federal Reserve Implements Monetary Policy, Finance and Economics Discussion Series 2020-092. Washington: Board of Governors of the Federal Reserve System.

[7] Odysseus is the hero of Homer's epic poem *Odyssey*. He went through a committed journey back home, an "Odyssean journey," and reasserted himself as the rightful king of Ithaca.

[8] Delphi is the ancient Greek sanctuary for the oracle who was consulted about important decisions such as whether to wage a war.

[9] Junhui Qian, 2016, The 2015 Stock Panic of China, SSRN Working paper available at `https://dx.doi.org/10.2139/ssrn.2795543`.

Appendix A

Math Tools

A.1 Total Differential

Consider a multivariate function $F(x_1, \ldots, x_n)$. The total differential of F at the point $(x_1^*, \ldots, x_n^*)$ is given by

$$dF = \frac{\partial F}{\partial x_1}(x_1^*, \ldots, x_n^*)dx_1 + \cdots + \frac{\partial F}{\partial x_n}(x_1^*, \ldots, x_n^*)dx_n.$$

The total differential characterizes the change of F at the point $(x_1^*, \ldots, x_n^*)$ using partial derivatives. To us, the total differential is useful in obtaining a *linear representation* of a change in a nonlinear multivariate function.

For example, consider an aggregate production function $Y = F(K, L)$ and an economy at the point (K^*, L^*). Then ΔY (a change in Y), if it is small compared to Y, can be well approximated by

$$\Delta Y = \frac{\partial F}{\partial K}(K^*, L^*)\Delta K + \frac{\partial F}{\partial L}(K^*, L^*)\Delta L.$$

That is, the change in output has to come from the change in inputs, given the marginal product of capital and labor.

Often we denote the partial derivative $\frac{\partial F}{\partial x_i}(x_1^*, \ldots, x_n^*)$ by $F_i(x_1^*, \ldots, x_n^*)$, meaning the partial derivative of F with respect to the ith argument. Or even simpler, we may omit the arguments and write F_i, when there is no confusion over the point where the total differential is taken. Using the shorthand notation, we may write the total differential formula as follows:

$$dF = F_1 dx_1 + \cdots + F_n dx_n.$$

A.2   Implicit Function Theorem

The implicit function theorem is very useful for the analysis of single-equation models. First consider the simplest case involving an equation of two variables, x and y:

Implicit function theorem: Let $\Theta(x, y)$ be a differentiable function around (x^*, y^*). Suppose that $\Theta(x^*, y^*) = 0$ and consider the equation $\Theta(x, y) = 0$. If $\frac{\partial \Theta}{\partial y}(x^*, y^*) \neq 0$, then there exists a differentiable function $y(x)$ defined on an interval around x^* such that $\Theta(x, y(x)) = 0$ for all $x \in I$, $y(x^*) = y^*$, and

$$y'(x^*) \equiv \frac{dy}{dx}\big|_{x=x^*} = -\frac{\frac{\partial \Theta}{\partial x}(x^*, y^*)}{\frac{\partial \Theta}{\partial y}(x^*, y^*)}.$$

If $\Theta(x, y) = 0$ represents a model, x is an exogenous variable, and y is an endogenous variable, then we can use the theorem to calculate the effect of a change in x on y.

The theorem can be easily extended to accommodate more variables. If the model is $\Theta(x_1, \ldots, x_n, y) = 0$, then it defines an implicit function $y = y(x_1, \ldots, x_n)$, and

$$\frac{\partial y}{\partial x_i}\big|_{x_1=x_1^*,\ldots,x_n=x_n^*} = -\frac{\frac{\partial \Theta}{\partial x_i}(x_1 = x_1^*, \ldots, x_n = x_n^*, y = y^*)}{\frac{\partial \Theta}{\partial y}(x_1 = x_1^*, \ldots, x_n = x_n^*, y = y^*}.$$

Or, using the shorthand notation,

$$\frac{\partial y}{\partial x_i} = -\frac{\Theta_i}{\Theta_y},$$

where Θ_i represents partial derivative of Θ with respect to the ith argument, which is x_i, and Θ_y is the partial derivative of Θ with respect to y.

A.3   Dealing with Multiple Equations

Implicit functions may be defined by multiple equations or a set of equations. For example, the following model is a set of equations:

$$\begin{aligned} F(x_1, x_2, y, z) &= 0 \\ G(x_1, x_2, y, z) &= 0. \end{aligned}$$

This set of equations defines an implicit function $y = y(x_1, x_2)$. Here, we may understand that x_1 and x_2 are exogenous variables, and y and z are endogenous variables. To analyze the effects of x_1 and x_2 on y, for example, we need to calculate

$\partial y/\partial x_1$ and $\partial y/\partial x_2$. For this purpose, there is a multiple-equation version of the implicit function theorem, but it is difficult to remember. Instead, we may first linearize the model using the total differential and apply Cramer's rule to calculate the partial effects.

First, we apply the total differential to each equation and obtain the following:

$$
\begin{aligned}
F_1 dx_1 + F_2 dx_2 + F_y dy + F_z dz &= 0 \\
G_1 dx_1 + G_2 dx_2 + G_y dy + G_z dz &= 0.
\end{aligned}
$$

Now we have a linearized model. Moving all exogenous variables to the right-hand side, we may represent the model as

$$
\left[\begin{array}{cc} F_y & F_z \\ G_y & G_z \end{array} \right]
\left[\begin{array}{c} dy \\ dz \end{array} \right]
=
\left[\begin{array}{c} -F_1 dx_1 - F_2 dx_2 \\ -G_1 dx_1 - G_2 dx_2 \end{array} \right],
$$

which is a linear system of equations with dy and dz as unknown variables. Then we can apply Cramer's rule to obtain $\partial y/\partial x_1$, $\partial y/\partial x_2$, $\partial z/\partial x_1$, and $\partial z/\partial x_2$. For example, if we want to calculate $\partial y/\partial x_1$, then we force $dx_2 = 0$, meaning that x_2 is fixed. Cramer's rule has

$$
dy = \frac{\left| \begin{array}{cc} -F_1 dx_1 - F_2 dx_2 & F_z \\ -G_1 dx_1 - G_2 dx_2 & G_z \end{array} \right|}{\left| \begin{array}{cc} F_y & F_z \\ G_y & G_z \end{array} \right|} = \frac{\left| \begin{array}{cc} -F_1 & F_z \\ -G_1 & G_z \end{array} \right|}{\left| \begin{array}{cc} F_y & F_z \\ G_y & G_z \end{array} \right|} dx_1.
$$

Hence

$$
\frac{dy}{dx_1} = \frac{\left| \begin{array}{cc} -F_1 & F_z \\ -G_1 & G_z \end{array} \right|}{\left| \begin{array}{cc} F_y & F_z \\ G_y & G_z \end{array} \right|}.
$$

Note that since we force $dx_2 = 0$, the derivative $\frac{dy}{dx_1}$ is in fact partial derivative $\partial y/\partial x_1$. Similarly, we can calculate $\partial y/\partial x_2$, $\partial z/\partial x_1$, and $\partial z/\partial x_2$. And the method can be extended to deal with higher-dimensional models.

Note that Cramer's rule is formally stated as follows.

Cramer's rule: Consider an n-dimensional system of linear equations, $Ax = b$, where

$$
A = \left[\begin{array}{cccc} a_{11} & a_{12} & \cdots & a_{1n} \\ a_{21} & a_{22} & \cdots & a_{2n} \\ \vdots & & \ddots & \vdots \\ a_{n1} & a_{n2} & \cdots & a_{nn} \end{array} \right], \quad
x = \left[\begin{array}{c} x_1 \\ x_2 \\ \vdots \\ x_n \end{array} \right], \quad
b = \left[\begin{array}{c} b_1 \\ b_2 \\ \vdots \\ b_n \end{array} \right].
$$

Then the solutions to x_1, x_2, etc., are given by

$$x_1 = \frac{\begin{vmatrix} b_1 & a_{12} & \cdots & a_{1n} \\ b_2 & a_{22} & \cdots & a_{2n} \\ \vdots & & \ddots & \vdots \\ b_n & a_{n2} & \cdots & a_{nn} \end{vmatrix}}{A}, \quad x_2 = \frac{\begin{vmatrix} a_{11} & b_1 & a_{13} & \cdots & a_{1n} \\ a_{21} & b_2 & a_{23} & \cdots & a_{2n} \\ \vdots & & & \ddots & \vdots \\ a_{n1} & b_n & a_{n3} & \cdots & a_{nn} \end{vmatrix}}{A} \quad \cdots$$

In other words, the solution to x_i is given by a fraction. On the denominator is the determinant of A. On the numerator is the determinant of A with its ith column replaced by the vector b.

References

Chapter 1

[1] Akerlof, G. A., 2002, Behavioral Macroeconomics and Macroeconomic Behavior. *American Economic Review*, 92 (3): 411–433.

[2] Friedman, M., 1953, The Methodology of Positive Economics. In *Essays in Positive Economics*. Chicago: University of Chicago Press, pp. 3–43.

[3] Hayek, F. A., 1945, The Use of Knowledge in Society. *American Economic Review*, 35(4), 519–530.

[4] Hoover, K. D., 2001, *The Methodology of Empirical Macroeconomics*. Cambridge: Cambridge University Press.

[5] Lin, J. Y., 2011, *Demystifying the Chinese Economy*. Cambridge: Cambridge University Press.

[6] Keynes, J. M., 1936, *General Theory of Employment, Interest and Money*. New York: Harcourt, Brace & World.

Chapter 2

[7] Bureau of Economic Analysis, 2015, Measuring the Economy: A Primer on GDP and the National Income and Product Accounts. Available online at `www.bea.gov/resources/methodologies/measuring-the-economy`.

[8] Landefeld, J. S., E. P. Seskin, and B. M. Fraumeni, 2008, Taking the Pulse of the Economy: Measuring GDP. *Journal of Economic Perspectives*, 22(2), 193–216.

Chapter 3

[9] Card, D., and A. B. Krueger, 1994, Minimum Wages and Employment: A Case Study of the Fast-Food Industry in New Jersey and Pennsylvania. *American Economic Review*, September, 84(4), 772–793.

[10] Liu, H., 1999, *Research on China's Central Banking* (in Chinese, 中国中央银行研究). Beijing: Economic Press China.

[11] Akerlof, G. A., and J. L. Yellen, 1986, *Efficiency Wage Models of the Labor Market*. Cambridge: Cambridge University Press.

[12] Fisher, I., 1930, *The Theory of Interest (as Determined by Impatience to Spend Income and Opportunity to Invest It)*. New York: Macmillan. Available online at `https://fraser.stlouisfed.org/title/theory-interest-6255`.

[13] Marshall, A., 1920, *Principles of Economics*. London: Macmillan.

Chapter 4

[14] Barry, J., 2018, *The Chinese Economy: Adaptation and Growth*. Cambridge, MA: MIT Press.

[15] Lewis, A. W., 1954, Economic Development with Unlimited Supplies of Labour. *The Manchester School*, 22 (2), 139–191.

[16] Romer, D., 2018, *Advanced Macroeconomics* (5th ed.). New York: McGraw-Hill Education.

[17] Romer, P. M., 1986, Increasing Returns and Long-Run Growth. *Journal of Political Economy*, 94 (5), 1002–1037.

[18] Romer, P. M., 1994, The Origins of Endogenous Growth. *The Journal of Economic Perspectives*, 8 (1), 3–22.

[19] Schumpeter, J. A., *The Theory of Economic Development*. Cambridge, MA: Harvard University Press.

[20] Schumpeter, J. A., 1942, *Capitalism, Socialism and Democracy*. New York: Harper and Brothers.

[21] Solow, R., 1956, A Contribution to the Theory of Economic Growth. *Quarterly Journal of Economics*, 70 (1), 65–94.

[22] Solow, R., 1957, Technical Change and the Aggregate Production Function. *Review of Economics and Statistics*, 39 (3), 312–320.

[23] Wu, J., 2010, *Understanding and Interpreting China's Economic Reform* (in Chinese, 当代中国经济改革教程). Shanghai: Shanghai Far East Publishers.

Chapter 5

[24] Bewley, T. F., 1999, *Why Wages Don't Fall in a Recession*. Cambridge, MA: Harvard University Press.

[25] Blinder A. S., 1994, On Sticky Prices: Academic Theories Meet the Real World. In N. G. Mankiw, ed., *Monetary Policy*. University of Chicago Press, 117–154.

[26] Dillard, D., 1948, *The Economics of John Maynard Keynes: The Theory of a Monetary Economy*. New Jersey: Prentice Hall.

[27] Fleming, J. M., 1962. Domestic Financial Policies under Fixed and Floating Exchange Rates. *IMF Staff Papers*, 9, 369–379.

[28] Mankiw, N.G., 2016, *Macroeconomics* (9th ed.). New York: Worth Publishers.

[29] Minsky, H. P., 1986, *Stabilizing an Unstable Economy*. New Haven: Yale University Press.

[30] Mundell, R. A., 1963, Capital Mobility and Stabilization Policy under Fixed and Flexible Exchange Rates. *Canadian Journal of Economics and Political Science*, 29 (4), 475–485.

[31] Rothermund, D., 1996, *The Global Impact of the Great Depression 1929–1939*. New York: Routledge.

[32] Samuelson, P. A., 1948, *Economics*. New York: McGraw-Hill.

[33] Stiglitz, J. E., 2002, *Globalization and Its Discontents*. New York: W. W. Norton.

[34] Su, G., and Qian, J., 2021, Structural Changes in the RMB Exchange Rate Mechanism. *China & World Economy*, 29 (2), 1–23.

Chapter 6

[35] Ihrig, J., and Wolla, S., 2020, *Let's Close the Gap: Revising Teaching Materials to Reflect How the Federal Reserve Implements Monetary Policy*. Finance and Economics Discussion Series 2020-092. Washington: Board of Governors of the Federal Reserve System.

[36] Lerner, A., 1943, Functional Finance and the Federal Debt. *Social Research*, 10, 38-51.

[37] Qian, J., 2016, The 2015 Stock Panic of China. SSRN Working paper available at `https://dx.doi.org/10.2139/ssrn.2795543`.

[38] Wang, J. J., 2020, *Central Banking 101*. Self published, available at Amazon and Google Books.

[39] Yi, G. (the governor of the People's Bank of China), 2021, China's Interest Rate System and Market-Based Reform of Interest Rate. *Financial Research* (in Chinese, 金融研究), 495 (9), 1–11.

Index

Printed in the United States
by Baker & Taylor Publisher Services